# Annals Information Systems





For further volumes:
http://www.springer.com/series/7573

Satish Nambisan
Editor

# Information Technology and Product Development

Springer

*Editor*
Satish Nambisan
Rensselaer Polytechnic Inst.
Lally School of Management & Technology
110 8th Street
Troy NY 12180
Pittsburgh Bldg.
USA
nambis@rpi.edu

ISBN 978-1-4419-1080-6 e-ISBN 978-1-4419-1081-3
DOI 10.1007/978-1-4419-1081-3
Springer New York Dordrecht Heidelberg London

Library of Congress Control Number: 2009910482



Printed on acid-free paper

Springer is part of Springer Science+Business Media (www.springer.com)

# Preface

Sometime in mid-2007, I received an invite from Professor Ramesh Sharda of Oklahoma State University, the Series Editor of the Annals of Information Systems (AoIS), to guest edit a volume in the AoIS series. I had just finished writing my new book on collaborative innovation, *The Global Brain* (Wharton School Publishing, 2007) and one of the topics I had dealt with in that book related to the role of information technology (IT) in facilitating inter-organizational collaborative innovation. I had also written an opinion piece on the topic of IT and product development in *MIS Quarterly* in 2003. As such, I was quite interested in exploring this topic further and an AoIS edited volume seemed a natural vehicle for that. I submitted a proposal outlining this idea and it was readily accepted by the Series Editor at Springer.

Given the broader organizational and business context in which IT applications support product development activities, it was clear to me from the proposal stage onward that to truly explore the different research issues on IT and product development the edited volume would need to seek out and include diverse disciplinary ideas and theoretical perspectives. So the Call for Chapters was sent out to a wide range of electronic mailing lists and other online venues representing varied academic fields and areas. Chapter submissions were due in early 2008. By the due date, I received many worthwhile papers from researchers in different fields including information systems, marketing, strategy, communications, and organizational behavior. I also received submissions from a few leading practitioners with keen interest on this topic. The final set of chapters selected for this volume represents such diversity in thought, ideas, and disciplinary background.

The chapter submissions went through a double blind review process. The reviews focused on evaluating the manuscripts on their research orientation, relevance and value addition of the theoretical perspective(s) employed, and their overall rigor and validity. Based on the reviews, the authors were invited to revise and resubmit their chapters. Most chapters that were accepted went through two rounds of such revision and some of the submissions were rejected after the first round of review. The final manuscript for this volume was submitted to Springer in April 2009.

I would like to thank Professor Ramesh Sharda and Gary Folven, the former area editor at Springer, for encouraging me to work on this edited volume and for readily accepting my proposal. I also wish to thank Neil Levine, the current area editor at

Springer, as well as Carolyn Ford and Matthew Amboy, both of Springer, for their help in producing this volume in a timely manner. I am also grateful to all those who volunteered to review the various chapters. Finally, I wish to thank the chapter authors without whose contribution this volume would not have been possible.

Troy, NewYork Satish Nambisan

# Contents

# Contributors

**Robert G. Fichman** Carroll School of Management, Boston College, 410A Fulton Hall, 140 Commonwealth Ave, Chestnut Hill, MA 02467, USA, fichman@bc.edu

**Elisa Fredericks** College of Business, Northern Illinois University, DeKalb, IL 60115-2897, USA, elisa@niu.edu

**Darren Harris** Enterprise Research Centre, ER1030, University of Limerick, Plassey, Limerick, Ireland, darren.harris@ul.ie

**Andrew Hewett** Director, PRTM, Ste. 600, Mountain View, CA 94041, USA, ahewett@prtm.com

**Aggelos Liapis** Vrije Universiteit, 522 Brugmann Avenue, Uccle 1180, Brussels, Belgium, aggelos@arkaos.net

**Julian Malins** Gray's School of Art, The Robert Gordon University, Garthdee Road, Aberdeen, Scotland, j.malins@rgu.ac.uk

**Satish Nambisan** Lally School of Management, Rensselaer Polytechnic Institute, Troy, NY 12180, USA, nambis@rpi.edu

**Emma O'Brien** Enterprise Research Centre, ER1030, University of Limerick, Plassey, Limerick, Ireland, emma.obrien@ul.ie

**Dawn R. Schneider** College of Business Administration, University of Illinois at Chicago, Chicago, IL 60607-7124, USA, dschne@uic.edu

**Mark Southern** Enterprise Research Centre, ER1030, University of Limerick, Plassey, Limerick, Ireland, mark.southern@ul.ie

**Priya Nambisan** Department of Health Policy, Management and Behavior, School of Public Health, University at Albany, SUNY, One University Place, Rm 185, Rensselaer, NY 12144, USA, pnambisan@albany.edu

**Ikenna S. Uzuegbunam** School of Management, Gatton College of Business & Economics, University of Kentucky, Lexington, KY 40506, USA, iuz222@email.uky.edu

# About the Authors

**Robert G. Fichman** is an Associate Professor of IS at the Carroll School of Management at Boston College. His main research stream examines the diffusion and assimilation of IT innovations, and draws implications for adopters and suppliers about how to better manage the introduction of new technologies. Current areas of interest include Web 2.0 technologies, healthcare IT, and the linkage between IT investments and realized business value. He has published broadly on these and other topics in *CACM*, *California Management Review*, *Decision Sciences Journal*, *Information Systems Research*, *Journal of AIS*, *Management Science*, *MIS Quarterly*, *Sloan Management Review* and other scholarly journals. Dr. Fichman currently serves as Associate Editor at *Management Science*, Senior Editor at *Journal of the Association of Information Systems*, and will join *Information Systems Research* as Senior Editor in 2010. Dr. Fichman holds a Ph.D. in Information Technology from the MIT Sloan School of Management.

**Elisa Fredericks** is an Associate Professor at Northern Illinois University. Her teaching and research interests include product development and management and cross-functional integration. She is currently researching how teams develop new products and what makes for a successful introduction into the marketplace. She has published in *Industrial Marketing Management*and *Qualitative Marketing Research* as well as being an active conference participant. She has received the Best Paper Award at the Winter American Marketing Association Conference, Technology and Marketing Track. Dr. Fredericks is also a member of the American Marketing Association, the Product Development and Management Association, and the Academy of Marketing Science.

**Darren Harris** is a manufacturing process engineer in Stryker Orthopaedics Limerick. In 2005, he graduated from the University of Limerick with a first class honors degree in Manufacturing Engineering and received the IEEE manufacturing engineering award. In January 2009, he graduated with an MEng by research in the field of process optimization using design of experiments and variation mode and effect analysis. Darren has undertaken many innovative process optimization initiatives in a number of Ireland's top medical device manufacturing organizations which has proved extremely beneficial to the storage of vital process critical information.

**Andrew Hewett** is a lead partner in the Product Development and Innovation practice for global management consultancy PRTM. He works primarily with technology-based companies developing and implementing software applications and systems for product development, portfolio management, resource management, operations, and call center operations. Andrew's experience with global companies has involved everything from application interface architecture, database structure, complex BOM designs, design for complexity and cost, engineering change management, master data management, part reuse, collaboration, deliver to promise, configuration, and retirement. Working with senior management teams, he has led the implementation of new products, processes, and systems for many, product development organizations, operations departments, and technical support groups. Andrew graduated from the University of Chicago with BA in Economics. In addition to his work at PRTM, he is a professional musician winning numerous music awards in his original band Evolution Eden. Andrew Hewett is located in the Mountain View, California office of PRTM.

**Aggelos Liapis** is product development manager at Arkaos, a major interactive visual technologies company based in Brussels. Dr. Liapis originates from Athens, Greece. He is a computer scientist, having been educated in Greece and in the UK. He completed his PhD in Computer Mediated Collaborative Design Environments at the Robert Gordon University, Aberdeen in 2007. His research focused on the development of a prototype collaborative environment that was designed to assist professional product designers during the early stages of the design process. Following completion of his PhD he undertook post-doctoral research at the University of Brussels (VUB) in the field of ontology engineering and computer-supported collaborative working.

**Julian Malins** is currently the Director of the Centre for Design and Innovation Management (www.c4di.org.uk) at Robert Gordon University, Scotland. He originally trained as a ceramist and ran his own studio ceramics business for a number of years. He later returned to full-time education to complete a Masters degree and a PhD. On completion of his PhD he undertook post-doctoral research at the Robert Gordon University, Aberdeen becoming a Professor of Design in 2007. The Centre for Design and Innovation Management is an ERDF and Scottish Government funded project that aims to assist businesses in Scotland through the application of design and innovation methodologies. Dr. Malins' published papers cover topics including approaches to research in art and design, the design of virtual learning environments, and collaborative design tools.

**Satish Nambisan** is a globally-recognized researcher and thought leader in the areas of innovation management and technology strategy. He has done pioneering research work on network-centric innovation, customer co-innovation, and IT-enabled product development. His research publications have appeared (or are forthcoming) in premier management journals such as the *Harvard Business Review*, *Management Science*, *Organization Science, Academy of Management Review*, *MIT Sloan Management Review, and Stanford Social Innovation Review.*

His new book *The Global Brain: Your Roadmap for Innovating Faster and Smarter in a Networked World* was published by the Wharton School Publishing in October 2007. Dr. Nambisan is an associate Professor of Technology Management & Strategy in the Lally School of Management at Rensselaer Polytechnic Institute, NY. He has held visiting faculty appointments at the at the Kellogg School of Management, Northwestern University and at the Institute for Entrepreneurship & Innovation, Vienna University of Economics and Business Administration, Vienna, Austria.

**Priya Nambisan** is an Assistant Professor of Healthcare Management at the Department of Health Policy, Management & Behavior, School of Public Health, University at Albany, SUNY. Prior to joining the University at Albany, she was a Post-Doctoral Fellow at the Centre for Health Systems Research and Analysis (CHSRA), University of Wisconsin–Madison. Dr. Nambisan's research focuses on the broad area of health information technologies (HIT) and their impact on the delivery and management of health information and healthcare services. Her recent research projects have examined patient-driven innovation and knowledge co-creation in healthcare, the role of online patient communities in health care, and the management of HIT adoption. Her publications have appeared in journals such as *MIT Sloan Management Review*, *International Journal of Internet Marketing and Advertising*, and *International Journal of Electronic Marketing and Retailing*. Dr. Nambisan holds a Masters degree in Nutrition Science from Syracuse University, NY and a PhD in Communication and Technology from Rensselaer Polytechnic Institute, Troy, NY.

**Emma O'Brien** is a research fellow at the University of Limerick where she is actively involved in working closely with industry to address issues of over dependence on staff through knowledge management. She received a primary degree in Business Computing and a Masters Degree in Computing in Education from Limerick Institute of Technology in 2000 and 2003, respectively. In 2005 she graduated with a PhD from the University of Limerick. Dr. O'Brien has previously worked on many EU-funded projects. Areas of research include e-learning, training models for SMEs, and knowledge management applications for innovation.

**Dawn R. Schneider** is a PhD student at the College of Business Administration University of Illinois of Chicago. She holds an Undergraduate Degree in Marketing from the University of Illinois at Urbana-Champaign and an MBA from DePaul University. Her research focuses on the intersection of three primary areas of interest: innovation, technology, and teams.

**Mark Southern** is a senior research fellow in the University of Limerick. He works closely with industry to make process and product innovations within SMEs. He graduated from Nottingham Trent University in 1989 with a degree in Industrial Studies and obtained his Doctorate in 2004 by researching the application of innovative wireless technology applications into SMEs. Dr. Southern is an experienced manager with a proven track record in project team management in both multinationals and SMEs. He has significant experience in managing teams in research, design, development, procurement, and installation of complex manufacturing systems in these environments.

**Ikenna S. Uzuegbunam** is an assistant professor in the management area at the Gatton College of Business & Economics, University of Kentucky. He earned his Ph.D. in management from Lally School of Management & Technology, Rensselaer Polytechnic Institute and M.Sc. from the University of Sussex. His primary research interests are technology strategy, network-centric innovation management, and entrepreneurship. He is a member of the Academy of Management and the Strategic Management Society and frequently presents his research at premier management conferences. In 2006, Dr. Uzuegbunam was honored at the Southern Management Meetings, Clearwater Beach, Florida for his co-authored paper "A Theory of Interfirm Niche Competence in Radical Technological Regimes." His previous industry and consulting experience spans a number of industries including medical devices, oil & gas, electronics, software, and the non-for-profit sector.

# Chapter 1
# The Role of Information Technology in Product Development: An Introduction

**Satish Nambisan**

**Abstract** Innovation has assumed considerable importance in the contemporary business world. In most industries, the very survival of firms is increasingly dependent on their ability to rapidly develop and introduce innovative products and services. At the same time, information technology (IT) has emerged as a critical resource for companies to enhance the efficiency and effectiveness of their product development activities. This chapter provides an introduction to the book by tracing the evolution of research on product (service) development and the increasing focus on IT-related issues in this context. Both traditional and emerging areas of research on IT and product development are identified. The motivation for the book is set out in detail, and the chapter concludes by describing the organization of the book and the various chapters.

## 1.1 Introduction

Innovation has assumed considerable importance in the contemporary business world. In most industries, the very survival of firms is increasingly dependent on their ability to rapidly develop and introduce innovative products and services (Cooper, 2001; Schilling & Hill, 1998). On average, more than one-third of a corporation's revenue comes from products and services that did not exist 5 years ago. That figure is much higher in certain technology industries (Griffin, 1997). The nature and the process of innovation have also undergone significant change in the past several years as more and more firms open up their organizational boundaries to seek out innovative ideas and expertise from a wide range of external entities including customers, suppliers, academic researchers, serial innovators (Nambisan & Sawhney, 2007). All of this has brought the research and the practice of innovation to the forefront of management dialog.

At the same time, it is also evident that the issues related to both product and service innovation will require the adoption of a more interdisciplinary mode of

S. Nambisan (✉)
Lally School of Management, Rensselaer Polytechnic Institute, Troy, NY, 12180, USA
e-mail: nambis@rpi.edu

S. Nambisan (ed.), *Information Technology and Product Development*, Annals of Information Systems 5, DOI 10.1007/978-1-4419-1081-3_1,

inquiry and call for contributions from most business functional areas. Indeed, the field of product development (PD) has been defined as including the set of activities "beginning with the perception of a market opportunity and ending in the production, sales, and delivery of a product" (Ulrich & Eppinger, 2000, p. 2). Compared to other management areas such as marketing, operations, and strategy, the field of information technology (IT) has been a relatively late entrant in the domain of product and service innovation.

From the mid-1990s, the rapid infusion of information and communication technologies in product development has significantly enhanced the importance of IT for product development managers and practitioners. IT-enabled product development now has the potential to radically redefine the processes and outcomes of new product development (NPD). However, as is evident from the extant research on IT management, effective deployment of IT resources for product development will call for careful consideration of the complex interplay between IT applications and the product development context (Nambisan, 2003). Managers need to understand how IT shapes the NPD processes and their outcomes, the development and management of the product development team (including the norms, values, and the relational ties), the knowledge flows and the knowledge acquisition/creation strategies, the project management models, and the linkages of product development (PD) with other organizational functions/objectives.

The primary purpose of this book is to contribute toward such an understanding by serving as a platform for researchers from varied disciplines to develop new theoretical concepts and insights on the application of IT in product and service innovation activities. Specifically, the different chapters in this book draw on theoretical concepts and issues from varied management areas including information systems, technology management, marketing, operations, business strategy, and organizational behavior to redefine and discuss the role of IT in product and service development and the organizational and management issues that underlie the successful deployment of IT in innovation contexts. Overall, the book is intended to provide a foundation for future research on the diverse types of IT applications in product development and their potential impact on both product and service innovation.

In the remainder of this introductory chapter, I examine the motivation for this book in greater detail and then describe the organization of the book.

## 1.2 The Evolution of Product and Service Development Research

The interdisciplinary field of product development has evolved gradually over the last 30 years or so, bringing different reference disciplines into focus at different points in time. The roots of the PD field can be traced to the R&D and engineering management literatures of the 1960s and the early 1970s. These two fields gave early PD research a project- and innovation-management orientation (Rothwell, Freeman,

Jervis, Robertson, & Townsend, 1974; Mansfield, 1968). Initially, the primary focus was on managing and executing the R&D activity. However, as the need for the customer/market focus in product development activities increased over the following decade, the marketing discipline also became a key contributor to research on NPD. Themes such as the "voice of the customer" (Griffin & Hauser, 1993) and "lead user" (von Hippel, 1988) brought fresh insights to PD. An increased emphasis was also placed on the organizational processes and communication that underlie product development. Consequently, organization theories became relevant. The organizational perspective elicited many issues related to product development processes and activities including team structure and building, leadership, recognition and reward systems, team culture, conflict management, group decision making, and communication (Allen, 1970; Katz & Tushman, 1981; Ancona & Caldwell, 1992; Dougherty, 1992).

By the early 1990s, two other themes – operational integration and product development strategy – had assumed significance in product development research. Increased globalization and competition resulted in more dispersed product development activities and renewed emphasis on reducing development costs and time-to-market. Such enhanced operational efficiency in product development was made possible by the more effective integration of product development activities across the supply chain. Thus, issues such as supplier involvement in innovation, design for manufacturing, production process and schedule optimization, and process concurrency highlighted theoretical models and insights from the fields of operations management and production (Imai, Ikujiro, & Takeuchi, 1985; Clark & Fujimoto, 1991; Hayes, Wheelwright, & Clark, 1988).

At the same time, highly dynamic product technologies and competition based on core competencies forced most organizations to ensure tighter linkages between their product development projects and business strategy and to adopt coherent enterprise-wide product development strategy. This led to the application of various concepts from the strategy literature (e.g., strategic product planning, technology planning, portfolio management, product platform strategy, technology alliances) in devising product development strategies (Cooper, Edgett, & Eleinschmidt, 1999; Gawer & Cusumano, 2002; Meyer & Lehnerd, 1997).

While the early focus of the innovation research community has been on product innovation, in the past 10 years or so, there has been an emerging focus on service innovation. It has been estimated that the service sector accounts for approximately 70–80% of the gross domestic product (GDP) in many developed countries (Chesbrough & Spohrer, 2006; Rust & Chung, 2006; Vries, 2006). Considerable research effort has gone into defining service and identifying focus and the boundaries of service innovation. However, two critical shifts in the service sector indicate that research on product and service innovation has to go hand in hand.

The first shift is the increased complexity and the convergence in products and services, as well as in their design and production (Gomes-Casseres, 1994; Nambisan, 2001). In most cases, the contemporary offering is an embodiment of several specialized skills that integrates across product and services. Consider the services offered by a typical healthcare organization. The evaluation, diagnosis, treatment, referral, and the follow-up of a patient and his/her ailment incorporate a set of processes that involve a wide range of product and service components. Another example of the confluence of products and services is IBM's migration to the "on-demand" strategy. As IBM realized the potential global market for integrated end-user solutions, it adopted a technology strategy that focused less on differentiating between product innovation and service innovation and more on integrating the complementary features of products and services to address critical market needs.

The second major shift is the rise of the Internet and the rapid digitization of products and services (Tidd, Bessant, & Pavitt, 2001). The prevalence of Internet creates both new opportunities and challenges for both product and service innovation. The changing nature of product and service distribution to customers is one such example. For example, book publishers who sold hard copies of the books through physical retail outlets or stores now increasingly pursue distribution of digitized versions through online outlets such as Amazon and which can be "read" using digital devices such as Kindle. Similarly, the "software as service" model pursued by companies such as Salesforce.com has brought about radical changes in the enterprise software market.

Thus, as some researchers have already contended, we exist in an intertwined product–service environment that is characterized by an overarching demand for experience innovation (e.g., Prahalad & Ramaswamy, 2003). In such a context, competition will increasingly center on personalized co-creation experiences, resulting in value that is truly unique to each individual customer or user. This in turn translates into the need for firms to strive for new strategies and sources for innovation – one that is achieved through partnerships with other firms that have complementary products and/or services and by created an integrated set of offerings (Rothaermel, 2001; Tripsas, 1997).

As noted previously, several management disciplines including marketing, operations management, organizational behavior, finance and economics, and strategy have contributed to the field of product and service innovation. Agenda-setting articles have clarified the research issues and identified important theoretical perspectives that these different disciplines can contribute to this area – for example, marketing and product development (Griffin & Hauser, 1996; Mahajan & Wind, 1992), strategy and product development (Cusumano & Nobeoka, 1992), operations management and product development (Krishnan & Ulrich, 2001), and organization theory and product development (Brown & Eisenhardt, 1995). Review articles that bridge the contributions to product development of two or more disciplines have also appeared. Tatikonda and Montoya-Weiss (2001), for instance, combine marketing and operations research perspectives for managing product development. These and other such articles indicate the potential benefits from integrating theoretical perspectives from multiple disciplines to inform on key issues on product and service innovation. The missing link in this area so far has been perspectives related to IT. Before we discuss the key IT-related issues in more detail, it would be appropriate to develop a better understanding of the emergence of IT applications in product and service innovation.

## 1.3 The Role of IT in Product and Service Development

As mentioned previously, in the past 10 years or so, IT has come to play a critical role in several aspects of product and service development (Nambisan, 2003; Ozer, 2000). For example, most of the challenges involved in the shift toward network-centric or distributed innovation – wherein the product or service innovation activities are distributed in both space and time across a wide range of external partners – cannot be addressed without the coordination and collaboration facilitated by IT (Dahan & Hauser, 2001; McGrath & Iansiti, 1998; Ozer, 2000; Sawhney & Prandelli, 2000). Moreover, the managerial issues associated with the selection, deployment, and the use of IT have become central to the success of product development efforts in most industries.

> The aggressive implementation of information technology in the product development arena will reshape innovation as we know it. Unlike existing innovation processes, which are passive, the IT-enabled innovation processes . . . are active, directly supporting innovation activities. They will help in the analysis of data, enable more efficient communication and efficient problem solving, and achieve much higher levels of integration than possible earlier. They will make the organization more flexible and responsive, optimizing the process to fit the context of the project. (McGrath and Iansiti, 1998, p. 2)

Recent publications in major product development journals and conferences indicate the critical importance that both practitioners and researchers in this area have started placing on IT. The number of articles on IT applications in product development has increased significantly in most product development-focused journals (e.g., *Research-Technology Management, Journal of Product Innovation Management, Engineering Management Journal*). The number of vendors offering IT-based solutions for managing product development has also increased considerably in the last several years. Seminars and workshops exploring IT-enabled product development issues abound, while several large firms including Intel, Cisco, and Sun have issued white papers on how they have started redesigning their product development using IT.

Within the academic domain too, the focus on IT and product development has increased significantly in the past few years leading to important insights on the selection and use of new IT applications to support innovation activities. Early efforts focused on identifying the wide range of organizational and management issues that lie at the intersection of information systems and product development (e.g., Nambisan, 2003; Ozer, 2000). More recent studies have considered a number of issues ranging from the competitive advantage that could be gained from using IT applications in product development to the role of IT in virtual product development and in collaborative product development (e.g., Ali, Ki-Chan, Thomas, & MatthiasAli, 2004; Banker, Bardhan, & Asdemir, 2006; Bardhan, 2007; Dahan & Hauser, 2002; Denno & Thurman, 2005; Durmusglu, Calantone, & Sambamurthy, 2006; Ettlie & Pavlou, 2006; Joglekar & Yassine, 2002; Li & Qiu, 2006; Pavlou & Sawy, 2006; Sethi, Pant, & Sethi, 2003; Su, Chen, & Yung-Jye, 2007; Xu, Li, Li, & Tang, 2007).

These studies indicate the rapidly emerging interest in the academic community on IT applications in product development. At the same time, given the rich promise and potential of IT applications to enhance the overall quality of product development activities and outcomes, it is critical that we develop a more comprehensive and coherent understanding of how IT resources should be effectively deployed and managed in this context. This will require us to take a step back and re-evaluate our "state of knowledge" of this area and then create a common platform for the research community (including those from related areas such as operations, organizational behavior, and marketing) to come together and develop a shared understanding of the important IT management issues in product and service development. Such a shared understanding can help us pursue a more fruitful research agenda – an agenda that would lead to insights that are relevant as well as valuable to both IT and product/service development practitioners in the years to come. This forms the primary motivation for this book.

In particular, the effort in this book has been to bring together researchers with different disciplinary backgrounds and with diverse research interests in the broad area of IT and product/service innovation and facilitate the integration of theoretical concepts and constructs focused on a range of important topics in this area including product life cycle management (PLM), development processes, project management, customer co-innovation, open innovation, knowledge co-creation, and virtual teams.

## 1.4 Traditional and Emerging Research Areas in IT and product development

The application of IT in product and service development can be classified into four broad categories: process management, project management, information and knowledge management, and collaboration and communication. The first two – project management and process management – form the traditional areas of IT application in product/service development and much of the research effort so far has focused on these areas. The latter two – knowledge management and collaboration – have emerged in recent years as the most promising application areas for IT given the increasing emphasis on network-centric, collaborative innovation in most industries.

### *1.4.1 Traditional Areas of IT–PD Research*

Starting in the 1990s, there has been considerable focus on the adoption of structured product (and service) development management models to bring rigor and stability to the design and development activities. An early initiative in this regard was the capability maturity model (CMM) developed for the software industry by the Software Engineering Institute at Carnegie Mellon University (Paulk, Weber,

Curtis, & Chrissis, 1995). CMM provided a much needed thrust to the area of software quality and software development metrics and induced other industries to build similar frameworks and models to guide their design and development activities (Stage Gate, PACE, ISO 9000, etc.). Along the same lines, the focus on project management has led to the development and adoption of practices related to task coordination, scheduling, and resource management of product development projects. Sophisticated project management models have enabled firms to manage aggregate project portfolios and to implement cross-project resource management strategies based on real-time project data (Cooper & Kleinschmidt, 2001). They also support complex workflow management and coordination of dispersed task groups in real time.

Different types of IT tools have been deployed to support both project and process management. Broadly these tools have been referred to as product life cycle management (PLM) tools (Teresko, 2004). These IT tools support process management by either prescribing a comprehensive process model or enable firms to adopt a flexible process framework to configure their own unique process model (Elliott, Gill, & Nelson, 2001; Nahass, 2001). The IT support also extends to cross-enterprise process specification and management as well as integration with other organizational and supply chain processes (Joglekar & Yassine, 2002). Many of these tools offer sophisticated project management features including virtual command center (or dashboard) that provides access to all project information through a common interface and integrate project management with the firm's process management. Furthermore, the Internet, intelligent agents, and other emerging technologies facilitate enhanced online visibility of project data, automated task and resource monitoring, and control. These systems also facilitate sophisticated cross-project knowledge management critical for implementing enterprise-wide product platform and portfolio management strategies.

As noted previously, there have been a number of studies, particularly in the last 5 years or so, on how IT applications can support project and process management in product development contexts. However, as newer types of IT applications emerge in these areas, newer issues related to their deployment and adoption also emerge and thereby indicate the need to maintain the research focus on these IT applications.

### *1.4.2 Emerging Areas of IT–PD Research*

Most product development projects generate an extensive amount of information and knowledge. Techniques to support data and information sharing with multiple entities in a network-centric or collaborative innovation environment have assumed critical importance in recent years. Moving away from traditional product data management (PDM) and product information management (PIM) systems and standards (e.g., the ISO-STEP), the newer IT-based systems and tools are designed to support a wider variety of knowledge capture and sharing methods. They incorporate emerging data standards, database, and visualization technologies that can handle different types of information (including graphics, audio, and video). They also attempt to offer more versatile decision support facilities capable of combining structured and unstructured information in real time.

Further, an increasing number of firms (e.g., Boeing, IBM, GE, Microsoft) rely on virtual product development teams to minimize their product development costs and time-to-market (Boutellier, Gassman, Macho, & Roux, 1998; Dahan & Hauser, 2001; Hameri & Nihtila, 1997; Ozer, 2000). The added focus on virtual teams has raised several management issues including establishing IT-based support for virtual teams, developing trust in virtual team environments, structuring of knowledge-management systems (e.g., Majchrzak, Rice, Malhotra, Nelson, & Ba, 2000; Maznevski & Chudoba, 2000; Jarvenpaa & Leidner, 1999; Malhotra, Majchrzak, Carman, & Lott, 2001; Cramton, 2001).

At the same time, the nature and the extent of collaboration in product and service innovation have undergone radical changes in recent years. Firms now seek innovative ideas from a wide range of potential partners – customers, suppliers, complementors, etc. For example, customers can contribute to innovation and value creation activities including product conceptualization or ideation, product design and development, product testing, product marketing and diffusion, and product support through virtual customer environments (VCEs) (Nambisan, 2002). Recent research (e.g., Dahan & Hauser, 2002; Nambisan & Nambisan, 2008; Prahalad & Ramaswamy, 2003; Sawhney & Prandelli, 2000; Thomke & von Hippel, 2002) has identified several interesting issues for future research in this area including motivations for customer co-creation, customer co-creation experience, organizational design choices that enhance the effectiveness of customer co-innovation. The same holds true for collaborative innovation with other types of partners.

As such the need for IT-based support to collaborative innovation has become more critical. The new IT-based systems that support such network-centric or distributed innovation environments integrate a wide range of collaboration tools (Dahan & Hauser, 2001; Nambisan & Sawhney, 2007). Furthermore, such virtual collaboration systems have to cater to multiple partners who differ in their IT capabilities, their need to access the project/product knowledge base, the nature of their participation in NPD, and their regional/organizational culture. Thus, the IT-based collaboration and communication systems used must be flexible and well integrated with knowledge-management systems.

In sum, future research on IT and product/service development will need to adopt a dual focus. On the one hand, it has to maintain the focus on the role of IT in supporting project and process management. This is critical as newer types of IT applications emerge in these areas and companies find it challenging to incorporate those applications in their day-to-day product development practice. On the other hand, future research will also need to initiate a focus on addressing the issues and challenges related to newer models of collaborative innovation such as network-centric innovation and open innovation. Maintaining such a dual focus in research on IT and product development will be crucial to be able to offer valuable insights on diverse types of IT-enabled product development models and activities. As described in the following section, this book will attempt to layout a research agenda that would maintain such a dual focus and advance research on both fronts.

## 1.5 The Focus of the Book and Its Target Audience

Despite the critical role that IT has come to play in supporting product and service development, there have been very few books on this topic. Existing books that have dealt with IT and product/service development issues fall into two broad categories.

The first category consists of books with a general focus on IT strategy and applications. These books, written primarily for practitioners, offer only a passing mention of the potential for applying IT in product development and innovation activities (e.g., Pearlson, 2004; Clarke, 2007). However, there is no specific focus on product/service development or on research issues in that context. The second set of books has its origins in the engineering field and focus more on IT applications in project management, concurrent engineering, and related topics (e.g., Stark, 1992; Turner & Simister, 2000). However, these books have limited focus on management issues and, moreover, they are based primarily on the engineering management literature and as such do not draw on research in other management areas.

This book focuses solely on IT and product/service development, and the various chapters draw on a wide range of management disciplines including organizational behavior, strategy, marketing, and operations. As such, it is designed to address the above gap in the literature and to promote a more integrated research approach in this area.

This book is intended to appeal to two sets of audiences. The primary audience is academic researchers in the management field. For this audience, the book offers an in-depth theoretical analysis of the wide range of organizational and management issues associated with the application of IT in product and service development. By presenting a diverse set of theoretical perspectives and models, the book will hopefully serve as a reference source for researchers from different fields (including information systems, marketing, operations, and organizational behavior) who are currently pursuing (or plan to pursue) research in this area. Given the broad treatment of the subject, the proposed book could also serve as material for doctoral level courses in information systems, information management, NPD, innovation management, and other related areas.

The book is also intended to appeal to researchers and other thought leaders in consulting organizations such as PRTM, Gartner, and Accenture whose primary area of interest is product development and/or IT applications. For example, many such consulting companies have a practice that is devoted to guiding companies in the deployment of PLM solutions. The models and concepts discussed in this book could serve as the foundation for developing a set of practical guidelines and strategies for the management of PLM tools.

## 1.6 The Organization of the Book

The book is organized into three parts. Part I (comprised of four chapters) follows this introductory chapter and focuses on the traditional areas of project and process management. Part II (comprised of four chapters) focuses on the emerging areas of collaborative innovation and knowledge co-creation. Part III (comprised of one chapter) draws on the various chapters and identifies some of the important themes and issues for future research on the broad topic of IT and product development. The specific chapters and their brief descriptions are given below.

In Chapter 2, Robert G. Fichman and Satish Nambisan propose a complementarities-based theoretical framework to examine the business value of IT applications for product development. Many companies that have made considerable investments in IT applications to support their product development activities have realized limited value from such efforts. In this chapter, we argue that a deep understanding of the complementarities that exist in the product development context is critical to ensure that business value is derived from the IT applications. We propose a multi-level complementarities-based model of IT innovation and business value to explain the factors that shape the success of IT-enabled product development. Our model posits that firms will obtain more value from innovative IT investment initiatives when the resulting IT applications are fitted into a system of *initiative or product development context-specific* complementary organizational elements (strategies, structures, processes, etc.). Further, firms will get more value from IT initiatives when investment is combined with certain firm-level elements such as a business strategy that is especially amenable to IT support, strong IT capabilities, and a modern organizational architecture that incorporates a cluster of practices associated with "digital" organizations. The model can guide researchers and managers in identifying the firm-level pre-conditions for realizing value from investments in IT to support product development and specifying necessary complementary investments in organizational change associated with product development.

In Chapter 3, Emma O'Brien, Darren Harris, and Mark Southern emphasize the importance of experiments to develop a better understanding of product development processes. In today's dynamic business world, the ability to continuously innovate and respond to customers' needs is fundamental to success. To enable companies to do this a thorough understanding of their internal processes is required. Experiments can provide significant opportunities for companies to generate knowledge about their product development processes. This chapter examines the role of experimentation in designing robust product development processes and the role of IT in supporting this. It outlines an IT-based knowledge-management system to support the creation, transfer, and the use of knowledge amongst engineers in designing and conducting experiments that lead to robust product development processes. The authors conclude the chapter with a discussion of the key issues for future research on this topic.

In Chapter 4, Julian Malins and Aggelos Liapis focus on the application of IT-based tools in product design consultancy firms. Product design and development processes do not always proceed in a linear step-by-step manner, starting with the initial problem leading to a solution consisting of a number of clearly defined steps in between. As such the development of IT-based tools to support this process is also far from straightforward. It requires considerable creativity to design IT-based systems that can enhance product designer's capabilities without detracting from the creative process. In this chapter, the authors offer insights into the use of various IT-based systems that have been developed in response to the requirements of a contemporary design consultancy. Specifically, the chapter examines the various stages in the design process based on a case study of a London-based design consultancy, Studio Levien. The authors use the case study to illustrate the key IT-based elements required to support the design process and to discuss their implications for research and practice.

Chapter 5 brings the focus to PLM as the author Andy Hewett provides a view from the field of the critical challenges related to PLM implementation. As noted previously, PLM has emerged as perhaps the most important enterprise IT application for supporting product and service innovation. This chapter examines the unique challenges associated with implementing PLM. Specifically, the chapter focuses on three primary organizational challenges: (a) cultural issues around the "product engineer"; (b) a lack of standard engineering processes as a foundation for PLM; and (c) the failings of the PLM technology itself. The discussion enables a better appreciation of the value a strong resource like a "senior engineering fellow" adds to the project team and underlies the differences between truly standard functional activities (such as accounting) and product development processes, and how these differences could potentially reduce the repeatability of PLM implementations. The discussion also highlights the technical complexity in most PLM solutions that arises from bolting together diverse modules needed to address the different business functions associated with product development. The chapter concludes by identifying several important directions for future research on PLM implementation.

In Chapter 6, Satish Nambisan considers the role of IT in supporting customer value co-creation and co-innovation. The author introduces the concept of virtual customer environments (VCEs) – IT-enabled customer co-innovation platforms – and identifies the different issues and challenges related to the successful design and deployment of such VCEs. The varied roles that customers can play in innovation and value creation are identified and the specific ways in which VCEs can support each of those roles are also discussed. The author also considers the design aspects of VCEs that would enhance particular types of incentives for customers to participate in value co-creation and co-innovation. The chapter emphasizes the need to adopt specific strategies and practices to enhance customers' overall interaction experience in VCEs, to embrace customers as partners in innovation and value creation, and to derive value from their customers' innovative contributions.

In Chapter 7, Elisa Fredericks and Dawn R. Schneider emphasize the need for companies to redefine the structure and organization of their product (service) development teams as they shift from closed innovation practices to open innovation practices. External environmental pressures resulting from increasing globalization, rapid technological advancements, and a fluctuating marketplace force firms to continually rethink their innovation models. Newer models suggest more open collaboration, increased interdependence between firms, shared resources, and network-centric practices. As firms adapt to more openness, boundaries blur between intra- and inter-organizational teams. Challenges surface regarding how to manage new relationships within the firm as well as those with customers, suppliers, and even competitors involved in innovation. The authors characterize closed and more open innovation models and compare and contrast factors facilitating the use of each of the models. They explore the role of the team, a pivotal force spearheading innovation, and the role of IT in supporting both teams and teamwork. While IT makes it possible to structure, facilitate, and manage open innovation, increasing demand for alternative and more adaptive innovation models will spur an increased demand for new forms of technology that can make it all possible. Through in-depth case study analysis and an extensive review of the literature, the authors examine the key factors that are likely to shape innovation success in the future. The chapter ends with several suggestions for future research on this topic.

In Chapter 8, Priya Nambisan focuses on the role of online health information technologies in facilitating collaborative service innovation in the healthcare sector. In the past few years, consumer participation in health care has increased significantly with the ready availability of medical information on health web sites and the ability to interact in disease-focused online health communities. Importantly, such consumer participation also involves creating new knowledge based on consumers' direct experiences with particular diseases and treatments – new knowledge that could lead to new or improved services. Such consumer-driven service innovation has assumed critical importance as most healthcare organizations come under considerable pressure to enhance the value they offer to their consumers (or patients). The author argues that an important task for value-driven healthcare organizations is to facilitate consumer-driven service innovation in health care through appropriate use of online health information technologies. The author adopts a knowledge creation perspective and proposes a theoretical framework that explains how health web sites and online health communities together can facilitate creation of innovative service ideas through knowledge socialization, combination, externalization, and internalization. Implications for future research on the role of IT in service innovation in health care are discussed. The implications for strategies and practices adopted by healthcare organizations are also examined.

In Chapter 9, Ikenna S. Uzuegbunam focuses on IT-based virtual ties that assume importance in the development of complex product systems (CoPS). Specifically, the author examines the value of "virtual embeddedness" in the context of firms that develop CoPS. The development of CoPS usually involves many firms working together. Firms may choose to maintain arm's length relationships with their partners. But often they must coordinate product development through more embedded interactions because of the intricate nature of systems development in CoPS. Although embeddedness can be socially constructed, the rise of Internet and digital technologies have given way to the emergence of a new form of embeddedness – virtual embeddedness, which provides CoPS firms with unprecedented opportunities for learning economies in the process of product development. Based on a new typology of virtual embeddedness in organizational space, the author argues that virtual embeddedness is a good complementary vehicle to modularity in the management of product development among CoPS firms. The chapter concludes with a discussion of the important implications for future research in this area.

In the concluding chapter, Chapter 10, Satish Nambisan draws on the issues discussed in the different chapters and outlines an agenda for future research on IT and product/service development. It is evident that much of the focus is needed on understanding how IT can be intertwined with the structure and the processes that underlie the dominant innovation model of the future, namely, collaborative or network-centric innovation. This will require bringing together concepts and insights from different theoretical areas and perspectives to explain how varied IT capabilities may enhance the nature and process of collaborative innovation. A second emphasis of future research should be on the role of IT in increasing the rigor and discipline of product and service innovation. The different issues that fall within these two themes present a challenging but rewarding agenda for future research – one that could help redefine the role of IT in product and service innovation.

## References


Ali, Y., Ki-Chan, K., Thomas, R., & Matthias, H. (2004). Investigating the role of IT in customized product design. *Production Planning & Control, 15*(4), 422–435.

Allen, T. J. (1970). Communication networks in R&D laboratories. *R&D Management, 1*, 14–21.

Ancona, D. J, & Caldwell, D. F. (1992). Bridging the boundary: external activity and performance in organizational teams. *Administration Science Quarterly, 37*, 634–665.

Banker, R. D., Bardhan, I., & Asdemir, O. (2006). Understanding the impact of collaboration software on product design and development. *Information Systems Research, 17*(4), 352–374.

Bardhan, I. (2007). Toward a theory to study the use of collaborative product commerce for product development. *Information Technology and Management, 8*(2), 167–180.

Boutellier, R. Gassman, O., Macho, H., & Roux, M. (1998). Management of dispersed product development teams: The role of information technologies. *R&D Management, 28*(1), 13–25.

Brown, S. L., & Eisenhardt, K.M. (1995). Product development: Past research, present findings, and future directions. *Academy of Management Review, 20*, 343–378.

Chesbrough, H., & Spohrer, J. (2006). A research manifesto for services science. *Communications of the ACM, 49*(7), 35–40.

Clark, K. B., & Fujimoto. T. (1991). *Product development performance*. Boston: Harvard Business School Press.

Clarke, S. (2007). *Information systems strategic management: An integrated approach*. NewYork: Routledge.

Cooper, R. G. (2001). *Winning at new products*. Cambridge, MA: Perseus Publications.

Cooper R. G., & Kleinschmidt, E. J. (2001). Portfolio management for new product development: Results of an industry practices study. *R&D Management, 31*(4).

Cooper, R. G., Edgett, S. J., & Kleinschmidt, E. J. (1999). New product portfolio management: Practices and performance. *Journal of Product Innovation Management, 16*(4), 333–351.

Cramton, D. (2001). The mutual knowledge problem and its consequences for dispersed collaboration. *Organization Science, 12*(3), 346–371.

Cusumano, M., & Nobeoka, K. (1992). Strategy, structure, and performance in product development: Observations from the auto industry. *Research Policy, 21*, 265–293.

Dahan, E., & Hauser, J. R. (2001). Managing a dispersed product development process. In B. Weitz & R. Wensley (Eds.), *Handbook of marketing*. New York: Sage Publications.

Dahan, E., & Hauser, J. (2002). The virtual customer. *Journal of Product Innovation Management, 19*(5), 332–353.

Denno, P., & Thurman, T. (2005). Requirements on information technology for product lifecycle management. *International Journal of Product Development, 2*(1), 109–120.

Dougherty, D. (1992). Interpretive barriers to successful product innovation in large firms. *Organizafion Science, 3*, 179–202.

Durmusglu, S., Calantone, R., & Sambamurthy, V. (2006). Is more information technology better for new product development? *The Journal of Product and Brand Management, 15*(7), 435–445.

Elliott, S., Gill, R., & Nelson, B. (2001). How Web-enabled tools can help optimize new product initiatives. *Visions Magazine, 25*(4), 13–17.

Ettlie, J., & Pavlou, P. (2006). Technology-based new product development partnerships. *Decision Sciences, 37*(2), 117–140.

Gawer, A., & Cusumano, M. (2002). *Platform Leadership: How Intel, Microsoft, and Cisco drive industry innovation.* Boston, MA: Harvard Business School Press.

Gomes-Casseres, B. (1994). Group versus group: How alliance networks compete. *Harvard Business Review, 72*(4), 62–74.

Griffin, A. (1997). *Drivers of NPD success: The 1997 PDMA report.* Chicago, IL: Product Development & Management Association.

Griffin, A., & Hauser, J. (1993). The voice of the customer. *Marketing Science, 12*(1), 1–27.

Griffin, A., & Hauser, J. R. (1996). Integrating R&D and marketing: A review and analysis of the literature. *Journal of Product Innovation Management, 13*(3), 191–215.

Hameri, A., & Nihtila, J. (1997). Distributed new product development project based on Internet and the World-Wide Web. *Journal of Product Innovation Management, 14*(2), 77–87.

Hayes, R. H., Wheelwright, S. C., & Clark, K. (1988). *Dynamic manufacturing*. New York: Free Press.

Imai, K., Ikujiro, N., & Takeuchi, H. (1985). Managing the new product development process: How Japanese companies learn and unlearn. In R. H. Hayes, K. Clark, & Lorenz (Eds.), *The uneasy alliance: Managing the productivity-technology dilemma* (pp. 337–375). Boston: Harvard Business School Press.

Jarvenpaa, S. L., & Leidner, D. E. (1999). Communication and trust in global virtual teams. *Organization Science, 10*(6), 791–815.

Joglekar, N. R., & Yassine, A. (2002). Management of information technology driven product development processes. In T. Boone & R. Ganeshan (Eds.), *New directions in supply-chain management.* Amacon Press.

Katz, R., & Tushman, M. L. (1981). An investigation into the managerial roles and career paths of gatekeepers and project supervisors in a major R&D facility. *R&D Management, 11*, 103–110.

Krishnan, V., & Ulrich, K. T. (2001). Product development decisions: A review of the literature. *Management Science, 47*(1), 1–21.

Li, W. D. & Qiu, Z. M. (2006). State-of-the-art technologies and methodologies for collaborative product development systems. *International Journal of Production Research, 44*(3), 2525–2540.

Mahajan, V., & Wind, J. (1992). New product models: Practice, shortcomings, and desired improvements. *Journal of Product Innovation Management, 9*(2), 128–139.

Majchrzak, A., Rice, R., Malhotra, A., Nelson, K., & Ba, S. (2000). Technology adaptation: The case of a computer-supported inter-organizational team. *MIS Quarterly, 24*(4), 569–600.

Malhotra, A., Majchrzak, A., Carman, R., & Lott, V. (2001). Radical innovation without collocation: A case study at Boeing-Rocketdyne. *MIS Quarterly, 25*(2), 229–250.

Mansfield, E. (1968). *Industrial research and technical innovation.* New York: Norton.

Maznevski, M. L., & Chudoba, K. M. (2000). Bridging space over time: Global virtual team dynamics and effectiveness. *Organization Science, 11*(5), 473–492.

McGrath, M., & Iansiti, M. (1998, Fall/Winter). Envisioning IT-enabled innovation. *Insight Magazine*, 2–10.

Meyer, M., & Lehnerd, A. P. (1997). *The power of product platforms*, NewYork: The Free Press.

Nahass, P. (2001). Web-enabling the stage-gate process at Albany international: Lessons learned and benefits derived. *Visions Magazine, 25*(3), 14–16.

Nambisan, S. (2001). Why service businesses are not product businesses. *MIT Sloan Management Review, 42*(4), 72–80.

Nambisan, S. (2002). Designing virtual customer environments for new product development: Toward a theory. *Academy of Management Review, 27*(3), 392–413.

Nambisan, S. (2003). Information systems as a reference discipline for new product development. *MIS Quarterly, 27*(1), 1–18.

Nambisan, S., & Sawhney, M. (2007). *The Global Brain: Your roadmap for innovating faster and smarter in a networked world*. Pennsylvania: Wharton School Publishing.

Nambisan, S., & Nambisan, P. (2008, Spring). How to Profit from a Better "Virtual Customer Environment." *MIT Sloan Management Review*, 53–61.

Ozer, M. (2000). Information technology and new product development: Opportunities and pitfalls. *Industrial Marketing Management, 29*, 387–396.

Paulk, M. C., Weber, C., Curtis, B., & Chrissis, M. (1995). *The capability maturity model*. NewYork: Addison-Wesley.

Pavlou, P., & Sawy, O. (2006). From IT leveraging competence to competitive advantage in turbulent environments: The case of new product development. *Information Systems Research, 17*(3), 198–220.

Pearlson, K. (2004). *Managing and using information systems: A strategic approach*. Hoboken, NJ: Wiley.

Prahalad, C. K., & Ramaswamy, V. (2003). *The future of competition: Co-creating Value with customers*. Boston: HBS Press.

Rothaermel, F. T. (2001). Incumbents' advantage through exploiting complementary assets via interfirm cooperation. *Strategic Management Journal, 22*, 687–699.

Rothwell, R., Freeman, C., Jervis, P., Robertson, A., & Townsend, J. (1974). SAPPHO Updated – Project SAPPHO Phase 2. *Research Policy, 3*, 258–291.

Rust, R. T., & Chung, T. S. (2006). Marketing models and relationships. *Marketing Science, 25*, 560–580.

Sawhney, M., & Prandelli, E. (2000). Communities of creation: Managing distributed innovation in turbulent markets. *California Management Review, 42*(4), 24–54.

Schilling, M. A., & Hill, C. (1998). Managing the new product development process: Strategic imperatives. *Academy of Management Executive, 12*(3), 67–81.

Sethi, R., Pant, S., & Sethi, A. (2003). Web-based product development systems integration and new product outcomes: A conceptual framework. *The Journal of Product Innovation Management, 20*(1), 37–47.

Stark, J. (1992). *Engineering information management systems: Beyond CAD/CAM to concurrent engineering support*. New York: Van Nostrand Reinhold.

Su, C., Chen, Y., & Yung-Jye, D. (2007). Managing product and customer knowledge in innovative new product development. *International Journal of Technology Management, 39*(1), 105–110.

Tatikonda, M. V., & Montoya-Weiss, M. M. (2001). Integrating operations and marketing perspective of product innovation. *Management Science, 47*(1), 151–172.

Teresko, J. (2004). The PLM revolution. *Industry Week/IW, 253*(2), 32–37.

Thomke, S., & von Hippel, E. (2002). Customers as innovators: A new way to create value. *Harvard Business Review, 80*(4), 74–81.

Tidd, J., Bessant J., & Pavitt, K. (2001). *Managing innovation: Integrating technological, market and organizational change*. Chichester, England: John Wiley & Sons Ltd.

Tripsas, M. (1997). Unraveling the process of creative destruction: Complementary assets and incumbent survival in the Typesetter Industry. *Strategic Management Journal, 18*, 119–142.

Turner, R., & Simister, S. (2000). *Gower handbook of project management* (3rd ed.). Burlington, VT: Gower.
Ulrich, K., & Eppinger, S. D. (2000). *Product design and development.* Boston, MA: McGraw-Hill.
von Hippel, E. (1988). *The sources of innovation*. New York: Oxford University Press.
Vries, E. J. (2006). Innovation in services in networks of organizations and in the distribution of services. *Research Policy, 35*, 1037–1051.
Xu, L., Li, Z., Li S., & Tang, F. (2007). A decision support system for product design in concurrent engineering. *Decision Support Systems, 42*(4), 2029–2034.

# Part I
# IT and Project and Process Management

# Chapter 2
# Deriving Business Value from IT Applications in Product Development: A Complementarities-Based Model

**Robert G. Fichman and Satish Nambisan**

**Abstract** Many companies that have made considerable investments in IT applications to support their product development activities have realized limited value from such efforts. In this chapter, we argue that a deep understanding of the complementarities that exist in the product development context is critical to ensure that business value is derived from the IT applications. We propose a multi-level complementarities-based model of IT innovation and business value to explain the factors that shape the success of IT-enabled product development. Our model posits that firms will obtain more value from innovative IT investment initiatives when the resulting IT applications are fitted into a system of *initiative or product development context-specific* complementary organizational elements (strategies, structures, processes, etc.). Further, firms will get more value from IT initiatives when investment is combined with certain firm-level elements such as a business strategy that is especially amenable to IT support, strong IT capabilities, and a modern organizational architecture that incorporates a cluster of practices associated with "digital" organizations. The model can guide researchers and managers in identifying the firm-level pre-conditions for realizing value from investments in IT to support product development and specifying necessary complementary investments in organizational change associated with product development.

## 2.1 Introduction

In recent years, IT applications that support product life cycle management (PLM) have assumed critical importance as companies focus on enhancing the efficiency and effectiveness of their innovation processes across the enterprise. PLM applications provide a common information backbone for all of the company's product development initiatives and also offer connectivity with other business operations through seamless integration with enterprise IT applications such as enterprise

---

R.G. Fichman (✉)
Carroll School of Management, Boston College, 410A Fulton Hall, 140 Commonwealth Ave, Chestnut Hill, MA, USA
e-mail: fichman@bc.edu

S. Nambisan (ed.), *Information Technology and Product Development*, Annals of Information Systems 5, DOI 10.1007/978-1-4419-1081-3_2,

resource planning (ERP) and customer relationship management (CRM) (Grieves, 2006; Saaksvuori, 2008).

The promise and the potential of PLM applications to reduce product development cost and time and enhance product quality have led companies to invest heavily in PLM applications. Indeed, the PLM market was approximately $25 billion in 2007 and is expected to grow up to $40 billion by 2012 (CIM, 2008). Despite these large investments in PLM applications, however, few companies have realized the set of benefits that have been predicted. To certain extent, the failure to realize value from PLM applications could be traced to the lack of maturity or quality of the PLM solutions themselves. However, it also points to a larger issue that is plaguing investments in other enterprise IT applications too – the lack of "fit" between the elements of IT and other organizational resources and the resulting disconnect between IT investments and the business value from such investments.

In this chapter, we formalize one important kind of "fit" between IT and organization and inform on the linkages between IT innovation investments and business value by drawing on the *logic of complementarities* (Milgrom & Roberts, 1990, 1995). Specifically, we develop a multi-level, complementarities-based model of IT innovation investments and business value. Our model posits that firms will obtain more value from innovative IT investment initiatives when the resulting IT applications are fitted into a system of *initiative specific* – here, product development context specific – complementary organizational elements (strategies, structures, processes, etc.). In addition, we argue that firms will get more value from IT investment initiatives when they are combined with certain firm-level elements that are not specific to any particular initiative, but rather, complement IT investments more generally construed. These firm-level complements include a business strategy that is especially amenable to IT support, strong IT capabilities, and a modern organizational architecture that incorporates a cluster of practices associated with "digital" organizations (Brynjolfsson, 2003).

The integrated theoretical model of IT innovation investments and business value makes several important and timely contributions. First and foremost, it helps to enhance our understanding of the complementary organizational strategies and practices that would need to accompany the implementation of IT applications (such as PLM) to support product development. Recognition of the broader product development context in which these IT applications are situated also raises several interesting issues for future research in both IT and product development areas.

Second, we use the logic of complementarities to join two important streams of IT research that have proceeded largely in parallel: An *innovation stream* that has examined the determinants of innovative initiatives to adopt and deploy new IT (Fichman, 2000) and a *business value stream* that has examined the contribution of IT investments to organizational performance (Melville, Kraemer, & Gurbaxani 2004). In doing so, we contribute to a better understanding of both firm-level pre-conditions and initiative-level complementary investments that are required to generate business value from IT investments in general.

Finally, investments in IT have increased over the years to the point where IT now represents over half of all capital investments in most companies. Despite increasing evidence that IT investments pay off in aggregate, we still see that IT initiatives produce dramatically varying outcomes from firm to firm, and even from initiative to initiative within a given firm. Our model seeks to account for this variation by using the economic logic of complementarities to analyze why certain clusters of organizational elements should be observed in conjunction with more successful IT investment and deployment. Thus, we contribute to the domain of IT and organizational design by redefining (or, re-conceptualizing) the concept of "fit" between IT and organization and by providing a precise logic for generating eminently testable hypotheses that relate IT to other organizational elements.

The remainder of this chapter is organized as follows. In Section 2.2, we discuss the "disconnect" between the IT innovation investments and the IT business value literatures, and establish the critical need to develop an integrated theory of IT investments, IT innovation, and business value, and the promise of the "complementarities approach" for doing so. In Section 2.3, we review the literature on the logic of complementarities and its application in the innovation and IT literatures. Section 2.4 provides an overview of our research model, and in Sections 2.5 and 2.6, we present the micro-level (i.e., PLM or IT initiative-level) and the macro-level (i.e., firm-level) parts of our model respectively. We conclude the chapter by discussing the important implications of the model for future research and managerial practice.

## 2.2 IT Investments and Business Value of IT: The Missing Link

The streams of research on IT innovation and IT business value have proceeded largely in parallel. The IT innovation stream has primarily been the province of behavioral science researchers and has addressed two general questions (Cooper & Zmud, 1990; Swanson, 1994): (1) Why are some organizations more prone to exhibit innovative behaviors than others? and (2) Why do some innovations diffuse more widely and rapidly than others? The IT business value stream, on the other hand, has mainly been the province of economics researchers, who have been concerned with establishing whether investments in IT produce business value and under what conditions this value will be greatest (Barua & Mukhopadhyay, 2000; Brynjolfsson & Hitt, 1996; Kohli & Devaraj, 2003; Melville et al., 2004).

The central goal of the IT innovation research stream has been to identify the determinants of IT adoption and implementation. This research has been guided by a number of theoretical perspectives, including the traditional communications-based diffusion of innovation model (Rogers, 2003), adaptive structuration (DeSanctis & Poole, 1994), the technology acceptance model and related approaches (Venkatesh, Morris, Davis, & Davis, 2003), organizational learning (Nambisan & Wang, 2000; Purvis, Sambamurthy, & Zmud, , 2001), network effects (Markus, 1987), institutions (Teo, Wei, & Benbasat, 2003), power and influence (Hart & Saunders,

1997), and mindfulness (Swanson & Ramiller, 2004) to name a few of the more prominent ones. This research has identified scores of different variables that influence organizational innovation with IT – variables pertaining to characteristics of the technologies themselves (e.g., compatibility), characteristics of leaders (e.g., degree of top management support), organizational structural characteristics (e.g., size), characteristics of the workforce (e.g., level of technical knowledge), environmental influences (e.g., competitive pressures), and implementation processes and tactics (e.g., innovation champions) (Fichman, 2000).

While the IT innovation stream has been concerned with whether organizations thoroughly deploy the innovations they have adopted, the ultimate organizational impacts that flow from deployment have been viewed as generally falling outside the scope of this stream, possibly because innovation behaviors are viewed as of intrinsic interest regardless of their specific impacts, or because their impacts are presumed to be generally beneficial (the so-called pro innovation bias), or because of the difficulty of examining both IT deployment and IT impacts within the confines of a single study. Whatever the reason, the absence of work that relates business value to innovation antecedents and behaviors leaves some important questions unanswered, such as how does the extent of deployment relate to business value? Besides the extent of deployment, what conditions at (a) the IT initiative-level and (b) the firm-level affect business value? How can we specify and measure these conditions so as to lead to actionable insights?

One might expect that the natural place to look for answers to the above questions would be the research on the business value of IT. However, with some notable exceptions to be discussed shortly, this research is generally conducted at a level of abstraction and aggregation that precludes answering these specific sorts of questions. Business value research tends to view IT as monolithic: Studies will often link firm-level IT spending or accumulated IT capital stock to firm-level business value (e.g., multi-factor productivity or accounting measures of profits and costs). Such measures of IT investment represent only a partial view of what has actually been spent on IT, and more to the point, do not capture what specific kinds of IT were invested in, when and how the investments occurred, or to what extent such investments can even be viewed as being "innovative."

So, unlike IT innovation research, IT business value research tends not to be contextualized to particular kinds of IT or organizational adopters, and this research does not usually link IT investment and business value to specific innovative behaviors, such as investment timing or extent of deployment. Despite this general stance, there are some notable exceptions. Dos Santos and Peffers (1995) showed that banks that had adopted ATM networks earlier gained a competitive advantage, thus linking an innovation concept (i.e., adoption timing) to business value (i.e., profitability). Hitt, Wu, and Zhou (2001) showed that greater operational improvements occurred for firms that had implemented ERP earlier and more thoroughly. Devaraj and Kohli (2003) linked the extent of IT use in a hospital setting to operational performance improvements. Karimi, Somers, and Bhattacherjee (2007) studied the impact of the extent of ERP implementation (functional scope, geographic scope, organizational scope, etc. of the solution) on business process outcomes (such as process flexibility, process efficiency). Similarly, Mishra, Konana, and Barua (2007) found that the extent of Internet use in procurement order initiation and completion had positive impact on the organization's overall procurement performance.

Despite the just-mentioned empirical work, there is as yet no systematic theoretical model that joins IT innovation and IT business value. Nevertheless, a fair question to ask at this point is why do we need a theory that spans these two domains, and supposing one is needed, why should this integration be based on complementarities? We suggest the following points in answer to these questions.

First, managers need to understand the whole chain of causation from investment to IT deployment and to business value. The bulk of innovation research cannot distinguish instances of IT deployment that produce value from instances that do not. The business value research stream, on the other hand, tends to treat the organization as a black box: IT investment comes in, and business value comes out, but specific causal mechanisms are usually left unspecified. By providing an integrated theory based on complementarities, we not only identify or specify the IT and the organizational design elements that fall inside such a "black box," but also explain how one element or factor "catalyzes" another factor and contributes to the generation of business value. Further, while we do not develop a process perspective of how the IT and the complementary organizational elements come into existence or co-evolve, our specification of an integrated model is a first step in that direction.

An additional advantage of the complementarities approach is that it provides a broad, but still, manageable theoretical scope and allows a clear specification of the model's theoretical boundaries. More importantly, the complementarities approach suggests that many of the same variables affect both IT innovation and IT business value, thus resulting in a true theoretical integration, rather than a "bolting together" of a model of innovation with a model of business value.

## 2.3 The Logic of Complementarities

Complementarities exist when doing more of one thing increases the returns to doing more of another. Thus, complementarities refer to a synergy between two variables as they impact a third variable. In a landmark paper that formalizes some key mathematical foundations of complementarities, Milgrom and Roberts (1990) provide an extended example of complementarities in action using a stylized description of computer-aided design (CAD). They recount how CAD has automatic links to programmable manufacturing equipment, and hence increases the returns to use of such equipment. CAD also makes it easier to update products more frequently and thereby encourages a broader product line. This, in turn, encourages shorter production runs, lower inventories, and a switch to more flexible manufacturing equipment that is cheaper to change over. They sum up their argument like so: "Thus CAD equipment, flexible manufacturing technologies, shorter production runs, lower inventories, increased data communication, and more frequent product redesigns are complementary" (1990). However, the complementarities are not limited to manufacturing, but spill over into marketing (e.g., faster delivery cycles and a higher emphasis on quality are encouraged) and engineering (e.g., design-for-manufacturability is encouraged).

Given the enormity of the potential benefits extending across multiple functions and indeed the entire enterprise, one might expect that manufacturing firms would have been especially quick to adopt and deploy this technology. However, the actual history of CAD adoption followed a much different story line. The technology was indeed rapidly acquired by manufacturing firms, but many years elapsed before it was actually utilized in a way consistent with the vision of the technology's designers. Liker et al. report that as late as in 1992, a decade after CAD was introduced, "true CAD/CAM [utilization was] still quite rare" (Liker, Fleischer, & Arnsdorf, 1992).

A variety of explanations could account for the slow deployment of CAD, such as technological immaturity, the difficulty of organizational learning, and incentive conflicts. However, the logic of complementarities itself provides an additional compelling explanation: If the majority of CAD's benefits only arise when the technology is combined into a complementary system of elements, this fact would actually serve to *magnify* the ill-effects of technological immaturity, learning barriers, local incentive conflicts, etc. An immature technology tends to have "bugs" (features that are missing, underdeveloped, or just do not work as they should). If benefits are not materializing, how does an organization sort out which problems are due to "bugs" in the technology, or "bugs" in the design of the surrounding organization? If the technology itself is hard to understand due to knowledge barriers, it will be that much more difficult to anticipate the best configuration of complementary organizational elements to build around it. If the technology poses incentive conflicts, that will make it more difficult to rally the whole organization around the need to make complementary organizational changes. Thus, in what might be seen as a supreme irony, complementarities not only magnify the beneficial effects of innovation investment when things go favorably, but may well make it less likely that things will go favorably by magnifying the effects of typical implementation barriers.

### *2.3.1 Complementarities-Based Studies in Innovation and IT Business Value Research*

As the CAD example shows, IT investment entwines with organizational innovation and business value in a manner consistent with the logic of complementarities. Thus, it is not surprising that complementarities have been receiving increasing attention from both innovation scholars and IT business value researchers. In this section, we step back to formalize the logic of complementarities and briefly survey some important empirical work.

According to Milgrom and Roberts, two activities are "Edgeworth" complements if "doing (more of) one thing increases the returns to doing (more of) the others" (1995: 181). A necessary condition for the existence of complementarities is that the effects of two variables (A, B) on a third variable (C) be *supermodular*; that is, the total effects of A and B together must be greater than the sum of the effects of A individually plus B individually. For example, in the CAD case, more investment in and usage of CAD equipment (A) increases the value generating potential of "design-for manufacturability" (B), and vice versa. Thus, value produced from the combination of CAD usage together with design-for manufacturability is greater than the sum of the returns to either taken individually, meaning these two elements are supermodular.

Several alternative statistical approaches have been used to infer the presence of complementarities, including pairwise partial correlations (Colombo & Mosconi, 1995; Hitt & Brynjolfsson, 1997), interaction terms (Bresnahan, Brynjolfsson, & Hitt, 2002; Powell & Dent-Micallef, 1997; Zhu, 2004), and second-order factors (Laursen & Foss, 2003; Tanriverdi & Venkatraman, 2005). Brynjolfsson and Hitt (2003) take a different approach, and infer the presence of complementarities by demonstrating multi-year lags in the arrival of productivity improvements.

In empirical work by organizational innovation researchers, complementarities have been used to explain the linkage between a cluster of a system of "new" human resource practices and greater innovation performance (Laursen & Foss, 2003); the synergy between technological and product market experience in promoting new product development in the pharmaceutical industry (Nerkar & Roberts, 2004); and the effects of business knowledge synergies on performance in multi-business firms (Tanriverdi & Venkatraman, 2005).

Empirical work by IT business value researchers has demonstrated that firm performance is enhanced by combining IT investment with the following complementary sets of elements: flexible culture, strategic planning–IT integration, and strong supplier relationships (Powell & Dent-Micallef, 1997); and decentralization of decision authority, emphasis on subjective incentives, and a greater reliance on skills and human capital (Hitt & Brynjolfsson, 1997). In other notable work, Zhu (2004) found that e-commerce capabilities and IT infrastructure were complementary in their effects on firm-level performance.

Complementarities have also been the subject of theorizing by IT business value researchers. Melville et al. (2004) give a prominent treatment to complementarities in IT business value framework synthesized from a comprehensive review of the literature. In an earlier review of the IT business value literature, Barua and Mukhopadhyay (2000) suggest that complementarities represent the most promising route forward for business value research. They use complementarities to develop a sketch of a theory in which business strategies, IT applications, business processes, and organizational incentives/controls form a complementary system that enhances intermediate firm outcomes (e.g., customer service, time to market, and inventory turnover).

The growing streams of research linking complementarities to innovation and to business value suggest that complementarities hold considerable problem as a foundation for theory that joins both IT innovation and business value. In the following section, we use complementarities to develop a coherent theory of IT investment, innovation, and business value.

## 2.4 Model Overview: Complementarities, IT Innovation Investments, and Business Value

In this section, we summarize the structure of our complementarities-based model of IT innovation and business value. We also comment on some of the finer points of the model structure and the theoretical assumptions behind it. Then, in the following sections, we give a more detailed explanation of our theoretical constructs and linkages.

Our proposed model operates at two levels of analysis: a *micro-level* that concerns the details of a specific innovative initiative and a *macro-level* that concerns firm-level variables affecting a whole class of IT. We envision four separate chains of causation in the model, labeled A–D in Fig. 2.1. One of these chains operates at the micro-level (A), while the other three (B, C, D) involve macro-level variables.

The micro-level of our model concerns a specific initiative to deploy some emerging IT – for example, PLM to support product development projects, where deployment refers to the breadth and depth of use of the technology itself (see Table 2.1 for suggested measures for IT deployment).

In our first causal chain (link A in Fig. 2.1), we argue that organizations will be better positioned to gain business value from such initiatives when they have coupled the deployment of the technology with a complementary set of initiative-related organizational elements: organizational strategies, structures, processes, policies, skills, and so forth. These initiative-related organizational elements could be pre-existing, co-implemented with the technology, or introduced after implementation.

Many scholars have argued that the scope of "technology" implementation should be expanded to include associated organizational changes (Leonard-Barton, 1988; Orlikowski, 1996). We contribute to this prior work by providing a formal and comprehensive argument relating complementarities to organizational design and change. More specifically, we posit that IT deployment and certain initiative-specific organizational elements will be supermodular, i.e., their combined impacts on business value will be greater than the sum of their individual impacts.

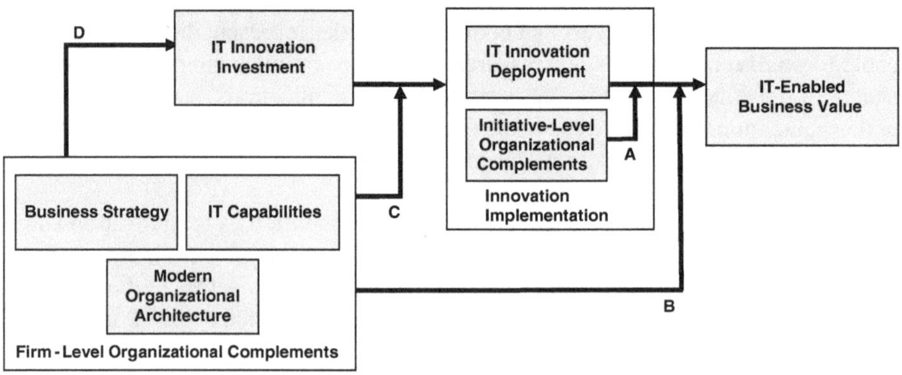


**Fig. 2.1** A complementarities-based model of IT innovation and firm value

**Table 2.1** Measuring IT investment, deployment, and business value

| Construct | Definition | Measures |
|---|---|---|
| IT investment | Extent of IT investment has traditionally been defined as actual capital expenditures on IT hardware (and sometimes, also software and/or labor). We depart from this practice and define the extent of investment in terms of timing, commitment, and scope. | We propose three measures for this construct:<br>(a) Investment timing: Organizations that make earlier investments can be viewed as investing more aggressively. Also, early vintages of a technology are generally more complex and less mature, and so cost more to implement.<br>(b) Organizational commitment to deployment: Organizations that are more certain in their intention to deploy a technology can be viewed as more aggressive than those that are less committed.<br>(c) Intended scope of deployment: This captures the intended breadth and depth of deployment. Organizations that aim for a greater scope of deployment can be viewed as making more aggressive investments. |
| IT innovation deployment | IT innovation deployment refers to the extent to which the IT artifacts comprising the innovation have been implemented throughout the receiving organization in a complete and sophisticated way | We propose two sub-dimensions of IT deployment:<br>Breadth of deployment refers to pervasiveness of technology use in the organization and could be measured as the frequency and extent of technology use across whatever organizational units are most relevant given the nature of the technology (e.g., across people, groups, projects, tasks, and process stages).<br>Depth of deployment refers to the quality of technology use within an organization and could be measured as the number and sophistication of functions in use, the number of inputs/outputs covered by the system, or the variety of information contained with in it. |
| IT-enabled business value | Business value researchers have divided IT-enabled business value into two broad categories: business process level value and firm-level value. Process level measures are specific to the processes affected by the particular IT in question, while firm-level measures transcend any given process or business function. | Measuring process level value requires that the affected business process be identified. Using new process development (NPD) as an example process, these measures could include the following:<br>Return on investment<br>Reduced NPD cycle time and costs<br>Increased speed of requirements and specification changes<br>Increased NPD project performance<br>Increased new product performance<br>Increased product–market fit<br>Increased number of products, services, or businesses launched in a period<br>Increased percent of revenues from new products in a period<br>Firm-level measures are not specific to a particular business process. Possible measures include the following:<br>Improved relative performance on firm-level accounting profit (e.g., ROA, ROS) or cost (e.g., COGS, SGA).<br>Improved relative growth of sales or market share<br>Increased market value or Tobin's Q |

The macro-level of our model pertains to the influence of firm-level variables. As noted in the reviews of empirical research on innovation and business value provided earlier, several organizational elements have been found to complement innovation and IT investment in general. Variables that enhance the effects of IT "in general" would also tend to enhance the effects of IT "in particular" unless there is reason to believe the focal IT is in some way unusual.

In our model, we organize these elements into three categories pertaining to strategy, IT capabilities, and organizational architecture. While prior work has empirically linked many of these firm-level complements to either innovation or IT business value, our contribution is to combine them in an integrated model with well-specified chains of causation. In particular, we posit two different causal chains linking firm-level variables to IT business value, designated by letters B and C in Fig. 2.1.

In the causal chain B, we posit that certain firm-level elements will increase the returns to any given level of IT deployment. For example, when a technology complements the firm's overall strategy, returns from deployment will be higher than when it does not. As a separate causal chain (link C in Fig. 2.1), we argue that these firm-level elements will actually promote more successful innovation deployment through complementarities with the level of IT investment. For example, firms with greater IT capabilities should be better able to plan and manage complex implementations of any given scope. Thus, according to this line of thinking, IT capabilities will magnify the level of IT deployment produced from any given level of IT investment.

As a final causal mechanism (link D in Fig. 2.1), we posit that firms will recognize (explicitly or implicitly) when they hold complementary positions on firm-level elements and will therefore be generally more aggressive when it comes to investing in emerging IT. This does not mean they will necessarily spend more on any given investment initiative. In fact, we can expect that firms that are well positioned (e.g., have strong IT capabilities) will generally have to spend less to achieve any given level IT deployment and business value. Furthermore, other things being equal, deployments that go smoothly should cost less than those that go badly, and ones that go smoothly should produce more business value. As a result, we depart from the traditional practice in IT business value research and suggest that the level of IT investment be measured using variables such as the timing of investment, extent of commitment to deployment, and the intended scope of deployment (see Table 2.1). These measures avoid the paradoxes just mentioned and also have strong linkages with the sorts of innovative behaviors examined in the IT innovation stream.

To wrap up our model overview we discuss three caveats. First, the scope of our model has been intentionally constrained by our interest in complementarities. Therefore, we focus on variables that are plausibly involved in complementary relationships with IT innovation or business value, and even with regard to those variables, we focus on interaction effects consistent with complementarities and give less attention to direct effects. Of course, there are many other variables that potentially affect IT innovation or business directly (as noted in the survey articles cited earlier), but these variables are specifically excluded from the scope of our model.

Second, for each higher-order factor in our model we suggest a representative typology of its potential sub-factors. Our suggestions are not meant to be the only or the "best" typology for each factor, rather just a typology that is representative enough to support more concrete theoretical arguments.

As a third and final caveat, our use of the economic logic of complementarities should not be taken to imply that we have adopted a pure rational-choice perspective on organizational decision making. Our model only requires that when certain organizational elements are present, innovation deployment and business value will be enhanced due to complementarities. While our model does not specify any particular mechanism for how these elements come to be present, we briefly comment on a few possibilities. One mechanism could be an explicit rational-choice process of considering the firm's strategy, IT capabilities, etc., as exemplified in implementation methodologies such as the matrix of change (Brynjolfsson, Renshaw, & Van Alstyne, 1997).

Alternatively, organizational behavior that resembles a rational-choice process could result from implicit assumptions and routines that determine an organization's general innovation posture (more aggressive and less aggressive) toward IT innovation. These implicit assumptions and routines should be more likely in organizations with favorable positions on organizational complements. As a third possibility, it could be assumed that most organizations do little in the way of preplanning, but rather, obtain a fit between technology and organization through cycles of adaptation and learning (Leonard-Barton, 1988). Even so, organizations whose cycles bring them to more favorable systems of complements will be more likely to sustain deployment and will be more likely to gain business value from any given level of deployment. Those that do not will be more likely to have low levels of deployment and business value.

So, our model does not require rational choice. However, there are reasons to believe that a rational-choice process is more likely to maximize business value. A key point made by Milgrom and Roberts (1995) is that partial systems of complements can be sub-optimal or even dysfunctional, and so there is no guarantee that an organization will evolve in an unguided fashion to the best or even a good configuration of complements.

With these caveats out of the way, we now proceed with a detailed development of our model. We begin with the micro-level of the model, and then proceed to the macro-level.

## 2.5 The Micro-level of the Model: Initiative-Specific Organizational Complements

The micro-level of our model specifies that organizations will obtain greater business value from innovative IT when technology deployment is joined with complementary positions on related organizational elements, including strategies, structures, processes. Unlike the macro-level of the model to be described in Section 2.6, the micro-level must be contextualized to a particular technology. Here, we will consider the context of PLM applications. As noted previously, PLM seeks to consolidate all the activities across the NPD life cycle (ideation, design, development, engineering, manufacturing process management, service, maintenance, product line growth, and retirement) under a common application umbrella, with a shared repository of product data (Bylinsky, 2004).

## 2.5.1 Linking IT Deployment and Business Value

In the end, IT can only provide business value based on how – and, how much – it is actually deployed. Despite this fact, comparatively few studies of IT business value have actually incorporated IT use:

> Perhaps one of the most serious issues [pertaining to studies of IT business value] has been that few studies have captured the actual usage of the IT. In addition, merely examining the dollars invested in IT may not be an accurate reflection of the effectiveness of IT because the extent of its usage may vary across industries, firms, or processes. Thus, there is a void in the IT payoff literature in evaluating the impact of individual technology usage on organizational performance. (Devaraj & Kohli, 2003, p. 27)

However, there are exceptions. Devaraj and Kohli (2003) consider the direct effects of IT use on performance, as does Hitt et al. (2001). Also, some work by innovation researchers has posited direct links from innovation to organizational performance (Dos Santos & Peffers 1995; Karimi et al., 2007; Mishra et al., 2007; Ramamurthy, Premkumar, & Crum, 1999; Subramanian & Nilakanta, 1996). While we do not doubt that these direct links are extremely important, we are more interested in specifying how the presence of complementary, initiative-specific organizational elements magnifies the value producing potential of any given level of IT deployment.

## 2.5.2 Complementarities Between Organizational Elements and IT Deployment

> The full advantages of [information] technologies cannot simply be purchased off the shelf; they are won by patiently and carefully tailoring the technology to fit a given firm's organizational and strategic context. At the same time, organizational skills, procedures, and assumptions within the firm need to be adapted to fit the new technology. (Tyre & Orlikowski, 1993, p. 13)

The idea that technology and organization must be fitted to each another in some fashion is a consistent theme that can be seen in such diverse perspectives on technology implementation as socio-technical design (Lyytinen & Mathiassen, 1998), business process reengineering (Davenport & Short, 1990), structuration (Orlikowski, 1992), and mutual adaptation (Leonard-Barton, 1988). However, despite almost universal agreement on this basic point, considerably less agreement exists on what "fit" actually means and exactly why it is important. Sometimes, the nature of "fit" is simply left unspecified, which limits the ability to make specific predictions or to give managerial guidance. This is where the logic of complementarities provides value: It gives an explicit definition of what *constitutes* fit (complementarities), it gives an explicit test for the *presence* of fit (i.e., supermodularity), and it provides a clear specification for the organizational *impacts* of fit (i.e., magnification of the performance-enhancing potential of IT on some variable related to business value).

So far as we are aware, there is no definitive list of organizational elements that can or should be fit to technology. Therefore, based on our review of the literature, we have developed the following representative set of organizational elements: strategies, structures, culture, processes, practices, policies, knowledge and skills, roles, and incentives. To formalize the link between these elements and business value (link A in Fig. 2.1), we offer the following proposition:

**Proposition 1:** *The effects of IT innovation deployment on business value will be reinforced by the presence of complementary initiative-specific organizational elements (strategies, structures, culture, processes, practices, policies, knowledge and skills, roles, and incentives).*

As stated, this proposition is essentially tautological because complementarities, by definition, reinforce effects on the focal performance variable. However, the tautology falls away when the general proposition is contextualized to a particular technology, as it must be. This process of contextualization can be accomplished by studying technology artifacts, examining accounts of the technology's nature and goals, meeting with experts, and conducting field studies of actual implementations.

For example, in the case of PLM application, a complementary strategy may relate to product portfolio management (Cooper & Kleinschmidt, 2001). Companies that invest in portfolio-level capabilities may find that their portfolio management processes reinforce the PLM solution and enable better utilization of critical organizational resources and assets across different projects. Similarly, adoption of process maturity models (such as the capability maturity model) could create a proactive environment for product development projects and enable better utilization of data and information sourced through the PLM application. Another complementary strategy relates to product platforms. A product platform strategy (Gawer & Cusumano, 2002; Meyer & Lehnerd, 1997) emphasizes modularity and the sharing of components across multiple products. Such a strategy would complement the data standardization and the cross-project information sharing capabilities achieved through PLM implementation and that, in turn, would likely enhance the value the organization derives from the IT solution.

We can identify four specific features that distinguish the complementarities approach from other theoretical approaches to linking organizational variables to technology implementation. First, complementarities require the specific designation of a *performance* or output variable whose levels increase in the presence of complements. By contrast, it would probably be a misuse of complementarities as an explanation for non-performance related impacts of technology and innovation. Second, the focus in a complementarities analysis is on explaining *synergies* between technology and organization as they relate to performance, rather than the effects of each variable directly on performance. Third, complementarities often involve *symmetry* between two elements, where not only A reinforces the effect of B on C, but B reinforces the effect of A on C. While we focus on how organizational elements reinforce the effects of IT, we can often reverse the argument to explain how IT reinforces the effects of the organizational elements. Finally, complements often come in *systems* (or clusters) of three or more elements, where each element of the system reinforces the returns to every other element in the system.

A careful analysis of the product development context would reveal a number of other complementary initiative-specific organizational elements that could potentially magnify the business value that the organization derives from the deployment of the PLM application. Thus, overall, the above analysis not only demonstrates how initiative-level complements would reinforce the impact of IT deployment on business value, but also shows how through a careful evaluation of the four features of complementarities-style analyses (focus on a performance variables, synergies, symmetry, and systems of variables), we can isolate the complementarities effect from other kinds relationships in such contexts.

## 2.6 The Macro-level of the Model: Firm-Level Organizational Complements and IT Business Value

The organizational complements we examined in the prior section were specific to a particular type of IT investment initiative. We now move from this micro-level to the macro-level and consider the organizational complements that generalize to an entire class of IT investments rather than a particular type of IT.

We posit three categories of firm-level organizational complements: business strategy, IT capabilities, and organizational architecture. Unlike the micro-level of the model, where complementarities have received less attention, there is considerable prior work that considers complementarities at the macro-level, and our selection of these three categories of variables is based in part on this prior work. We also build on this literature by adding more precision to the consideration of the complementarities effects involving these variables. More importantly, by combining their complementarities effects with regard to IT investment and with regard to IT deployment, we contribute toward a more holistic understanding of the role of firm-level organizational complements in IT innovation and use.

We use a well-known business case to illustrate our arguments, in this instance, Cisco Systems. In so doing, we follow the example of Milgrom and Roberts (1995) who used a reanalysis of the classic Lincoln Electric business case to illustrate the role of complementarities in modern manufacturing.

### 2.6.1 Cisco Systems

In the mid-1990s, Cisco was facing a crisis: Its existing IT infrastructure was becoming increasingly inadequate in the face of the firm's hypergrowth. In a bold maneuver, Cisco conceived and executed a $15 million ERP implementation in only 9 months that, while not without problems, was a remarkable success compared to most ERP implementations of the day (Austin, Nolan, & Cotteleer, 2002). However, this was just the beginning. In the ensuing 2 years Cisco invested $85 million more toward a more ambitious objective, which was to replace all of Cisco's major systems worldwide with a standard Internet-based architecture, i.e., it "web enabled" all major processes in the firm. This involved making all internal systems available through the company intranet, including executive support systems (EIS), decision support systems (DSS), systems to support communication and distance learning, and systems to support collaboration and workflow (Nolan, 2001). Cisco also web-enabled a set of outward facing systems, including supply chain management, customer self-service, e-commerce, and marketing through the web.

In the wake of this implementation, Cisco did an analysis that attributed over $1 billion in cost savings to the web-enablement initiative as a whole. While most of this savings came from improvements in supply chain performance, considerable savings were also attributed to improved customer service, improved workforce productivity, and efficiencies due to the use of the Internet to support commerce. Beyond cost savings, it can be assumed that Cisco also benefited considerably on the revenue side; by serving as an exemplar for business use of the Internet, they no doubt encouraged other firms to do likewise.

### 2.6.2 Business Strategy

A long line of research has argued for the need to align business strategy and IT strategy in order to maximize the value of IT investments (Chan, Huff, Barclay, & Copeland, 1997). However, only recently has the logic of complementarities entered into the discussion of the link between business strategy and IT investment. For example, Lee, Barua, and Whinston (2000) develop an analytical model that suggests complementarities between e-commerce and a strategy of mass customization. Dehning, Richardson, and Zmud (2003) rely on the logic of complementarities, in part, to explain why IT investments that enable a strategic transformation should produce greater business value than investments that automate or informate individual processes.

Just as initiative level complements cannot be identified until the model is contextualized to a particular technology, the potential complementarities with firm strategy cannot be identified until the model is contextualized to a particular type of firm. Thus, we use a case example, Cisco Systems, to describe the rationales in support of the following generic propositions:

**Proposition 2a:** *The effects of IT innovation deployment on business value will be reinforced by complementary business strategies.*

**Proposition 2b:** *The effects of IT investment on IT innovation deployment will be reinforced by complementary business strategies.*

While we do not require that the *same* business strategy be involved in both Propositions 2a and 2b, it can indeed turn out this way. Cisco's primary strategy was to become the dominant supplier of Internet infrastructure worldwide. Through both internal development and an aggressive program of acquisitions, Cisco sought to assemble a broad product line that would permit "one stop shopping" for business network equipment. This *Internet leadership strategy* reinforces the effects of deployment on business value (Proposition 2a), in that it leads to especially rapid sales growth; this, in turn, allows the benefits of Cisco's web-enabled systems to leverage across a larger scale of business activities. Further, as a more diverse set of acquisitions are made, it also allows Cisco to more tightly integrate the business processes by enforcing the same web-enabled systems throughout the extended enterprise, thereby further enhancing the extent of business value derived from it.

The *Internet leadership strategy* also reinforces the effects of Cisco's web-enablement investment (Proposition 2b), because the deep knowledge of the Internet that Cisco gained in the execution of this strategy can be applied to the task of designing and deploying internal systems based on the Internet. The reinforcing relationships go the other way as well (i.e., the relationship is symmetrical). Deployment of web-enablement facilitates the effects of Cisco's Internet leadership strategy by providing a unique marketing asset: Cisco can demonstrate firsthand the potential benefits of Internet use for business, and thereby encourage Internet adoption and increase the demand for their routers. Because they are the dominant Internet infrastructure provider, they capture most of the benefits of demand increases.

In addition, through their own web-enablement deployment, Cisco engages in a cumulative learning process that can be shared with their customers. Cisco's acquisition of KPMG as a consulting arm can be seen as a means to capture and replicate this learning for the benefit of customers. To the extent that customers are more willing to follow Cisco's example and web-enable their own systems, this will increase the demand for the infrastructure that Cisco sells and thereby enhance their business performance.

### *2.6.3 IT Capabilities*

Several authors have noted IT capabilities as a critical determinant of a firm's "conversion effectiveness," i.e., the ability to translate any given level of investment into business value (Weill, 1992; Markus & Soh 1993; Soh & Markus 1995). In empirical work, Bharadwaj (2000) found that firms with high capabilities performed better than a set of matched firms on various firm-level profit and cost measures. While they relied on a proxy for IT capabilities (i.e., ratings of the most innovative users of IT by Information Week's editors), several typologies have been offered to provide a more systematic measure of what constitutes IT capabilities (Bharadwaj Sambamurthy, & Zmud, 1999; Wade & Hulland, 2004).

For the purpose of this discussion, we adopt the typology proposed by Ross and Beath (1996), who argue that IT capabilities ultimately derive from strong positions on three types of IT assets: human, technical, and relationship. They define IT capability as "the ability to control IT-related costs, deliver systems when needed, and effect business objectives through IT implementations" (p. 31). Ross and Beath define the assets that enable this capability as follows:

- The technology asset refers to shareability of technical platforms and databases. Two distinguishing characteristics of a valuable technology asset are well-defined technology architecture, data, and platform standards.
- The human asset refers to the ability of the IT staff to consistently solve business problems and addresses business opportunities through IT. Three distinguishing features of valuable IT human assets are technical skills, business understanding, and a problem-solving orientation.
- The relationship asset refers to the extent that IT and business unit management share the risk and the responsibility for the effective application of IT in the firm. A valuable relationship asset is distinguished by business partner ownership of IT projects and top management leadership in establishing IT priorities.

At the most abstract level, it is nearly self-evident that firms with stronger IT capabilities would be better able to translate any given level of investment into more thorough IT deployment (suggesting complementarity with IT investment) and would be better able to translate any given level of IT deployment into greater business value (suggesting complementarity with IT deployment). In fact, the three parts of Ross and Beath's definition go to these exact points. Firms that have greater ability to "deliver systems when needed" will, other things equal, be better able to convert IT investment into higher levels of deployment. Firms that are "better able to control costs" and "effect business objectives through IT implementations" will find that any given level of IT deployment will cost less and will be more likely to operate IT in a way that produces business value.

This suggests the following two propositions:

**Proposition 3a:** *The effects of IT innovation deployment on business value will be reinforced by stronger IT capabilities.*

**Proposition 3b:** *The effects of IT investment on IT innovation deployment will be reinforced by stronger IT capabilities.*

To further develop the rationales in support of these two propositions, we examine more fine-grained complementarities involving each of the three assets that underlie strong IT capabilities, namely technology, human, and relationship assets. In Table 2.2, we provide a rationale for how each asset reinforces the IT investment $\Rightarrow$ IT deployment relationship and the IT deployment $\Rightarrow$ business value relationship. We illustrate these rationales with examples taken from Cisco Systems, particularly the account of Cisco's ERP implementation (Austin et al., 2002).

**Table 2.2** IT capabilities, IT deployment, and business value

| Type of IT asset | How the asset reinforces relationships | Examples from the Cisco case |
|---|---|---|
| Technology asset | Reinforcement of IT investment ⇒ IT deployment: A robust physical infrastructure can better accommodate a major addition in the form of a major new IT implementation. A poor infrastructure has to be retrofitted first, at additional cost and risk. Reinforcement of IT deployment ⇒ business value: A robust physical infrastructure allows deployed systems to be operated and maintained more cheaply. Users will find it easier to locate and access information contained in the deployed systems, thus enhancing the value of those systems. | Cisco established 100% standardization at each level of their architecture: hardware, operating systems, databases, networking, and most applications. This allowed them unusual speed in rolling out new applications (essentially replacing all applications over a 2 year period) and integrating acquisitions (usually completed in 60–100 days). |
| Human asset | Reinforcement of IT investment ⇒ IT deployment: Large-scale IT deployment requires considerable knowledge and skills to orchestrate the project successfully. IT staff must not only master the technologies to be implemented (technical skill), but also understand how the technology can be best configured to support the business (business understanding) and to be able to solve the problems that inevitably arise in any major implementation (problem-solving orientation). Reinforcement of IT deployment ⇒ business value: Firms with strong IT human assets will be able to operate and maintain any level of deployed systems more efficiently, thus lowering the costs. | Cisco was able to successfully implement ERP in 9 months and replace most of the rest of their IT infrastructure in 2 years, which gives a clear indication of the strength of their IT human assets. Indications of the skill of the IT staff can be seen in their attention to recruiting top-quality implementation partners, the decision to aggressively control the project scope, and their quick and effective responses to setbacks on the project. |
| Relationship asset | Reinforcement of IT investment ⇒ IT deployment: Any major IT implementation today requires enthusiastic support and participation from other departments and from senior management. Their participation is required to ensure that the right systems and features are chosen and to mobilize the organization. | |

**Table 2.2** (continued)

| Type of IT asset | How the asset reinforces relationships | Examples from the Cisco case |
|---|---|---|
| | Reinforcement of IT deployment ⇒ business value: When strong relations exist there will be free flow of information about how well systems are suiting user needs. In this climate, necessary fixes and improvements are more likely, rather than users suffering along with inadequate systems or avoiding use of systems entirely. Also users are more likely to understand how best to use systems as they are. | During Cisco's ERP implementation they took the unprecedented step of reassigning 80 of their "best and brightest" to work full time on the implementation. CEO Chambers made clear his support for the implementation by including successful completion of the project as one of the corporation's top seven objectives for the year. |

As explained in Table 2.2, each of these assets has complementarities with IT investment and deployment. However, they also reinforce one another, suggesting a system of complements. Ross and Beath note that

> [T]he relationship asset is heavily dependent on mutual respect, which means that business partners must view the IT staff as competent (human asset), which is partly dependent on the quality and cost of the existing technology base (technology asset). At the same time, competent IT staff members can develop a strong technology infrastructure only if business partners accept some accountability for IT projects (relationship asset) and top management provides sufficient investment for constant reskilling of the IT staff (human asset). The architecture is valuable only if it supports business needs, as articulated by senior business managers (relationship asset), and is effectively and efficiently managed by competent IT staff (human asset). (Ross & Beath, p. 35)

## *2.6.4 Modern Organizational Architecture*

Organizational architecture refers to a firm's organization of labor and related human resource practices (Hitt & Brynjolfsson, 1997). Considerable prior work has examined the question of how certain aspects of modern organizational architectures might complement technology and innovation (Bresnahan et al., 2002; Brynjolfsson & Hitt, 2003; Hitt & Brynjolfsson, 1997; Laursen & Foss, 2003; Milgrom & Roberts, 1995). In this section, we adopt a typology offered by Brynjolfsson (2003) for a set of practices that comprise the "digital" organization.

This typology, based on decade of empirical studies in this area, identifies a collection of five elements[1] of modern organizational architectures that complement IT

[1] Brynjolfsson's (2003) typology identifies six factors, but for brevity we combine two closely related factors – skilled labor, and an emphasis on recruitment and training, into a single factor.

use: (1) automation of routine tasks, (2) emphasis on the use of skilled labor and an increased emphasis on recruitment and training, (3) decentralization of decision making, (4) increased vertical and lateral information flow, and (5) emphasis on performance-based incentives.

We propose two distinct causal chains linking these elements and business value. In the first chain, we propose that some of these elements reinforce the effects of IT deployment on business value (link B in Fig. 2.1). In the second chain, we propose that these practices also reinforce the effects of IT investment on the level of IT deployment (link C in Fig. 2.1). These proposed causal chains are captured in the following two propositions:

**Proposition 4a:** *The effects of IT innovation deployment on business value will be reinforced by modern organizational architectures.*

**Proposition 4b:** *The effects of IT investment on IT innovation deployment will be reinforced by modern organizational architectures.*

Brynjolfsson (2003) gives a nice discussion of how modern organizational architecture reinforces the relationship between IT investment and business value. We expand on that by bringing IT deployment into the analysis. In particular, in Table 2.3 we provide rationales for how these five elements each reinforce the IT deployment ⇒ business value relationship, and in some cases, the IT investment ⇒ IT deployment relationship. We also provide examples, where possible, from the Cisco System case.

### *2.6.5 Firm-Level Complements as a Driver for IT Investment*

A large number of studies have confirmed a strong positive association between the aggregate level of IT investment and realized business value, thus dispelling the myth that IT investments do not pay off (Barua & Mukhopadhyay, 2000).

We posit two explanations for the strong relationship between IT investment and business value. First, as we have been arguing all along, firms often join IT investment with organizational elements (complementary strategies, IT capabilities, and modern organizational architectures) that magnify or reinforce the value of those investments. Payoffs do not result from IT investment per se, but rather from how those investments are combined with other organizational elements.

However, perhaps more importantly, we suggest that firms that are well positioned in terms of organizational complements will be likely to invest more in IT to begin with. That is, we posit that these firm-level organizational complements can also drive the decisions related to IT investments. For example, senior managers will recognize when they have business strategies that have potential synergies with IT use and may formulate or support plans for specific IT investments. Similarly, they will recognize when their IT capabilities are strong and the potential synergies this has with IT use may create environments conductive for IT investment.

**Table 2.3** Modern organizational architecture, IT deployment, and business value

| Practice | How the practice reinforces relationships | Examples from the Cisco case |
|---|---|---|
| Automation of routine tasks | Reinforcement of IT investment ⇒ IT deployment:<br>Routine tasks, which require little human judgment, are particularly suitable for automation, thus reinforcing the link between IT investment and IT deployment.<br>Reinforcement of IT deployment ⇒ business value<br>Automation of routine tasks, when it can be accomplished successfully, provides a very direct route to business value. IT systems are the means by which white-collar work is automated. | Cisco's web-enablement initiative allowed automation of virtually any routine task. This can be seen in how Cisco's architecture supports extensive self-service by both employees and customers. None of this self-service would be possible without automating the underlying tasks. |
| Highly skilled labor, training, and recruitment | Reinforcement of IT investment ⇒ IT deployment:<br>Modern IT is complex and requires higher skill to understand and implement than prior technologies. This suggests that a more highly skilled labor force will increase the level of deployment achieved for any given level of IT investment.<br>Reinforcement of IT deployment ⇒ business value:<br>Much of modern IT can be seen as a tool to amplify human skill by "informating" processes. The more skill that exists to begin with, the greater the productivity benefits that will accrue from amplifying that skill. Also, IT itself is an important tool to facilitate skill acquisition. | Cisco is a high-technology company with a particularly high ratio of white-collar workers (due to outsourcing of manufacturing).<br>It used its web-enabled architecture to implement a robust world-wide program of distance learning, thus reinforcing the value of its skilled workforce. |
| More decentralized decision making | Reinforcement of IT deployment ⇒ business value:<br>Decentralized decision making has the advantage of being more responsive, and it allows decisions to take into account local conditions. Modern IT enhances the value of decentralization by moving | Senior Cisco managers are equipped with "digital dashboards" that allow them to monitor key performance indicators at lower levels of the organization. All employees are given a personalized "my Yahoo" page that "pushes" |

**Table 2.3** (continued)

| Practice | How the practice reinforces relationships | Examples from the Cisco case |
|---|---|---|
| | knowledge and skill down to line workers that was once the sole preserve of senior managers and by allowing monitoring of decision quality by senior managers. | relevant corporate and industry information to their desktops, including live broadcasts of the CEO's address to Cisco's Quarterly Meeting. |
| Improved vertical and lateral information flow | Reinforcement of IT deployment ⇒ business value:<br>Increased information flow makes organizations more responsive to changing conditions. IT enables more efficient and effective information flow, thus reinforcing the positive impact of any given level of information flow on business value. | Cisco's web-enabled architecture calls for a one-to-one ratio of networked PCs to employees. The above-mentioned "digital dashboards" and "my Yahoo" pages reinforce information flows up and down the organization. Cisco's online directory, which gets millions of hits per year, promotes vertical and lateral communications. |
| Strong performance-based incentives | Reinforcement of IT investment ⇒ IT deployment:<br>Workers with performance-based incentives will be more willing to adopt new IT tools that could enhance their performance.<br>Reinforcement of IT deployment ⇒ business value:<br>Performance-based incentives are the optimal motivational tool, but only when based on accurate information about performance. Modern IT automatically captures raw data related to performance as workers use it to perform their jobs. Thus, performance data can be captured more accurately and efficiently. | Cisco uses its web-enabled architecture to track individual performance, to give broad access to performance information, such as sales and customer satisfaction, and to allow employees to measure their performance against company goals. Seventy percent of the employees have a very significant bonus related to annual customer surveys. |

Finally, they will also recognize when their organizational architecture includes the kinds of modern elements that support – and are supported by – greater IT use and provide added impetus to IT investment decisions. In short, we argue that the very recognition of complementary organizational elements may shape or drive the decisions regarding IT investments in the firm. This rationale leads to our final set of propositions:

**Proposition 5a:** *Organizations that have business strategies that possess greater potential complementarities with IT use will have higher levels of IT investment.*

**Proposition 5b:** *Organizations with strong IT capabilities will have higher levels of IT investment.*

**Proposition 5c:** *Organizations with a modern organizational architecture will have higher levels of IT investment.*

## 2.7 Contributions of the Model

In this chapter, we have developed a complementarities-based model of IT innovation investments and business value and illustrated its application in the context of PLM. In so doing, we join two robust streams of research – IT innovation and IT business value – that despite important overlaps, have proceeded largely in parallel. The IT innovation stream explains why firms make innovative investments in IT, and how these investments can be translated into greater deployment; the business value stream explains the conditions under which IT investments and deployment lead to business value.

Our use of complementarities as the unifying logic allows us to do much more than simply join existing models of IT innovation and business value "at the hip" with a simple linear sequence from innovation antecedents to innovation deployment to business value. Rather, our approach focuses on variable interactions and illustrates how many of the same variables that interact to increase the business value flowing from IT deployment also have separate effects that increase the level of IT deployment flowing from any given level of IT investment. Indeed, our model goes even further to explain why some firms are more prone to invest in innovative IT to begin with, a question not empirically examined in the business value literature. At a holistic level, our model provides an explanation of the otherwise puzzling *strength* of the observed correlation between IT investment and business: Firms that are best positioned to derive value from IT due to potential complementarities are most likely to invest more aggressively; then these same potential complementarities, when realized, serve to magnify the ability to translate both investment into deployment and deployment into value. Prior work on IT complementarities and business value has not always been precise about whether complementarities reinforce business value directly, or indirectly by reinforcing IT deployment; we show how they do both.

Another key contribution of our model is that it highlights the *importance of initiative-level complements*. These complements have received comparatively less attention from IT business value researchers owning the tendency to treat IT as a monolith, yet at this level the richness and power of the complementarities for informing managerial practice becomes especially apparent. This level of the model allows us to move beyond generic (though no doubt, still very useful) innovation deployment guidance (e.g., pertaining to the need for top management support, innovation champions, attention to organizational learning) to develop rich, technology-specific prescriptions for practice. For example, the model brings a focus to specific product development strategies and capabilities that complement

PLM applications and indicate how organizations can achieve a genuine synergy between deployment of the technology and the related organizational elements.

A final contribution of our model is that it provides a *fourth perspective* on the nature of the causal relationship between technology and organizational change, beyond the three perspectives (technology imperative, organizational imperative, and emergence perspective) identified in Markus and Robey's (1988) influential article. The complementarities perspective shares with the technology imperative the notion that we should tend to see certain clusters of technology and organizational elements, but rejects the notion that technology deployment has "caused" organizational elements in these clusters any more than the organizational elements have "caused" the technology elements.

Furthermore, complementarities reject the technology imperative notion of certain necessary organizational changes that span all adopters, in that the optimal configuration of organizational elements can vary from organization to organization depending on their history and context. The complementarities approach shares with the organizational imperative the idea that organizations often take a rational approach to implementation planning, but rejects the notion that organizations have complete discretion in how the organization is designed around a technology; in that only complementary design elements will lead to enhanced business value.

Finally, the complementarities perspective shares with the emergent perspective the idea that technology and organization can co-evolve in an emergent fashion, but rejects the notion that this process is necessarily chaotic and unpredictable. Rather, it posits that technology and organization tend to be jointly determined according to the logic of complementarities.

## 2.8 Implications for Research and Practice

Our model suggests three future lines of research. First, as noted previously the model needs to be *contextualized* and applied to specific instances of emerging IT, using a combination of case study and survey approaches. Our effort has been to illustrate the promise and potential for the model to inform on PLM implementation. Further research would be required to identify all the possible organizational elements that complement the PLM application.

PLM researchers applying our model would contextualize the model by identifying (through a literature search, examination of PLM system features, interviews with experts and early adopters, etc.) those specific strategies, structures, processes, skills, etc., that complement use of PLM at the initiative level, and also the nature of the potential synergies between PLM and overall firm strategies, IT capabilities, and modern organizational architectures. The contextualization process would also involve developing measures of the extent of IT deployment (based on what it actually means to deploy PLM more broadly and deeply) and of business value (based on those aspects of organizational performance that should be most affected by PLM deployment – for example, product development cost, time).

While we believe the model as proposed achieves a nice balance between richness and parsimony as it is, we see some especially promising ways to extend the model. One such extension is to add *non-IT functional capabilities* to the macro-level of the model. This would be particularly appropriate for those emerging IT systems used primarily within a particular functional area. To return to the PLM example, we expect that product development capabilities, broadly defined, will have complementarities with PLM deployment.

Another intriguing extension would be to incorporate the idea of *innovation-path complementarities*. Just as a technology can possess complementarities with organizational features, they can also possess complementarities with other technologies that already exist, or more interestingly, are yet to come. Smith (2004) develops these ideas in an examination of the adoption of "linked technologies," where adoption of a technology in one period has complementarities with technologies introduced later.

The study by Zhu (2004) can be seen as illustrating the structure of innovation-path complementarities. This study demonstrates complementarities between IT infrastructure – operationalized primarily as the installed base of IT equipment – and e-commerce capabilities – measured as the sophistication of firm's website and the degree of integration between the website and the back-end systems. Innovation-path complementarities could exist either because one technology interacts with another on a technical level, or because the *knowledge* gained during implementation of one technology pertains to another.

Returning to the PLM example, we might posit innovation-path complementarities with the prior deployment of related technologies (e.g., CAD/CAM, PDM). We might also posit innovation-path complementarities with the deployment of systems that require similar kinds of implementation strategies and knowledge, such as CRM or ERP. It is worth noting that the kernel of this idea does already reside in our proposed model, in that IT technology assets are posited as a dimension of IT capabilities. However, we see the potential for greater development of this concept, and the opportunity to draw interesting connections between innovation-path complementarities and other innovation concepts, such as absorptive capacity (Zahra & George, 2002) and the real-options perspective on new technology investment (Fichman, 2004).

Our model holds implications for managerial practice. First, our model provides a rationale for investing in IT capabilities that support product development in conjunction with investments in other types of product development capability (for example, development process maturity). Such investments can be particularly difficult to justify based on directly observable benefits, and as such, the insights from our model will likely contribute toward adopting a more holistic IT investment decision-making framework. Further, the often found "symmetry" in complementarities effects also imply the potential contribution of IT deployment toward enhancing the returns from investments in other organizational elements (e.g., product development team management practices). This implies the need for IT managers as well as senior business managers to include such considerations while evaluating innovative IT investment opportunities.

Finally, our model also provides a rationale for a concerted strategic role in IT resource commitments. Milgrom and Roberts (1995) have argued that central strategic direction of fully coordinated moves will be especially valuable in the presence of complementarities because partial configurations are not necessarily complementary and may even be counterproductive. As a result, organizations cannot be expected to automatically evolve toward the optimal configuration of complementary elements.

The research implication is to reinforce the importance of robust planning processes that link IT to strategy and that examine the link between technology and organization during implementation. It also suggests that organizations that do choose to engage in a less directed process of adaptation or even improvisation (Orlikowski, 1996) should take special pains to avoid having the implementation "freeze" (Tyre & Orlikowski, 1994) prematurely, before the optimal configuration of complementary elements has been discovered in situ.

Orlikowski (1996) describes how the use of groupware to support help desk incident reports came to be surrounded by system of changes pertaining to employee roles, employee training, worker evaluation policies, and distribution of work among call specialists. The combined effects of these changes were greater than the sum of their parts, suggesting complementarities.

The implication for managers is to enlarge the scope of technology implementation planning to consider complementarities; to be wary of concluding that a technology has no benefits based on partial configurations; and to continually revisit an implementation for the addition of new complementary elements, rather than seeking to rapidly "freeze" some particular configuration.

## References

Austin, R. D., Nolan, R. L., & Cotteleer, M. J. (2002). *Cisco systems, Inc.: Implementing ERP*. Boston: Harvard Business School, Case #9-699-022.

Barua, A., & Mukhopadhyay, T. (2000). Information technology and business performance: Past, present and future. In R. W. Zmud (Ed.), *Framing the domains of IT management: Projecting the future through the past*. Cincinnati, OH: Pinnaflex Educational Resources.

Bharadwaj, A. S. (2000). A resource-based perspective on information technology capability and firm performance: An empirical investigation. *MIS Quarterly, 24*(1), 169–196.

Bharadwaj, A. S., Sambamurthy, V., & Zmud, R. W. (1999). *IT capabilities: Theoretical perspectives and empirical operationalization*. Proceedings of the Twentieth International Conference on Information Systems, Charlotte, NC.

Bresnahan, T., Brynjolfsson, E., & Hitt, L. M. (2002). Information technology, workplace organization, and the demand for skilled labor: Firm-level evidence. *Quarterly Journal of Economics, 117*(1), 339–376.

Brynjolfsson, E. (2003). The IT productivity gap. *Optimize*, 21.

Brynjolfsson, E., & Hitt, L. (1996). Paradox lost? Firm-level evidence on the returns to information systems spending. *Management Science, 42*(4), 541–558.

Brynjolfsson, E., & Hitt, L. M. (2003). Computing Productivity: Firm Level Evidence. *Review of Economics & Statistics, 85*(4), 793–808.

Brynjolfsson, E., Renshaw, A. A., & Van Alstyne, M. (1997). The Matrix of Change. *Sloan Management Review, 38*(2), 22–40.

Bylinsky, G. (2004). Not Your Grandfather's Assembly Line. *Fortune, 150*(1), 136B–136H.

Chan, Y. E., Huff, S. L., Barclay, D. W., & Copeland, D. G. (1997). Information Systems Research. *Business Strategic Orientation, Information Systems Strategic Orientation, and Strategic Alignment, 8*(2), 125–150.

CIM. 2008. *CIM Data Predicts Strong PLM Market Growth for 2007.*http://parts.ihs.com/news/2008/cimdata-plm-market-growth-2007.htm

Colombo, M. G., & Mosconi, R. (1995). Complementarity and cumulative learning effects in the early diffusion of multiple technologies. *Journal of Industrial Economics, 43*(1), 13–48.

Cooper, R. G., & Kleinschmidt, E. J. (2001). Portfolio management for new product development: Results of an industry practices study. *R&D Management, 31*(4).

Cooper, R. B., & Zmud, R. W. (1990). Information technology implementation research: A technological diffusion approach. *Management Science, 36*(2), 123–139.

Davenport, T. H., & Short, J. E. (1990). The new industrial engineering: information technology and business process redesign. *Sloan Management Review, 31*(4), 11–27.

Dehning, B., Richardson, V. J., & Zmud, R. W. (2003). The value relevance of announcements of transformational information technology investments. *MIS Quarterly, 27*(4), 637–656.

DeSanctis, G., & Poole, M. S. (1994). Capturing the complexity in advanced technology use: Adaptive structuration theory. *Organization Science, 5*(2), 121–147.

Devaraj, S., & Kohli, R. (2003). Performance impacts of information technology: Is actual usage the missing link? *Management Science, 49*(3), 273–289.

Dos Santos, B. L., & Peffers, K. (1995). Rewards to investors in innovative information technology applications: First movers and early followers in ATMs. *Organization Science, 6*(3), 241–259.

Fichman, R. G. (2000). The diffusion and assimilation of information technology innovations. In R. B. Zmud (Ed.), *Framing the domains of IT management: Projecting the future through the past*. Cincinnati, OH: Pinnaflex Educational Resources, Inc.

Fichman, R. G. (2004). Real options and IT platform adoption: Implications for theory and practice. *Information Systems Research, 15*(2), 132–154.

Gawer, A., & Cusumano, M. (2002). *Platform Leadership:* How Intel, Microsoft, and Cisco drive industry innovation. Boston, MA: Harvard Business School Press.

Grieves, M. (2006). *Product lifecycle management: Driving the next generation of lean thinking.* New York: McGraw-Hill.

Hart, P., & Saunders, C. (1997). Power and trust: Critical factors in the adoption and use of electronic data interchange. *Organization Science, 8*(1), 23–42.

Hitt, L. M., & Brynjolfsson, E. (1997). Information technology and internal firm organization: An exploratory analysis. *Journal of Management Information Systems, 14*(2), 81–101.

Hitt, L. M., Wu, D. J., & Zhou, X. (2001). Investment in enterprise resource planning: Business impact and productivity measures. *Journal of Management Information Systems, 19*(1), 71–98.

Karimi, J., Somers T. M., & Bhattacherjee, A. (2007). The impact of ERP implementation on business process outcomes: A factor-based study. *Journal of Management Information Systems, 24*(1), 101–134.

Kohli, R., & Devaraj, S. (2003). Measuring information technology payoff: A meta-analysis of structural variables in firm-level empirical research. *Information Systems Research, 14*(2), 127–145.

Laursen, K., & Foss, N. J. (2003). New human resource management practices, complementarities, and the impact on innovation performance. *Cambridge Journal of Economics, 27*(2), 243–263.

Lee, C.-H. S., Barua, A., & Whinston, A. B. (2000). The complementarity of mass customization and electronic commerce. *Economics of Innovation & New Technology, 9*(2), 81–109.

Leonard-Barton, D. (1988). Implementation as mutual adaptation of technology and organization. *Research Policy, 17*(5), 251–267.

Liker, J. K., Fleischer, M., & Arnsdorf, D. (1992). Fulfilling the promises of CAD. *Sloan Management Review, 33*(3), 74–86.

Lyytinen, K., & Mathiassen, L. (1998). Attention shaping and software risk – a categorical analysis of four classical risk management approaches. *Information Systems Research, 9*(3), 233–255.

Markus, M. L. (1987). Toward a "Critical Mass" Theory of interactive media: Universal access, interdependence and diffusion. *Communications Research, 14*(5), 491–511.
Markus, M. L., & Robey, D. (1988). Information technology and organizational change: Causal structure in theory and research. *Management Science, 34*(5), 583–598.
Markus, M. L., & Soh, C. (1993) Banking on information technology: Converting IT spending into firm performance. In R. Banker, R. Kauffman, & M. A. Mahmood (Eds.), *Strategic information technology management* (pp. 375–403). Harrisburg, PA: Idea Group Publishing.
Melville, N., Kraemer, K., & Gurbaxani, V. (2004). Review: Information technology and organizational performance: An integrative model of IT business value. *MIS Quarterly, 28*, 283–322.
Meyer, M., & Lehnerd, A. P. (1997). *The power of product platforms*. New York: The Free Press.
Milgrom, P., & Roberts, J. (1990). The economics of modern manufacturing: Technology, strategy and organization. *American Economic Review, 80*(3), 511–528.
Milgrom, P., & Roberts, J. (1995). Complementarities and fit: Strategy, structure, and organizational change in manufacturing. *Journal of Accounting & Economics, 19*(2/3), 179–208.
Mishra, A. N., Konana, P., & Barua, A. (2007). Antecedents and consequences of Internet use in procurement: An empirical investigation of U.S. manufacturing firms. *Information Systems Research, 18*(1), 103–120.
Nambisan, S., & Wang, Y. (2000). Web technology adoption and knowledge barriers. *Journal of Organizational Computing & Electronic Commerce, 10*(2), 129–147.
Nerkar, A., & Roberts, P. W. (2004). Technological and product–market experience and the success of new product introductions in the pharmaceutical industry. *Strategic Management Journal, 25*(8/9), 779–799.
Nolan, R. L. (2001). *Cisco systems: Web-enablement*. Boston: Harvard Business School, Case #9-301-056.
Orlikowski, W. J. (1992). The duality of technology: Rethinking the concept of technology in organizations. *Organization Science, 3*(3), 398–427.
Orlikowski, W. J. (1996). Improvising organizational transformation over time: A situated change perspective. *Organization Science, 7*(1), 63–92.
Powell, T. C., & Dent-Micallef, A. (1997). Information technology as competitive advantage: The role of human, business, and technology resources. *Strategic Management Journal, 18*(5), 375–405.
Purvis, R. L., Sambamurthy, V., & Zmud, R. W. (2001). The assimilation of knowledge platforms in organizations: An empirical investigation. *Organization Science, 12*(2), 117–135.
Ramamurthy, K., Premkumar, G., & Crum, M. R. (1999). Organizational and interorganizational determinants of EDI diffusion and organizational performance: A causal model. *Journal of Organizational Computing and Electronic Commerce, 9*(4), 253–285.
Rogers, E. M. (2003). *Diffusion of Innovations* (5th ed.). New York: The Free Press.
Ross, J. W., & Beath, C. M. (1996). Develop long-term competitiveness through IT Assets. *Sloan Management Review, 38*(1), 31–42.
Saaksvuori, A. (2008). *Product lifecycle management* (3rd ed.). NewYork: Springer.
Smith, M. (2004). A model of the linked adoption of complementary technologies. *Economics of Innovation and New Technology, 13*(1), 91–99.
Soh, C., & Markus, M. L. (1995). How IT creates business value: A process theory synthesis. In G. Ariav, C. Beath, J. I. DeGross, R. Hoyer, & C. F. Kemerer (Eds.), *Proceedings of the sixteenth international conference on information systems* (pp. 29–41). Amsterdam: ACM.
Subramanian, A., & Nilakanta, S. (1996). Organizational innovativeness: Exploring the relationship between organizational determinants of innovation, types of innovations, and measures of organizational performance. *Omega-International Journal of Management Science, 24*(6), 631–647.
Swanson, E. B. (1994). Information systems innovations among organizations. *Management Science, 40*(9), 1069–1092.
Swanson, E. B., & Ramiller, N. (2004). Innovating mindfully with information technology. *MIS Quarterly, 28*(4), 553–583.

Tanriverdi, H., & Venkatraman, N. (2005). Knowledge relatedness and the performance of multibusiness firms. *Strategic Management Journal, 26*(2), 97–119.

Teo, H. H., Wei, K. K., & Benbasat, I. (2003). Predicting intention to adopt interorganizational linkages: An institutional perspective. *MIS Quarterly, 27*(1), 31.

Tyre, M. J., & Orlikowski, W. J. (1993). Exploiting opportunities for technological improvement. *Sloan Management Review, 35*(1), 13–26.

Tyre, M. J., & Orlikowski, W. J. (1994). Windows of opportunity: temporal patterns of technological adaptation in organizations. *Organization Science, 5*(1), 98–118.

Venkatesh, V., Morris, M. G., Davis, G. B., & Davis, F. D. (2003). User acceptance of information technology: Toward a unified view. *MIS Quarterly, 27*(3), 425–478.

Wade, M., & Hulland, J. (2004). Review: the resource-based view and information systems research: review, extension, and suggestions for future research. *MIS Quarterly, 28*(1), 107–142.

Weill, P. (1992) The relationship between investment in information technology and firm performance: A study of the valve manufacturing sector. *Information Systems Research, 3*(4), 307–333.

Zahra, S. A., & George, G. (2002). Absorptive capacity: A review, reconceptualization, and extension. *Academy of Management Review, 27*(2), 185–203.

Zhu, K. (2004). The complementarity of information technology infrastructure and e-commerce capability: A resource-based assessment of their business value. *Journal of Management Information Systems, 21*(1), 167–202.

# Chapter 3
# IT-Based Knowledge Management Systems to Support the Design of Product Development Processes

**Emma O'Brien, Darren Harris, and Mark Southern**

**Abstract** In today's dynamic business world, the ability to continuously innovate and respond to customers' needs is fundamental to success. To enable companies to do this a thorough understanding of their internal processes is required. Experiments can provide significant opportunities for companies to generate knowledge about their product development processes. This chapter examines the role of experimentation in designing robust product development processes and the role of information technology in supporting this. It outlines an IT-based knowledge management system to support the creation, transfer, and the use of knowledge amongst engineers in designing and conducting experiments that lead to robust product development processes. The chapter concludes with a discussion of the key issues for future research in this area.

## 3.1 Introduction

In today's dynamic business world the ability to continuously innovate and respond to customers' needs is fundamental to success. To enable companies to do this a thorough understanding of their internal processes is required. Experiments can provide significant opportunities for companies to generate knowledge about their product development processes. However, such experiments are not widely adopted by companies particularly in Europe (Gremyr, Arvidsson, & Johansson, 2003, Antony, 2002). This chapter examines the role of experimentation in designing robust product development processes and the role of information technology in supporting this.

Experiments have long been recognized as a method of creating knowledge (Fahey & Prusak, 1998, Nonaka, Toyama, & Konno, 2000). However, their potential has not yet been widely explored in the context of knowledge management. In designing product development processes, experiments can be used to explore the

---

E. O'Brien (✉)
Enterprise Research Centre, ER1030, University of Limerick, Plassey, Limerick, Ireland
e-mail: emma.obrien@ul.ie

S. Nambisan (ed.), *Information Technology and Product Development*, Annals of Information Systems 5, DOI 10.1007/978-1-4419-1081-3_3,

effect different factors have on the production processes as well as on the product outcomes. Knowledge management systems (KMS) can support this process by encouraging knowledge creation and transfer. There are few KMS that have focused on the area of knowledge creation, particularly on the use of experiments for defining development processes.

The objective of this chapter is to explore the potential for experiments as a knowledge creation exercise in the product development process. Furthermore, it outlines an IT-based KMS to support the creation, transfer, and use of knowledge amongst engineers in designing and conducting experiments that lead to robust product development processes.

This chapter is divided into a number of sections. Section 2, The Role of Experiments in Product Development, examines the potential of experimentation in developing robust products and processes. Section 3, Design of Experiments (DOE) and Robust Design in Product Development, examines traditional approaches to process design and investigates the use of DOE as an alternative approach. Section 4 focuses on the different types of knowledge used when creating knowledge via experimentation and relates to Nonaka's knowledge spiral. Section 5 identifies issues which need to be considered when managing knowledge to support the use of experiments. In Section 6, we describe a case study that outlines the design of an IT-based KMS to support the creation of knowledge related to design of product development processes. Section 7 deals with some of the issues for future research in this area.

## 3.2 The Role of Experiments in Product Development

The overall aim of product development is to create a high-quality product that meets customer's expectations and requirements. To ensure such an outcome, product development processes have to achieve a high level of consistency. Often this would be to very narrow specifications. Consistently producing a high-quality product is no accident. Production has associated with it many factors that might affect the quality of the product – factors such as the raw material, machinery, settings on the machines amongst others. Each of these factors has the ability to inhibit the product performance and thus affect its ability to satisfy customer requirements. In manufacturing, to identify the optimal settings needed to produce high-quality products, often experiments are run. A well-known and structured method of identifying such settings is the robust design method (RDM).

RDM uses statistical experiments to identify the optimum factors and their settings for product development processes. It allows the control of factors that may affect the variation of the product quality. It also allows the identification of the relationships between these factors and the outcomes. The design of robust processes for product development improves product quality, manufacturability, and reliability (Leung Tsui, 1992).

Robust design methodology uses an approach called the DOE that has been proven to be expensive to run in terms expertise and time (Breyfogle, 2003;

Shoemaker, Leung Tsui, & Wu, 1991). Thus it is important to store the knowledge obtained in these experiments for reuse later. The execution of such experiments requires a combination of tacit and explicit knowledge. An explicit knowledge of the methodology and tools is required but the tacit knowledge experience gained over time from conducting these experiments is invaluable. For example, based on knowledge gained over time by conducting experiments, an engineer may obtain significant tacit knowledge and intuitively know the relationships between the environmental factors (or process-related factors) and the product development outcomes. Thus it is important to capture this knowledge. The following section examines the use of DOE and RDM in greater depth.

## 3.3 DOE and Robust Design in Product Development

Engineers execute experiments to enhance their knowledge of a particular process or product. One of the most common techniques of doing so is by varying one factor or one variable at a time while holding the other factors constant. This method of experimentation is commonly known as one-factor-at-a-time (OFAT) and can be regarded as a form of "trial and error" requiring a mixture of luck, experience, and intuition for its success (Clements, 1995).

The OFAT approach to experimentation for determining main setting parameters is still very popular in today's organizations for several reasons (Antony & Tzu-Yao, 2003). It is commonly thought that the most accurate way of measuring the effect of a design change is to keep all the other factors fixed while one factor is being assessed. Furthermore, it is believed that OFAT techniques are easily conducted and do not need any advanced statistical knowledge in their application. The OFAT process also provides a "quick-fix" solution that managers are often content with. This is due to the fact that the significance of DOE is not stressed enough to engineers within academic institutions. Antony and Tzu-Yao (2003) highlights that many companies are not ready for the implementation of advanced quality improvement techniques such as DOE. However, the use of an easy-to-use information technology-based system to support the DOE process may address such issues.

Statistical experimentation such as the DOE and the analysis of variance (ANOVA) technique dates back to the 1930s (Fisher, 1935), "DOE" is one of the most powerful quality improvement techniques for reducing process variation, enhancing process effectiveness, and process capability (Antony, 2006). Fishers' approach to experimentation was a direct alternative to the OFAT approach. Since then, his approach has evolved into a number of techniques for improving process performance/capability and reducing process variation (Montgomery, 2001b).

DOE offers a number of advantages to experimentation over the OFAT approach (Antony & Tzu-Yao, 2003). First, DOE requires much less resources (i.e., a number of experiments, time, material cost) than OFAT experiments for the same amount of information (or insights) obtained. For example, with three factors at two levels, a full factorial design requires only eight runs compared to 16 runs for an OFAT experiment (Anderson, 2000). More importantly, the estimates of the factor effects from OFAT are less precise than DOE. In many situations, the effects of a factor would change when the conditions of other factors vary. Using DOE, one can vary all the factors simultaneously. This allows the experimenter to determine the effect of a factor when the levels of the other factors change. OFAT techniques do not determine the interactions among the different factors consequently leading to inaccurate test results. DOE provides better product or process optimization tools than traditional OFAT experimentation. This applies to experiments where the response function has to be maximized or minimized. A regression model can be created which highlights the relationship between key input factors and factor interactions, something which OFAT is unable to provide. Regression models can also provide engineers with extremely important or valuable information; for example, by studying the model the setting of factors can be manipulated to achieve a pre-determined target level for the variable of interest.

As mentioned previously, DOE is one of the most powerful quality improvement techniques for reducing process variation, enhancing process effectiveness and process capability. If implemented well, DOE can optimize the process or product under investigation "by exploiting the non-linear effects of the process parameters on the performance characteristics" (Simms & Garvin, 2002) and help determine the settings which would minimize variation within that product or process. However, what is the cause of this variation?

Common variation within a process is known as "noise." This noise can occur as a result of poorly maintained machinery, inconsistent operating conditions from operator skill levels, machine fluctuations, same batch raw material variation, etc. Optimizing a process through DOE involves determining the optimal setting conditions of each factor which would lead to a response which is least sensitive to this noise. If all the control and signal factors are optimized, the result is a robust process with significantly reduced non-conformance and variability. Taguchi and Clausing (1990) stated that "if a process performs well in adverse conditions (as a result of noise factors) it will perform considerably better in normal conditions." As the correct implementation of DOE is highly critical for the success of an experiment, a number of distinct steps following the plan-do-check-act procedure have been put forward (Antony & Knowles, 2001; Montgomery, 2001b; Simms and Garvin, 2002). Unfortunately, they all differ slightly and so the steps to completing a DOE are not as readily recognized. However, used within the context of a structured methodology, DOE approach such as RDM can lead to beneficial outcomes.

Since the 1980s engineers have gradually become more aware of the benefits of using DOE and as a result for this there has been many new opportunities for applying DOE. The most important of these is RDM – a methodology that was developed by Taguchi (Arvidsson & Gremyr, 2008). Its advantage over other techniques is that it enables robustness due to its emphasis on designing processes insensitive to uncontrollable factors known as noise.

RDM has been defined as "*Systematic efforts to achieve insensitivity to noise factors. These efforts are founded on an awareness of variation and can be applied in all stages of product design.*" (Arvidsson & Gremyr, 2008).

The main focus of RDM is on designing products and processes that are insensitive to potential environmental factors and variation to enable products to be manufactured as close to the desired specification as possible. Furthermore, RDM is concerned with identifying the optimal operating conditions so that variability is minimized (Montgomery, 2001a).

The main benefits that RDM can provide to product development are as follows (Antony, 2002):

- Improved understanding of products and processes and the factors which affect these (for example, humidity, raw material, temperature);
- Development of processes that are insensitive to factors which cause variation;
- Improves the quality of your products due to reduced defects; and
- Improves the efficiency of your process and reduce costs.

Due to these benefits RDM was used as a methodology to improve existing products and processes in the company outlined in the case study described later in this chapter. DOE formed a major step in this process.

Within RDM importantly, DOE is a technique that can readily be used in the design and development of new products and the associated processes (Ellekjaer, & Bisgaard, 1998). Furthermore, DOE can assist the modification of existing processes and lead to incremental improvements in such products. Thus it is useful for both radical and incremental innovation as well as for both product and process innovation.

Radical innovations are fundamental changes that represent revolutionary change in technology. They represent clear departures from existing practices. In contrast, incremental innovations are minor improvements or simple adjustments in current technology. This is significant in light of the way businesses operate today. Stalk (1993) highlights that with the fast moving pace of today's business world, product lifecycles are constantly shrinking and as a result it is important that companies develop the capability to rapidly replace products with better versions.

DOE focuses on the improvement and identification of new processes regardless. "Process creation is an innovation process that emphasises the need to design and redesign products in a way to match organisational needs with emergent technology" (Zumd, 1984). The importance of this is further emphasized by a study conducted by Yamin, Mavondo, Gunasekaran, and Sarros (1997) which found that process innovations were the stronger predictor of performance over product innovation.

Now that we have established the role of DOE in defining (or innovating) product development processes, we will examine the significance of knowledge in the DOE process.

## 3.4 Importance of Knowledge in DOE

Cambridge Dictionary defines knowledge as an "*u*nderstanding of or information about a subject which has been obtained by experience or study which is either in a person's mind or possessed by people generally." This definition supports the autopoietic view of knowledge, in which the brain constructs its own meaning from information as opposed to the traditional view which sees knowledge as "universal and objective and which can be used interchangeably with the terms data and information" (Vicari, Krogh, Roos, & Mahnke, 1996). This has major implications for the field of IT-based KMS. First, KMS should be systems that support knowledge sharing (not systems to generate knowledge). Second, explicit knowledge is information that needs to be interpreted. Thus, knowledge is gained by interpreting and interacting with information (Alavi & Leidner, 2001).

The use of DOE allows one to gather the maximum amount of knowledge while using the minimum amount of resources, the application of the technique itself provides a road map to improvement and the possibility of avoiding large amounts of capital expenditure as a result of a successful experiment (Goh, 2002).

DOE as with any form of experimentation is in itself a knowledge creation process. It is a method that allows an engineer to understand the product better in terms of factors that can influence its specification. This knowledge can be made explicit using a number of tools from the outputs of the analysis of the experimental data. Prior research suggests that the use of quality tools and methods can lead to knowledge creation (Choo, Linderman, & Schroeder, 2002. Structured method and motivational potential in knowledge creation: linking quality and knowledge. University of Minnesota Working Paper.).

Knowledge creation involves a number of phases consisting of tacit and explicit knowledge. Tacit and explicit knowledge are mutually dependant on each other, i.e., to understand explicit knowledge tacit knowledge is required (Alavi and Leidner, 2001). For example, to be able to read a document you need an understanding of the meaning of the symbols (words and numbers) on the page (Beijerse, 2000).

The knowledge creation process as outlined by Nonaka et al. (2000) is a spiral, consisting of four phases – externalization, combination, internalization, and socialization. It consists of a conversion process between tacit and explicit knowledge. As the creation process spirals through the interaction between tacit and explicit knowledge the amount of knowledge in the organization expands.

This process applies also equally well to the DOE context too – the design and execution of experiments increase an organization's knowledge of product development processes, resulting in new as well as improved products and processes. In applying Nonaka's spiral of knowledge creation, we can conclude that the DOE approach creates new knowledge as follows:

- Externalization (tacit to explicit) – documenting in some way the results or findings of the experiment.
- Combination (explicit to explicit) – selecting multiple sources of explicit knowledge and combining it into some form which the individual understands.
- Internalization (explicit to tacit) – using existing information to conduct additional experiments and further their knowledge.
- Socialization (tacit to tacit) – sharing what you have learned with other team members.

In terms of the DOE process, tacit and explicit knowledge are used at a number of levels. Specifically, tacit knowledge is developed at a social level and at the individual level. External explicit knowledge and internal explicit knowledge are also required for knowledge creation. Thus, this leads to tacit knowledge being created at the individual level and explicit knowledge being created at the organization level (i.e., internally within the organization).

### 3.4.1 Guidelines for DOE

Due to the lack of a universally accepted process for conducting DOE it was decided to adopt the guidelines identified by Montgomery (2001b). Figure 3.1 outlines the types of knowledge required to conduct a DOE, and furthermore explains the knowledge created as a result.

| | **Tacit** | **Explicit** | |
|---|---|---|---|
| **Social** | Meetings<br>Brainstorming | Reports<br>Training courses<br>Books | **External** |
| **Individual** | Conduct Experiments | Internal documents<br>Email<br>Knowledge artifacts | **Internal** |

**Fig. 3.1** Four types of knowledge use and output in DOE

We will now examine the types of knowledge in terms of the DOE model (Montgomery, 2001):

1. Problem identification: This step entails all concerned stakeholders identifying issues with the current product or process. A team approach is recommended for this step using brainstorming and meetings. Thus social tacit knowledge is used for this step. For social tacit knowledge to evolve individuals must also have tacit knowledge to contribute. Social tacit knowledge requires discussions and interactions which results in individuals developing their own understanding of the problem (i.e., the generation of individual tacit knowledge either during the brainstorming sessions or shortly thereafter).
2. Choice of factors: This involves selecting the factors which may have the greatest influence on the problem associated with the product or process. These factors will be measured in the experiments. It is usually conducted simultaneously with Steps 1 and 3. As it is conducted within meetings or brainstorming sessions, this step requires individual tacit knowledge to create social tacit knowledge from which individual tacit knowledge is reabsorbed.
3. Selection of response variable: This includes identifying suitable measures/responses to determine if the problem has been addressed. Again this

step is conducted simultaneously with Steps 1 and 2. As it employs the social medium, it requires the use of social tacit knowledge. This results in the generation of individual knowledge (i.e., individual tacit knowledge is created).
4. Choice of experiment design: This involves identifying appropriate methods for conducting the experiments (e.g., RDM, RSM). External explicit data is deployed here, such as participating in training courses and/or reviewing books. The result is the generation of individual tacit knowledge (as one interacts with the explicit data to form their own knowledge of the material).
5. Perform the experiment: This involves executing the experiment and calls for individual tacit knowledge which has been generated in Steps 1–4. This results in a greater understanding of the development processes in the organization.
6. Statistical analysis of the data: This step involves analyzing the results of the experiments. To analyze the data, a knowledge of statistical methods is required which is often obtained from external sources such as training courses, websites, and books. This results in internal explicit knowledge being generated via the recording and analysis of experimental data. Furthermore, individual tacit knowledge is also generated from the interpretation of the results.
7. Conclusions and recommendations: This involves making recommendations based on the findings from the analysis of the experimental data. When generating conclusions, the individual has to use the tacit knowledge created in Step 6. The outcome is the creation of internal explicit knowledge which is disseminated to the organization through a specific medium.

To enable the above process to occur, a platform must exist to facilitate it. Nonaka and Konno (2000) defined "Ba" as a shared place – physical, mental, or virtual – for knowledge creation. In the following few sections, we describe such a platform for knowledge creation – specifically, an IT-based KMS that was designed to facilitate the creation of knowledge in the DOE environment.

## 3.5 Knowledge Management in DOE

Fahey and Prusak (1998) highlight the importance of experimentation as a method of encouraging exploration and knowledge creation. However, to date, no research has been conducted into the development of KMS to support experimentation and exploit such data. This section will explore issues with regard to the use of KMS in the DOE context. The following section will then identify how these issues have been addressed through the implementation of an IT-based KMS in a company.

### *3.5.1 Need for Knowledge Management to Support DOE*

One might question why KMS is required to support the DOE. There are two reasons for this. First, as mentioned previously, DOE can be resource intensive to execute in terms of both time and money. Thus, it is important to capture as much of the information as possible for reuse and application. In addition, as can be seen from the previous section the DOE process is highly dependant on existing knowledge to enable experiments to be executed. Also in the different steps in the process several types of information are generated, reused, and re-absorbed. The whole DOE process is reliant on the use of existing knowledge and the generation of new knowledge. Thus, without the management of the knowledge creation process it would be impossible to conduct the DOE procedure. In short, KMS is critical to enable the diverse stakeholders to access existing information and to reuse them during DOE.

### *3.5.2 Issues for Knowledge Management in DOE*

DOE is a process of innovation as it discovers new development processes and methods. Several studies have highlighted the relationship between innovation and organizational performance and survival (Cavusgil, Calantone, & Zhao, 2003). Prajogo and Ahmed (2007) argue that "the most commonly held concept of innovation refers to the newness and novelty of products or processes." In terms of knowledge, innovation can be identified as "the application of knowledge to produce new knowledge" (Drucker, 1993).

However, over-reliance on existing information inhibits innovation (Darroch, 2005). Ozanne, Brucks, and Grewal (1992) stated that knowledge workers are often exposed to incomplete information and have the option to search for additional information in order to update. Thus it is important that a KMS to encourage innovation does not provide the complete picture. Traditional expert systems that provide complete answers to problems are inappropriate.

The IT-based KMS outlined in this chapter will take account of these issues as well as those identified by Cooper (2003) as supportive of innovation (given below):

- KMS should be integrated into current work practices and complement the individuals work rather than distract them. The IT system should enable the individual to work at different levels of abstraction scanning, brief evaluation, and in depth analysis. Furthermore, Grant (1996b) highlighted the role of embedding KMS into organizational routines to encourage knowledge use.
- KMS should take into consideration contextualization (i.e., what is relevant and when).

Much research has linked knowledge management to both radical and incremental innovation. Studies have found that there is a positive link between knowledge acquisition (internal and external) and innovation but not between knowledge dissemination and innovation (Darroch & McNoughton, 2002). This suggests that one should focus on models that facilitate the acquisition and creation of knowledge rather than dissemination or codification of knowledge. Experimentation is in effect a knowledge creation or acquisition activity. The following section examines the role of information technology in facilitating knowledge management for DOE.

### *3.5.3 Role of IT in Facilitating Knowledge Management for DOE*

As mentioned previously, Nonaka et al. (2000) highlighted the need for a shared space to enable knowledge to be changed from tacit to explicit, a critical part of the knowledge creation process. Information technology in the form of a KMS can provide such a space and facilitate the conversion of explicit knowledge into tacit knowledge (through interpretation by an individual or a group).

We now describe the case study and the IT-based KMS in greater detail.

## 3.6 An IT-Based Knowledge Management System for DOE/RDM

### *3.6.1 Case Study Overview*

The company is a small engineering company in the wire forming industry with 30 employees. They wished to move into the medical devices sector due to the increased demand of such products. To do so, they were required to have highly accurate product specification processes as this is a highly regulated industry.

This can be quite difficult given that wires can be as small as 25 μm. In addition, there is high level of uncertainty regarding the quality of the raw material as it composed of numerous materials, e.g., steel, platinum. For example, spring steel can have very severe variations. The company suspected that much of the variation was associated with incoming material. The company tended to rely on good engineering practice to find the process settings that resulted in stable processes. Thus, it was decided to adopt a DOE approach to improve existing product design and development processes.

### *3.6.2 Background*

The accuracy and the quality of micro design/manufacturing processes, particularly micro coiling, have become increasingly critical in today's medical device manufacturing industry. There is limited literature available in the micro-coiling industry concerning process robustness and machine optimization. Control factors, such as machine settings, contain sources of unwanted variation which can negatively affect the repeatability and quality of a product or process. At a micro-level these variations can hugely influence how the manufacturing process performs. Therefore, it is critical to determine which control factors can be manipulated in order to make the product or process insensitive to noise and unwanted variation.

Hence, DOE is utilized to optimize the design and manufacturability of a medical micro-coil used within the vascular system. DOE is applied to systematically determine noise factors that affect key product characteristics (KPCs). Results obtained enabled the practitioner to apply designed experiments in order to successfully achieve process optimization. The analysis of the data helps to understand how process characteristics (e.g., $KPC_1$, $KPC_2$, ..., $KPC_n$) are affected by exploiting the control factors. Experimental data obtained from this research provided vital information for the new and unexplored medical micro-coiling industry.

### 3.6.3 System Scope

The scope of the system is to capture explicit knowledge in a common place and disseminate this knowledge to enable the creation of tacit knowledge allowing components to be produced to an accurate specification. Furthermore, the system will encourage users to "think outside the box" by promoting users to conduct further experiments where existing information in the system does not support the requirements. The system will automatically interpret these experimental findings.

### 3.6.4 System Requirements

The focus of this chapter is on the use of experimentation as a method of knowledge creation and the design of an appropriate IT-based system to support and facilitate this activity. In previous sections, we discussed the meaning of knowledge and saw that there were several perspectives of knowledge. It was identified that knowledge is subjective and not objective as opposed to the traditional view.

As mentioned previously, to enable knowledge creation to occur it is important that the different stages in the knowledge spiral be facilitated. The scope of the IT system targeted three of the stages of the knowledge spiral:

- Externalization (or tacit to explicit conversion): The system will store all the tacit knowledge obtained as a result of these experiments in explicit form using a variety of media such as procedural documents, videos, and images.
- Combination (explicit to explicit conversion): The individual will be able to search for relevant explicit knowledge and the system will help combine it into a model that addresses the users' requirements.
- Internalization (explicit to tacit conversion): The system will allow the individual to use the explicit knowledge and apply it to their experimental work to further enhance their knowledge.

The KMS does not support the socialization phase of knowledge creation (tacit to tacit conversion). As part of the DOE process brainstorming and regular meetings take place. However, since the company described here is a small company with engineers working in close proximity to others there was not an urgent need for a virtual facility to facilitate this stage of the knowledge spiral.

### 3.6.5 System Design

To design the system, a combination of a knowledge management development life cycle and the common KADS approach (Schreiber) was used. Table 3.1 summarizes the steps taken to design the system.

**Table 3.1** A summary of the IT-based KMS for DOE

| | |
|---|---|
| Company strategy and context for DOE | The company's strategy is to identify a method of producing high-quality products with a narrow range of deviation from the required specification. Explicit knowledge is available to allow the production of the component to a specific point in the range, however, a more accurate specification is needed. The KMS should help capture explicit and tacit knowledge and employ that to develop better development processes. |
| Data collection | To collect data about the current development processes several interviews were conducted with key engineers. The developer also studied existing documents and reports. |
| Design and scope of the IT system | The scope of the IT system is to support engineers in generating new experimental data, and thereby improving existing processes. Both tacit and explicit knowledge is to be addressed. Tacit knowledge will be recorded using videos and pictures and documented where possible. Explicit knowledge will be automatically imported from existing documents and data files. The IT-based system will support externalization, combination, and internalization stages of knowledge creation. |

Earlier, we identified several issues related to knowledge management that any IT-based system should address. Below we explain how these issues were addressed by the current KMS:

- First, it was noted that KMS should be integrated into current work practices. Further, the role of embedding KMS into organizational routines to encourage knowledge use was also highlighted. There is a concern however that this may lead to static approaches with over-reliance on the system and not encouraging individuals to "think outside the box" (Darroch, 2005). To address this issue the KMS will be tied closely with the daily tasks of the R&D engineer/operator/technician. They will be able to search for knowledge associated with these tasks. This will be used as a reference for employees wishing to conduct their daily work. This, in turn, would result in the knowledge being embedded into their organizational routines. The system will only act as a guideline and a remedy for known issues and further experiments will be required in the event the prescribed remedies do not satisfy the user's requirements.

- Second, it was noted that the KMS should address analyzing the data rather than interpreting the findings. To address this issue, the system was designed to be responsible for storing explicit knowledge, fetching this knowledge, and displaying such knowledge to the individual. The individual will be responsible for interpreting this data and applying to their daily work.

The knowledge repository was updated with knowledge artifacts including experimental data, documentation, videos, and images. The R&D engineer had already created many of these sources of explicit knowledge. The knowledge system was then coded to allow the above functionality. The system operates by the user initiating all responses, through the query of existing explicit information or the update of existing information. The user can interact with the application in the following ways:

- View/update procedure: This allows the user to view/update any documents, images, and video associated with conducting a procedure; they can view purposes of the procedure, references, definitions, pre-requisites, or the procedure itself, images, and videos.
- Upload artifacts (video, images, and documents): The user can upload documents, images, and videos associated with a specific procedure.
- Upload experiment: The user can upload new experiments for analysis.
- Analyze experimental data: The user can analyze an experiment based on a customer specification. This will recommend machine and process settings to design and manufacture a product of such specifications.

To build the IT application a suite of software was used. A standalone DOE application was used for the recording of experimental data. A content management system (Joomla) was used to host the application due to its user-friendly capabilities. A combination of PHP and Javascript was used to enable the system to be interactive. This software was used to fetch, update, and query information. Apache server was used to host the application. The IT-based KMS was hosted on an intranet server in the company.

The KMS system supported the company's business objective by enabling them to operate in the highly regulated medical device sector. It enabled engineers to exploit explicit knowledge recorded in the system to further enhance their tacit knowledge (by conducting and interpreting additional experiments as required). The company now offers products in the medical devices sector which was not previously feasible with their old development and manufacturing processes.

The redesign of the development and manufacturing processes as a result of the KMS has led to reducing the company's innovation time as well as enabling it to be more flexible and adaptive to customer requirements. The company turns to experiments to address any issues which may arise and are not afraid of changing internal processes to enable them to identify new ways of doing things.

## 3.7 Future Research Directions and Conclusions

The objective of the chapter was to identify a model for developing an IT-based KMS that would facilitate knowledge creation in an organization through the exploitation of experimental data, with an emphasis on DOE. This chapter took account of the types of knowledge required to conduct a DOE and the resulting knowledge produced. We described an IT-based KMS that implemented Nonaka's knowledge spiral in the DOE context.

A number of areas of improvement of the system can be identified that in turn present opportunities for future research in this area. First, due to the nature of the company, the socialization aspect of Nonaka's knowledge spiral was not included here. However, this aspect may be addressed in a several ways.

- The use of e-mail to notify all stakeholders about the launch of new experiments.
- Additional capability to record and automatically synthesize information (and insights) from brainstorming sessions into audio and video files. Rather than codifying social tacit knowledge it merely records and hosts it, this can then be available for all employees to listen to and reabsorb into their own cognitive system for transfer to individual tacit knowledge.
- Discussion boards and forums have been researched as a form of socialization. Ruggles and Little's (1997) report proposed the use of weekly forums with outside experts and internal employees – as this provides opportunities for socialization both internal and external to the organization.

As outlined, graphical access to experimental findings would provide greater insight into the relationship between different factors and also further build users' tacit knowledge. Functionality that would allow employees to exploit the use of graphical mediums to display experimental findings would most certainly facilitate the generation of internal tacit knowledge. Future research should examine the impact of such IT-based features.

An additional feature where all employees synchronously interact with the findings of experiments via IT and discuss different issues would also encourage the socialization aspect of the knowledge spiral and present additional avenues for future research. In addition, there may be greater potential to exploit experimental data beyond the capabilities of the DOE software. Currently, the system only queries one experiment at a time; however, there is potential for the system to query multiple experiments (based on similarities in product specifications or findings). Furthermore, the IT system could highlight areas where knowledge is lacking and make recommendations for additional experiments based on this. Such a feature could be extended to address other areas of experimentation (i.e., outside the DOE context).

Acquisition of explicit knowledge can be time consuming. Search engines such as Google have capabilities that enable automating searches and features that integrate those capabilities with the KMS would be highly beneficial. However, this would require better understanding of the issues that underlie such knowledge integration and indicate potential issues for future research.

The above suggestions for further research are likely to lead to a deeper understanding of how IT can be used to support experimentation that enhances product development processes.

In conclusion, it is hoped that this chapter will provide valuable insights regarding the promise and potential of the IT-based KMS to facilitate and support improvement of development and manufacturing processes through experimentation. As noted in the beginning of this chapter, the use of experimentation in this context has received very limited attention from researchers. This chapter has hopefully provided a foundation to build further knowledge in this area.

## References


Alavi, M., & Leidner, D. (2001, March). Review, knowledge management and knowledge management systems: Conceptual foundations and research issues. *MIS Quarterly, 25*(1), 107–136.

Anderson, M. J. (2000). Success with DoE. *Quality, 39*, 38–44.

Antony, F. (2001). Simultaneous optimisation of multiple quality characteristics in manufacturing processes using Taguchi's quality loss function. *International Journal of Advanced Manufacturing Technology, 17*, 134–138.

Antony, J. (2002). Robust Design in new product development process: A neglected methodology in UK manufacturing organizations. *Work study, 51*(2), 81–84.

Antony, F. (2006). Taguchi or classical design of experiments: A perspective from a practitioner. *Sensor Review, 26*(3), 227–230.

Antony, F., & Knowles, G. (2001). 10 steps to optimal production. *Quality, 40*, 45–49.

Antony, F., & Tzu-Yao, C. (2003). Training for design of experiments. *Work Study, 52*(7), 341–346.

Arvidsson, M., & Gremyr, I. (2008, February). Principles of robust design methodology. *Quality and Reliability Engineering International, 24*, 23–35.

Beijerse, R. P. (2000). Knowledge management in small and medium-sized companies: Knowledge management for entrepreneurs. *Journal of Knowledge Management, 4*(2).

Breyfogle, F. W. (2003). *Implementing six sigma: Smarter solutions using statistical methods*(2nd ed.). Austin, TX: Wiley.

Cavusgil, S., Calantone, R., & Zhao, Y., (2003). Tacit knowledge transfer and firm innovation capability. *Journal of Business and Marketing, 18*(1).

Choo, A. S., Linderman, K., & Schroeder, R. S. (2002). *Structured method and motivational potential in knowledge creation: Linking quality and knowledge*. University of Minnesota Working Paper.

Clements, R. B. (1995). *The experimenter's companion*. Milwaukee, WI: ASQC Quality Press.

Cooper, L. P. (2003). A research agenda to reduce risk in new product development through knowledge management: A practitioner perspective. *Journal of Engineering and Technology Management, 20*, 117–140.

Darroch, J. (2005). Knowledge management, innovation and firm performance. *Journal of Knowledge Management, 9*(3).

Darroch, J., & McNoughton, R., (2002), Examining the link between knowledge management practices and types of innovation. *Journal of Intellectual Capital, 3*(3).

Dewar, R., & Dutton, J. (1986). The adoption of radical and incremental innovations: An empirical analysis. *Management Science, 32*(11).

Drucker, P. F. (1993). *Post capitalist society*. Harper Business, ISBN 0887306616.

Ellekjaer, M. R., & Bisgaard, S. (1998). The use of experimental design in the development of new products. *International Journal of Quality Science, 3*(3), 254–274.

Fahey, L., & Prusak, L. (1998, Spring) The eleven deadliest sins of knowledge management. *California Management Review, 40*(3), 265–276

Fisher, R. A. (1935). *The design of experiments*. Edinburgh: Oliver and Boyd.

Goh, T. N. (2002). The role of statistical design of experiments in six sigma: Perspectives of a practitioner. *Quality Engineering, 14*(4), 659–671.

Grant, R. M. (1996a). Toward a knowledge-based theory of the firm. *Academy of Management Executive, 17*, 109–122.

Grant, R. M. (1996b, Winter). Toward a knowledge-based theory of the firm. *Strategic Management Journal,*17, Special Issue: Knowledge and the Firm, 109–122.

Gremyr, I., Arvidsson, M., & Johansson, P. (2003). Robust design methodology: Status in the Swedish manufacturing industry. *Quality and Reliability Engineering International, 19*, 285–293.

Leung Tsui, K. (1992). An overview of Taguchi method and newly developed statistical methods for robust design. *IIE Transactions, 4*(5), 44–57.

Madhavan, R., & Grover, R. (1998, October). From embedded knowledge to embodied knowledge: New product development as knowledge management, *Journal of Marketing, 62*, 1–12.

Montgomery, D. C. (2001a). *Introduction to statistical quality control*(4th ed.). New York: Wiley.

Montgomery, D. C. (2001b). *Design and analysis of experiments*(5th ed.). New York: John Wiley & Sons.

Nonaka, I., & Konno, N. (2000). The concept of Ba building a foundation for knowledge creation. *Handbook of knowledge management 1999–2000*, 37.

Nonaka, I., Toyama, R., & Konno, N., (2000, February). SECI, *Ba*and leadership: A unified model of dynamic knowledge creation. *Long Range Planning, 33*(1), 5–34.

Ozanne, J. L, Brucks, M., & Grewal, D. (1992). A study of information search behavior during the categorization of new products. *Journal of Consumer Research, 18*, 452–463.

Phelan, K. (2004). *Evaluating the knowledge and support systems necessary to help first time users of statistically designed experiments achieve success*. (M. Tech), University of Limerick.

Prajogo, D., & Ahmed, P. K. (2007). The relationships between quality, innovation and business performance: An empirical study. *International Journal of Business Performance Management, 9*(4).

Ruggles, R., & Little, R. (1997). *Knowledge management and innovation: An initial exploration*, working paper. Ernst and Young, accessed 13th August 2008 http://www.providersedge.com/docs/km_articles/KM_and_Innovation.pdf

Ryan, T. P. (2000). *Statistical methods for quality improvement*(2nd ed.). New York: Wiley.

Schreiber, G., Akkermans, H., Anjewierden, A., De Hoog, R., Shadbolt, N., Van de Velde, W., et al., (1999). *Knowledge engineering and management: The common KADS methodology*. MIT Press

Shoemaker, A. C., Leung Tsui, K., & Wu, J. (1991, November). Economical experimentation methods for robust design. *Technometrics, 33*(4), 415–427.

Simms, C., & Garvin, J. S. (2002). It′s a black art: Design of experiments switches on the light. *Managerial Auditing Journal, 17*(1/2), 65–71.

Stalk, G., (1993) Time and innovation. *Canadian Business review, 20*(3).

Taguchi, G. & Clausing, D. (1990). Robust quality. *Harvard Business Review, (Jan–Feb)*, 65–75.

Genichi Taguchi, G., Elsayed, E. A., & Hsiang, T. C. (1989). *Quality engineering in production systems*. McGraw Hill.

Vicari, S., Krogh, G., Roos, J., & Mahnke, V. (1996). Knowledge creation through cooperative experimentation. In G. Von Krogh, & J. Roos (Eds.), *Managing knowledge: Perspectives on cooperation and competition*, 184.

Yamin, S., Mavondo, F., Gunasekaran, A., & Sarros, J. (1997). A study of competitive strategy, organisational innovation and organisational performance among Austrian manufacturing companies, International. *Journal of Production Economics, 52*(1).

Zumd, R. (1984, June). An examination of 'Push –Pull' theory applied to process innovation in knowledge work. *Management Science, 6*.

# Chapter 4
# IT-Based Tools to Support New Product Design: A Case Study of a Design Consultancy Firm

**Julian Malins and Aggelos Liapis**

**Abstract** Product design and development processes do not always proceed in a linear step-by-step manner, starting with the initial problem leading to a solution consisting of a number of clearly defined steps in between. As such the development of IT-based tools to support this process is also far from straightforward. It requires considerable creativity to design IT-based systems that can enhance product designer's capabilities without detracting from the creative process. In this chapter, we offer insights into the use of various IT-based systems that have been developed in response to the requirements of a contemporary design consultancy. Specifically, we examine the various stages in the design process based on a case study of a London-based design consultancy, Studio Levien. The case study is used to illustrate the key IT-based elements required to support the design process and their implications for research and practice.

## 4.1 Introduction

Product design and development processes do not always proceed in a linear step-by-step manner, starting with the initial problem leading to a solution consisting of a number of clearly defined steps in between. Indeed, the reality is far more complex and unpredictable. The process may consist of many iterative steps and the progress may appear to be haphazard and idiosyncratic. Like the creative process itself, it resists clear definition (Brazier, 2001; Press & Cooper, 2003; Hudson, 2005). As such the development of IT-based tools to support this process is also far from straightforward. It requires considerable creativity to design IT-based systems that can enhance product designer's capabilities without detracting from the creative process. In this chapter, we use the case study of a product design consultancy firm to illustrate this and to emphasize the implications for research on IT and product development.

---

J. Malins (✉)
Gray's School of Art, The Robert Gordon University, Garthdee Road, Aberdeen, Scotland
e-mail: j.malins@rgu.ac.uk

S. Nambisan (ed.), *Information Technology and Product Development*, Annals of Information Systems 5, DOI 10.1007/978-1-4419-1081-3_4,

Product designers use IT systems in a variety of ways to support their practice, from the initial gathering of information surrounding a product concept to the use of advanced visualization and project management tools. The use of computer aided design (CAD) software has become standard in many design consultancies to help visualize new designs, communicate ideas to colleagues and clients, and create 3D models which can then be used to generate the machine code needed to drive rapid prototyping systems. There are, however, situations where a pencil and paper or a hand-made model has considerable advantage over an IT-based system. The advantage may come from the ability to communicate a concept more directly or to understand a form more completely as a result of handling a physical object.

Organizations may employ their own in-house professional designers. Alternatively, they may prefer to make use of design consultancy companies offering more specialized services. Making use of a design consultancy firm offers particular advantages. The independent nature of the consultancy can provide a new perspective to a company, allowing them to bring a more innovative approach, which may not be available in-house. All design consultancies are unique in some respect or the other; however, they all require sophisticated IT systems in order to track the development of projects and to assist in the product design process itself.

This chapter offers insights into the use of various IT-based systems that have been developed in response to the requirements of a contemporary design consultancy. This chapter examines the various stages in the product design process based on the case study of a London-based design consultancy company, Studio Levien. The case study is used to illustrate the key elements or features of the IT system required to support the design process and their implications for design practice. The chapter concludes by identifying some useful research directions based on the themes that emerged during the development and evaluation of the IT application described here.

## 4.2 Design Consultancies: Business Model and Processes

Design consultancy companies come in many different forms and sizes. They are businesses that offer specialized services to their clients ranging from advice on corporate and brand strategy to the conceptualization and design of whole product ranges, in some cases providing a company with an entire brand identity designed with the purpose of distinguishing them from their competitors. Many of the design consultancies that specialize in new product design have built their client base on the skill and reputation of highly talented individual designers.

One such company is the London-based design consultancy, Studio Levien. The company was founded in 1999 by Robin Levien and his partner Tricia Stainton. Levien graduated from Central St Martins School of Art and the Royal College of Art before specializing in the design of industrial ceramics. Stainton graduated in Printmaking at the RCA in 1977. On graduation, Levien worked for the design consultancy, Queensbury Hunt, becoming a partner in the firm a few years later (Queensbury Hunt Levien). In 1982, the company Ideal Standard Ltd. commissioned Queensberry Hunt Levien to design a range of sanitary ware.

Up until this point many sanitary ware manufacturers had not considered the design of a bathroom as a complete design in which all the elements complimented and harmonized with one another. Prior to this concept becoming main stream, the various products within the bathroom at this level in the market would bear little relation to each other in terms of form. Levien's designs had a transforming effect on the whole industry as other manufacturers adopted a similar holistic approach to their product ranges.

Since then Levien has built a worldwide reputation for excellence in design, establishing his own design consultancy, Studio Levien, in 1999. The company now employs a core team of full-time product designers, model makers, support staff, and freelance designers and consultants working on individual products, including tableware, sanitary ware, and other consumer products.

While all design consultancies are unique in terms of their internal design processes and the nature of the information technology systems they adopt, there are some common elements of the processes and the IT systems that can be identified. Specifically, there are some recognized stages in the design process that can be supported with the use of IT systems. Studio Levien provides a useful example to illustrate how IT systems can be used by a design consultancy and offers valuable insights on how IT systems add value to the design process.

Next, we describe the design process at Studio Levien. Figure 4.1 provides a simplified overview of the design process with the various IT systems used to support it. All projects at Studio Levien begin with a contract between the client and the consultancy firm. Project management software is used to keep track of the project from the contract signing stage through to its conclusion.

## 4.3 The Studio Levien Product Design Process

It may be that a manufacturer wishes to invigorate a product range or perhaps their competition has developed a new range of products that challenge the client's position in the marketplace. The manufacturer looks for a design consultancy company, beginning with an examination of the consultancy's portfolio of clients and successful product designs. An initial dialogue may lead to the company commissioning the design consultancy to undertake the design of a new product.

The design process begins with the development of a design brief. The brief may be developed in consultation with the design consultancy. The document may be highly detailed or may be deliberately vague and open. A typical design brief will contain information about the manufacturing company, a statement setting out the problem, information about the various constraints the new product has to meet, and an approximate budget and timescale. The brief may contain additional information regarding risks and benefits. In the best case scenario, the design brief is developed

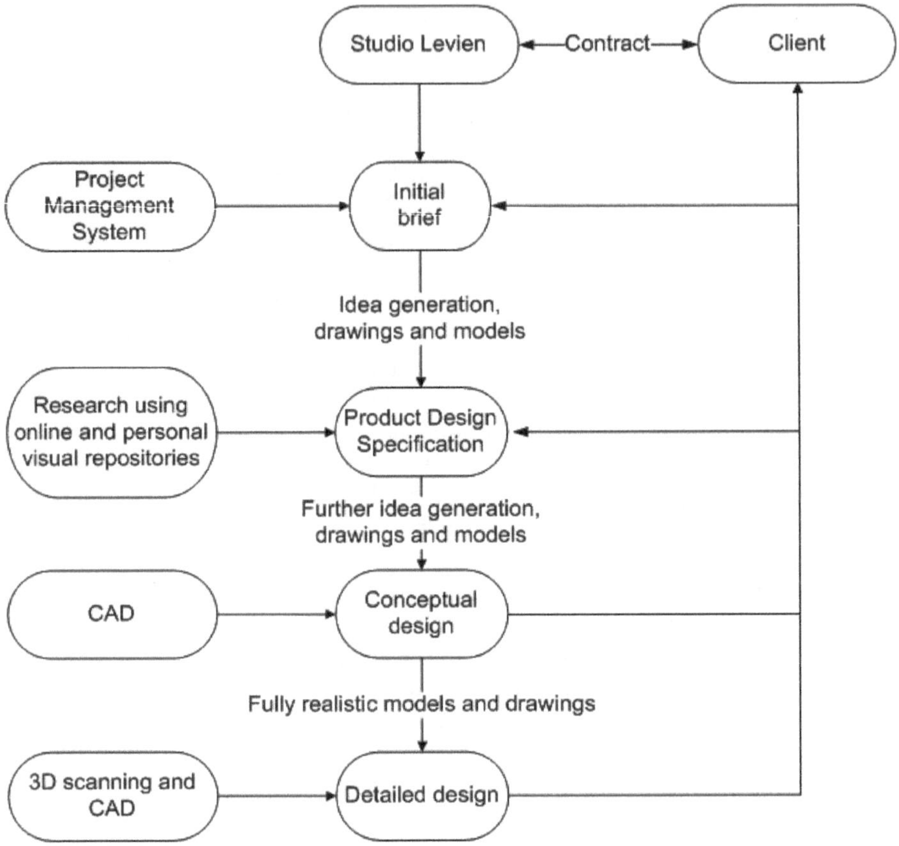


**Fig. 4.1** Stages in the design process supported by IT

in collaboration with the design consultancy which will then lead to a shared understanding of which of the constraints within the brief are priorities and which may be rephrased to avoid predetermining any possible solution.

The next stage is the development of the product design specification (PDS). The PDS is a document listing the problem in detail (Oren & Jin, 2002). The design consultancy will collaborate with the client in analyzing the marketplace in order to produce a list of requirements necessary to design and manufacture a successful product. This document is not limited to the functionalities associated with the product. It will also consider issues such as product performance, product weight and size, operating conditions throughout the product's life cycle, approximate retail cost, visual appearance, when the product should be available in the market, how long the product should last in the market, and how it will finally be disposed of (or retired). In addition, issues related to product safety, industrial standards, environmental regulations, manufacturing quality, and product maintenance would also be specified.

Product designers will constantly refer back to the PDS to ensure that the subsequent designs are appropriate and fulfill the brief. To produce the PDS the design team will research the problem and analyze competing products (Brazier, 2001; Hudson, 2005). Once the project is established, the details can be entered on to the design consultancy's database. The database may be a relatively simple stand-alone application containing basic information relating to the client or a more sophisticated project management system (PMS) designed to track the progress of the project, providing the project timeline, and critical path information. Microsoft's MS-Project and Merlin are two commercially available software packages used by designers for this purpose.

Before beginning work on a new project, a detailed contract is established between Studio Levien and the client. Studio Levien charges on the basis of royalties on each product sold and funds the design process based on an advance on future royalties.

The next stage is that of conceptual design, in which the broad or schematic concepts are proposed (Williams, 1997). With reference to the PDS, the design team produces a range of outline concepts (Verbeke, 2001). The conceptual design outlines some of the key product components (or modules) and their arrangement (i.e., configuration). More detailed information is provided at a later stage (Brazier, 2001). For example, the concept design for a car might consist of a sketch showing a car with four wheels and the engine mounted at the front of the car. The exact details of the components, such as the diameter of the wheels or the size of the engine, are determined at the detail design stage.

The degree of detail generated at the conceptual design stage will vary depending on the product being designed (Hudson, 2005). This stage of the design process involves drawing up a number of different concepts which satisfy the requirements of the product outlined in the PDS. They will then be evaluated to decide on the most suitable for further development (Günther, Frankenberger, & Auer, 1996).

The technique of "matrix evaluation" is one approach which can be used for the evaluation process (Oren & Jin, 2002). Matrix evaluation lists the important features required from a product. The list is developed using the PDS. The quality of the other concepts are compared against the benchmark concept for the required features, to help identify if the concept is better, worse than, or is the same as the benchmark concept. The design with the most "better than" features is likely to be the best concept to develop further.

The designers at Studio Levien capture their ideas by sketching them out on paper. Annotation helps identify key points so that their ideas can be communicated with the other members of the design team. There are a number of synectic techniques available to the designer to aid the development of new concepts. One of the standard techniques is brainstorming (Ivashkov, Souchkov, & Dzenisenka, 2000). This usually sparks ideas from other team members (Hymes & Olson, 1992). By the end of a brainstorming session there will be a list of ideas that may have the potential to be developed into a concept. Brainstorming works best when the members of the team have a range of expertise to draw upon.

Once a number of concepts have been generated, it is necessary to choose the design that would be most suitable to fulfill the requirements set out in the PDS. The PDS is used as the basis of any product decisions made. Ideally, a multifunction design team should perform this task so that each concept can be evaluated from a number of angles or perspectives (for example, market, technology, manufacturing). The chosen concept will then be developed in detail.

At Studio Levien, it is standard practice to develop a highly realistic 3D model usually made from high-density polyurethane foam. In some cases, this is given a resin coating to resemble glazed ceramic. The models will form the basis of the presentation to the client. The models often require considerable levels of hand finishing, which means that they may require to be 3D scanned in order to capture the physical dimensions for later manipulation within a CAD environment.

The final stage of the design process is that of detail design (Brazier, 2001). At this stage, the chosen concept is designed in detail with all the necessary dimensions and specifications (Hudson, 2005; Curtis, Krasner, & Iscoe, 1988). A large number of decisions need to be made relating to specific issues, and the precise work of detailed drawing, calculating and testing is carried out at this stage (Anderson, Button, & Sharrock, 1993). The earlier stages may be revisited if problems are encountered. The end result is a detailed product description containing all the necessary specifications for the product's manufacturer.

Studio Levien's approach is to present the client with an accurate 3D model of what the finished product would look like. It may then be necessary to work closely with the client to iron out any manufacturing anomalies. In the case of ceramics, considerable amount of distortion can occur during the firing process which needs to be accounted for in the design. For example, the design of a dinner plate would account for the dropping of the rim of the plate during the firing so that the final shape of the product is correct.

Next, we describe a set of IT-based applications that were developed to support the design processes described so far.

## 4.4 Virtual Design Environment

A virtual (i.e., IT-based) design environment was developed in collaboration with Studio Levien to support the company's design activities (Liapis, 2007). The environment consists of a series of tools and services designed to support the product conceptualization and design processes. These tools and the underlying principles that they are based on are described in more detail in the following sections.

Figure 4.2 illustrates how the new virtual design environment integrates into the design process, providing support for the design team particularly during the early stages of the development of the initial concept.

Once a contract is established between a client and Studio Levien details are entered into the design environment's database. The client's requirements, encapsulated in the design brief, are shared with the design team.

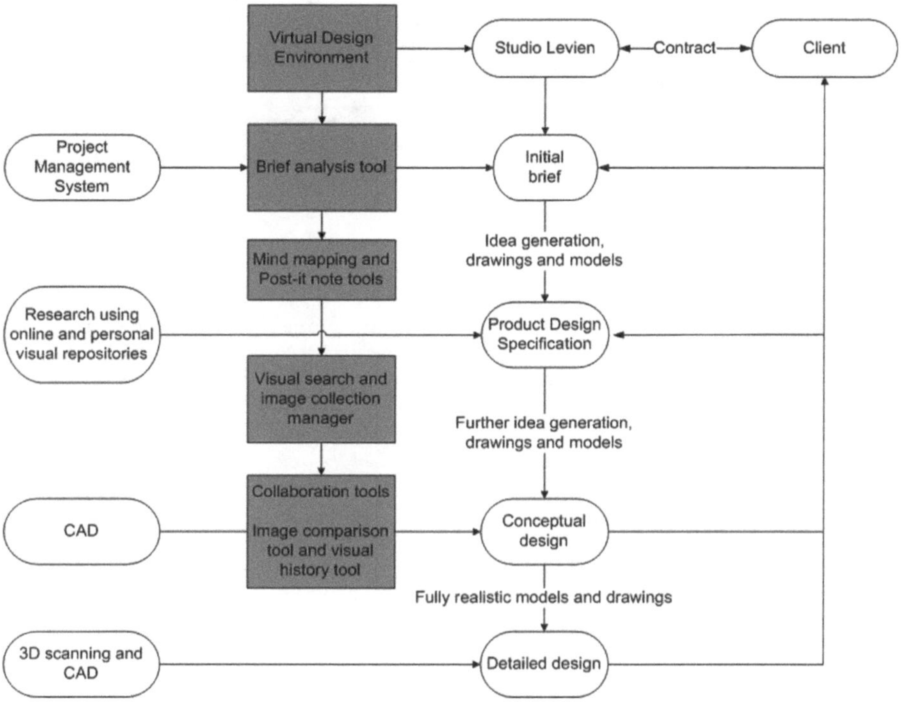


**Fig. 4.2** Virtual design environment and design process

## *4.4.1 "Design Brief" Analysis Tool*

The environment contains a brief analysis tool. Keywords in the design brief document can be identified automatically by the software, using an algorithm, which is then used to search a database. The brief analysis tool was initially designed to work automatically; however, it was subsequently found that better results were achieved if the designer identified the keywords manually. The tool helps the designers identify the main points in the design brief by locating related Web-based resources based on the keywords that they have identified.

The core of the analysis tool is founded on a database derived from the TRIZ algorithm. The Russian problem solving technique of TRIZ (http://www.mazur.net/triz/) aims to create an algorithmic approach to the invention of new systems and the refinement of old systems. In practice, TRIZ provides a large body of proven design heuristics, which offer set ways of transforming problems, and therefore, a sound basis for creative idea generation.

The tool integrates the TRIZ algorithm into a portable version of Open Office Writer, which combined with a C++ based agent running in the background, searches the Web allowing users to access a variety of third party online resources based on their inputs (keywords) as illustrated in Fig. 4.3.

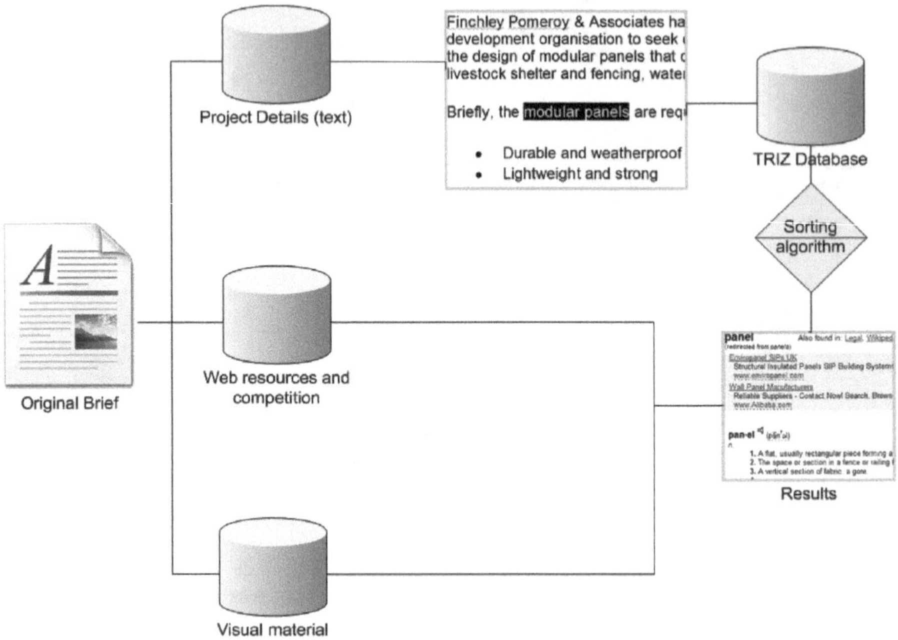


**Fig. 4.3** Architecture of the "design brief" analysis tool

The "design brief" analysis tool provides a lot of useful background information, which is stored in the central database. The use of the tool speeds up the necessary background research and provides information about rival products, new materials, manufacturing techniques, and any relevant legislation or government regulations.

The client's requirements may emerge following a series of conversations, either face-to-face or over the telephone. The environment uses voice recognition software to make transcripts of the telephone conversations. At present the accuracy of the transcription software is limited to 80% but this is considered to be sufficient in order to provide an overview of the conversation.

The environment also includes a "record meeting" tool that is designed to record the synchronous activity, which takes place when designers are working collaboratively, using the environment's collaboration tools. The core of the tool is developed in C++ and the video outputs are either in avi or swf format. If the user chooses to convert the output to swf format the tool automatically creates the HTML file for Web publishing purposes.

### *4.4.2 Support for Idea Generation*

The virtual design environment has a number of tools to support idea generation, including the use of mind maps and Post-it notes. The design process may begin by either referring to case-based design solutions (Domeshek, 1992) or by applying existing design knowledge to retrieve information from the designer's own resources (Fischer, 1997; Nakakojin, 1999).

Ideas can be generated by a wide range of intuitive and systematic creative problem-solving techniques. The techniques are designed to stimulate the mind into generating additional ideas. Besides brainstorming, techniques may include mind mapping, attribute listing, the use of checklists, and various forms of analogy-based techniques (i.e., based on other systems). In addition, support for more systematic approaches based on techniques such as morphological analysis is also available. Ideas can be generated by association, by analogy, by exploration, or by transformation (Diehl, 1987). Software tools exist which support all of these, although they are disconnected (Dartnall, 1994; Gardner, 1985). Figure 4.4 describes the mechanism behind the brainstorming tools included in the environment.

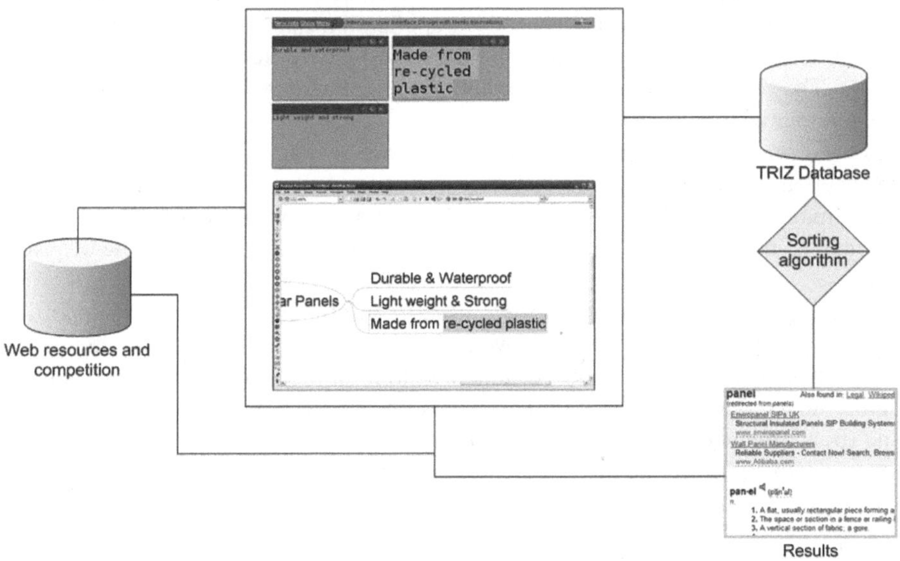


**Fig. 4.4** Architecture of the brainstorming tools

Figure 4.4 shows both tools using a TRIZ-based database combined with appropriate sorting algorithms, which allows users access to relevant third party online resources while brainstorming. The user is able to brainstorm using either the mind mapping or Post-it note tool to extend their original ideas, the software locating related sources using the integrated agent.

At Studio Levien it is standard practice to gather information from multiple sources so as to inform the design process. The designers use key words to search visual repositories, such as Google Images and Picsearch, which provide images that are used to assist the creative process. The virtual design environment provides a more sophisticated set of tools to accomplish this task by searching multiple visual repositories simultaneously.

### 4.4.3 The Importance of the Visual

The growth of online visual repositories makes it possible to search a vast amount of images very quickly. The images may be used to create mood boards or simply provide sources of inspiration. For example, designers tend to use mood boards to immerse themselves into a particular state of emotions associated with a task or product (Liapis, 2008). These mood boards consist of a collection of visual images (e.g., photographs, material samples) gathered together to represent an emotional response to a design brief (Dartnall, 1994; Gardner, 1985; Gero, 1993; Gross, 1996).

At Studio Levien, images are often used to convey a quality or suggest an association on behalf of the viewer that helps to emphasize the qualities of the designed object. For example, the image of a falling feather next to a new design may be used to convey a feeling of lightness.

Images are a powerful resource to convey meanings, particularly emotional values and experiences (Wycoff, 1991). Their application can serve as an important tool to communicate values that cannot be expressed easily through words (Sharples, 1994). The image can offer the designer and client a shared language, thus aiding the communication process.

Based on a cognitive process model there are two approaches to help product designers use visual images for their creative tasks, either by identifying and delivering images that might be useful for the designers, and/or by identifying properties that can be mapped from partially identified design requirements to those of visual images.

Both approaches are related to the issue of information delivery in supporting creative design. In response to this, two tools were developed and integrated into the virtual design environment: (a) An image search tool that searches all the popular online image databases based on key words and properties introduced by the user and (b) an image collection tool that allows the designer to create collections of the images gathered from the image databases (Liapis, 2008).

### 4.4.4 Image Search Tool

The image search service provided in the prototype is a What You See Is What You Get (WYSIWYG) tool. The tool illustrated in Fig. 4.5 provides access to every

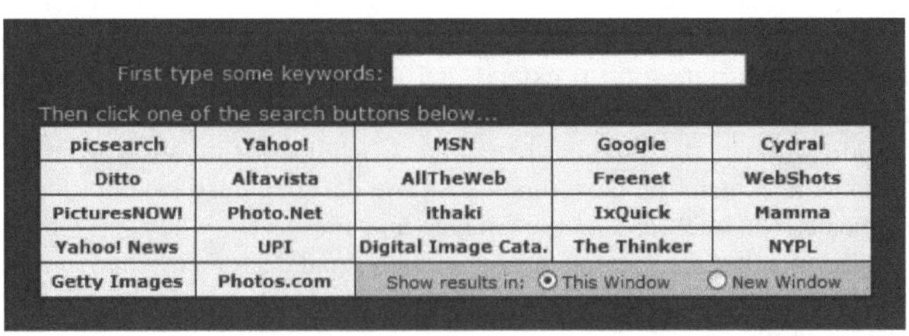


**Fig. 4.5** Interface of the image search tool

major free Web-based image database, delivering relevant pictures as thumbnails and links to the websites related to these images.

The algorithms used for the image search engine integration are commercially available. They might also look for clues from the image′s context (for example, words or phrases that are close to the image) or the meta-information found at the top of the HTML coding. Analysis of an image′s text and context is used to exclude images. This is the same principle used by Web image filters.

### 4.4.5 Image Collection Manager

The image collection manager is an advanced tool featuring a number of innovative content-based search techniques. The core of the tool is based on a series of prototype C++ and Python-based searching algorithms. These make use of a multi-resolution wavelet decomposition algorithm to query image databases. Image search queries may be expressed in three different ways, either by using a rough sketch scanned or drawn directly into the computer using a sketching tool, or by using a similar image, or by using meta-data key words.

By clicking on the "Draw" tab the user can draw a brief sketch of the image or images that they are looking for. The color and shape are also used to narrow the search parameters. For example, by drawing a simple orange triangle using the sketch tool, the image collection tool returns ten best matches along with a score indicating how similar they are to the actual sketch, in this case, a picture of the pyramids (66.3% matched to original) from a collection of 404 images in total (see Fig. 4.6).

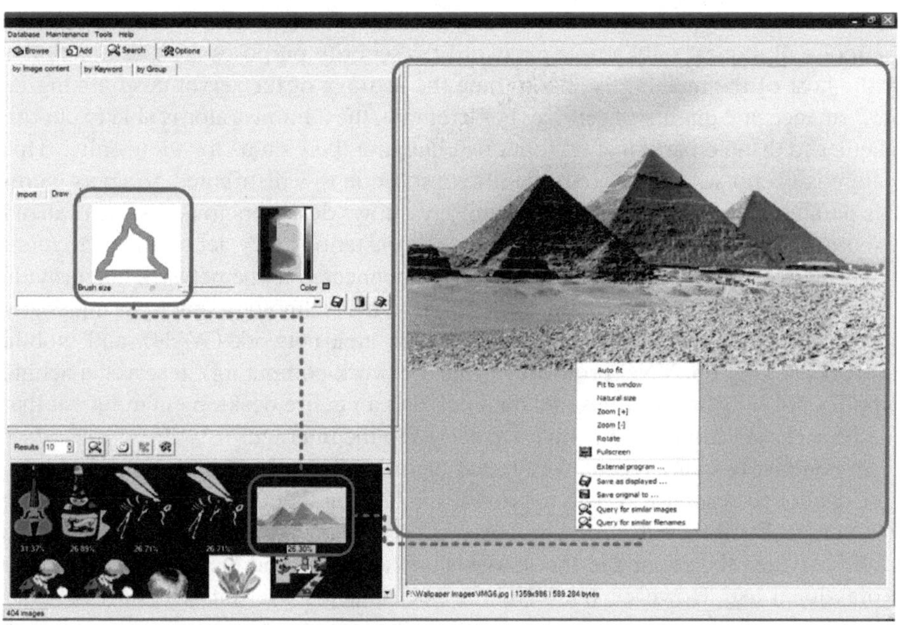


**Fig. 4.6** Interface of the image collection manager

The tool may be used to browse personal image collections by directory or by visual similarity in "Browse images." Users are able to automatically group images by color, date, time, and key features with the use of an adaptive clustering algorithm. The tool provides all the appropriate meta-information (description, size of the image, quality, name of the designer or the contributors, etc.). The system uses this information for the creation of HTML-based albums, storyboards or when searching for images.

In addition, users are able to search the database using key words, finding at the same time duplicate images based on user parameters (dimensions, file size, file name, and similarity). The virtual design environment also includes a tool designed to remove the Alpha channel from pixel-based images (background of an image), making it easier to collage images together for storyboard purposes.

### *4.4.6 Computer-Supported Collaborative Working*

Computer-supported collaborative working (CSCW) tools refer to applications that support the sharing of data between computers as well as communication tools that support both synchronous and asynchronous working (Dartnall, 1994; Gardner, 1985; Gero, 1993; Gross, 1996). IT-based applications that allow two or more users to work simultaneously on a design are available. These tools allow users to share desktops using remote desktop applications. This facility is already part of both Mac and PC operating systems. This technology transmits keyboard and mouse events from one computer to another.

A tool that simplifies the operation of setting up a shared desktop was incorporated into the virtual design environment at Studio Levien. The default settings of the tool will request only a user password for security purposes. The administrator or the host of the meeting is able to tune the settings of the server customizing its performance and quality of service. For example, the administrator is able to choose whether to disable participants' input by changing their status to "view only." This feature is useful when you are presenting a solution to a distributed group as it creates an interaction protocol. This technology allows designers to access centralized resources from remote workstations. These workstations may act as clients to more powerful distributed server machines that are connected to the network and provide users with appropriate tools, data, and storage. This technology functions under any network type local area network (LAN), wide area network (WAN), and mobile networks. Using the VNC protocol (virtual network computing), a server machine supplies not only applications and data but also an entire desktop environment that can be accessed from any machine connected to the internet.

In contrast to many recent Web-based or Internet applications VNC uses a random challenge-response system to provide the basic authentication when connecting to a server. Even though this is reasonably secure, once the user is connected the traffic between the client and the server is unencrypted, and therefore is unsafe for professional use. However, the VNC may be tunneled over an SSH or VPN connection which adds an extra security layer with stronger encryption. This approach encrypts all traffic between the two machines using public key encryption techniques, making it very difficult for anyone else to access the data. It can also be used as a reliable way to penetrate firewalls delivering data securely.

If product designers are working on a single design, a tool that can highlight changes made to the design by different people is very valuable. These changes may be quite subtle and may occur asynchronously. It is also valuable to be able to provide a visual history, which illustrates the development of a design, making it possible to track back through the various changes that have occurred. In this way, it is possible to observe how a design has evolved over time (and based on inputs from multiple team members).

The virtual design environment at Studio Levien includes tools that allow for the quick comparison of images, allowing significant changes to be noted. These features are used to provide users with information on the progress being made in a project and can also be used to identify the contributions made to a project by individual contributors.

The image comparison tool creates three image forms: source, operator, and result. Each form always keeps one image in the computer's memory. In order to locate the differences between two images the user has to open the image that they wish to compare in the source and operator windows. This service uses a C++ and Python algorithm, as well as wavelet decomposition, to break the two images into pieces and then searches for similarities, producing the remaining parts in the "results" window. Such a feature allows a large team that may be dispersed geographically as well as in terms of time zone to work on a single design efficiently and effectively.

Overall, the virtual design environment at Studio Levien offers a portfolio of IT-based tools that support the various aspects or stages of the design process, and more importantly, collaborative design. Next, we examine some of the implications for future research based on the experience in developing and implementing the virtual design environment at Studio Levien.

## 4.5 Research Implications and Conclusions

The research which has gone into the design and development of the virtual design environment indicates some promising avenues for future research. One area of particular interest is the development of the environment to support the education of new product designers. Design students and lecturers require a range of tools and technologies that can mirror the professional context, whilst simultaneously allowing students the maximum range in their creativity, encouraging experimentation and a reflective approach to learning. Educators need to be able to track students' individual progress and provide meaningful and timely feedback. Future studies may consider how such a virtual environment may enhance the learning process in product design.

Another area of research relates to the development of a visual search engine tool that can aid product designers. Future studies may consider the desired attributes and features of such a tool and the varied product design contexts where it may be useful.

Another key problem that IT-based tools could address in the design process relates to the lack of a common language of expression between clients and designers. One possible solution to this would be the application of computer-based ontologies. Tools implementing such ontologies could be integrated into a semantically driven version of the virtual design environment. Future studies should examine the design of such tools and the factors that may impact their effectiveness.

Information technology can play a critical role in supporting the product design process. The tools described in this chapter, some of which are still at the prototype stage, have considerable potential to increase the productivity and effectiveness of the design process. They are underpinned by a number of principles and techniques in common use by design professionals and as such these tools present limited learning curve for designers. The complex nature of the product design process requires creative and innovative solutions capable of enhancing the designers' capabilities, particularly integrating the communication, idea generation, and idea evaluation processes, so that more effective design solutions may result.

It is hoped that this chapter would lead to greater focus from both researchers and practitioners on the development and implementation of IT-based tools that support product design.

## References

Anderson, B., Button, G., & Sharrock, W. (1993). Supporting the design process within an organisational context. In S. S. De Michaelis (Ed.), *Third European conference on computer-supported cooperative work.* Milan, Italy, Netherlands: Kluwer.

Brazier, N. (2001). *Designing creativity*. Intelligent Interactive Distributed Systems Group, Faculty of Sciences, Vrije University, Amsterdam.

Curtis, B., Krasner, H., & Iscoe, N. (1988). A field study of the software design process for large systems. *Communications of the ACM, 31*(11), 1268–1287.

Dartnall, T. (1994). *Artificial intelligence and creativity.* Kluwer Academic Publishers.

Diehl, V. (1987). Productivity loss in brainstorming groups: Toward the solution of a riddle. *Journal of Personality and Social Psychology, 53*, 497–509.

Domeshek, E. A. (1992). A case-based design aid for architecture. *Artificial intelligence in design'92.* The Netherlands: Kluwer Academic Publishers.

Fischer, S. G. (1997). Computational environments supporting creativity in the context of lifelong learning and design. *Knowledge-Based Systems Journal, 10*(1), 21–28.

Gardner, H. (1985). *New science: A history of the cognitive revolution.* Basic Books, Inc.

Gero, J. (1993). *Creativity and knowledge-based creative design.* Lawrence Erlbaum Associations Inc.

Gross, M. D. (1996). Ambiguous intentions: a paper like interface for creative design. *ACM Conference on User Interface Software Technology (UIST) '96.* Seattle, WA, pp. 183–192.

Günther, J., Frankenberger, E., & Auer, P. (1996). Investigation of individual and team design processes. *Analyzing design activity.* Chichester: Wiley Press.

Hudson, P. (2005). *The design process*, available from: http://www.ider.herts.ac.uk/school/courseware/design/index.html accessed at: 10/09/2005.

Hymes, C. M., & Olson, G. M. (1992). Unblocking brainstorming through the use of a simple group editor. *ACM conference on computer-supported cooperative work (CSCW'92)*. ACM Press.

Ivashkov, M., Souchkov, V. & Dzenisenka, S. (2000). *A Triz based method for intelligent design decisions*. ETRIA European TRIZ association.

Liapis, A. (2007). *Computer mediated collaborative design environments*, Published PhD Thesis, The Robert Gordon University, Aberdeen, UK.

Liapis, A. (2008). Synergy: A prototype collaborative environment to support the conceptual Stages of the Design Process. In *Proceedings of the International Conference on Digital Interactive Media in Entertainment and Arts, DIMEA 2008*, Athens, Greece, ACM/IEEE Digital Library.

Nakakojin, K. (1999) A framework that supports collective creativity in design using visual images. *Creativity and cognition*. Loughborough, UK: ACM Press.

Oren, B., & Jin, Y. (2002). Creative stimulation in conceptual design. *ASME 2002 Design Engineering Technical Conferences and Computer and Information in Engineering Conference*. Montreal, Canada.

Press, M., & Cooper, R. (2003). *The design experience: The role of design and designers in the twenty-first century*. Aldershot, England: Ashgate Publishing Limited.

Sharples, M. (1994). *Cognitive support and the rhythm of design, artificial intelligence and creativity*. Kluwer Academic Publishers.

Verbeke, G. (2001). *A future focus on collaborative design*. Hogeschool voor Wetenschap & Kunst, Saint Lucas Architecture, Brussels, Belgium, Technical Design & Informatics, Faculty of Architecture, Delft University of Technology, the Netherlands.

Williams, A. (1997). *A project to incorporate remote collaboration into a design process for technology teacher trainees*. University of Newcastle, Australia, Edith Cowan University, Australia.

Wycoff, J. (1991). *Mind mapping: Your personal guide to exploring creativity and problem solving*. New York: Berkeley Books.

# Chapter 5
# Product Lifecycle Management (PLM): Critical Issues and Challenges in Implementation

**Andrew Hewett**

**Abstract** Product life cycle management (PLM) has emerged as perhaps the most important enterprise IT application for supporting product and service innovation. This chapter examines the unique challenges associated with implementing PLM. Specifically, the chapter focuses on three primary organizational challenges: (a) cultural issues around the "product engineer"; (b) a lack of standard engineering processes as a foundation for PLM; and (c) the failings of the PLM technology itself. The discussion enables a better appreciation of the value a strong resource like a "senior engineering fellow" adds to the project team and underlies the differences between truly standard functional activities (such as accounting) and product development processes, and how these differences could potentially reduce the repeatability of PLM implementations. The discussion also highlights the technical complexity in most PLM solutions that arises from bolting together diverse modules needed to address the different business functions associated with product development. The chapter concludes by identifying several important directions for future research on PLM implementation.

## 5.1 Introduction

Managing the end-to-end process – or life cycle – of new product development efforts is a critical function of a product company's operations. However, the systems and practices that underlie such product life cycle management (PLM), commonly referred to as PLM, has undergone significant changes in recent years. New and emerging information technologies, rapid globalization of businesses, and evolving core functions such as collaborative design and outsourced manufacturing have forced companies to re-examine their product development practices. A significant part of such a change in the management of new product development has been the introduction and adoption of a new type of enterprise-class IT application referred to simply as PLM.

---

A. Hewett (✉)
Director, PRTM, Mountain View, CA 94041, USA
e-mail: ahewett@prtm.com

S. Nambisan (ed.), *Information Technology and Product Development*, Annals of Information Systems 5, DOI 10.1007/978-1-4419-1081-3_5,

Just like in the late 1980s and early 1990s when the enterprise resource planning (ERP) application was emerging, in the 2000s, the PLM application has assumed considerable importance in most corporate IT budgets and activities. There are many parallels that can be drawn between some of the initial ERP implementations and the current PLM implementations: improperly set executive management expectations, high application implementation costs, frustrated end-users, armies of IT consultants, and evasive returns on investment.

For many years, there was healthy skepticism and debate on how successful ERP implementations and the resulting business solutions actually were. PLM application implementations are drawing many of these same criticisms. Similar to the history of the ERP project, some of these PLM implementation problems will disappear with the growing maturity of the software solution and the increase in the exposure and experience of the product development management team. At the same time, the challenges related to implementing a successful PLM solution are still considerable. In fact, there are surprisingly few truly successful PLM implementations in existence today! While there has much effort expended on installing PLM solutions in companies across industries, the business value these applications have delivered is still debatable. And, much of that can be traced to poor PLM implementation and an inability to boldly address the critical challenges associated with PLM implementation.

This chapter identifies some of the more important challenges related to implementing a PLM application. Our discussion does not address the common IT implementation challenges such as lack of project sponsorship or poor project team management. Instead, the chapter focuses on the nuances of implementing PLM.

Specifically, the chapter is organized around three primary challenges: (a) cultural issues around the "product engineer"; (b) a lack of standard engineering processes as a foundation for PLM; and (c) the failings of the PLM technology itself. The discussion will contribute to a deeper understanding of the value as well as the challenges a strong resource like a "senior engineering fellow" will add to the PLM implementation team. This includes the potentially dysfunctional political influences that such an "end user" would bring to an implementation team. The discussion will also distinguish between a truly standard business process (for example, accounting process) and product development process and how the implications of this on the repeatability of PLM implementations. Finally, most PLM vendors have bolted together different applications (components or modules) to address all of the PLM functionalities and this has increased the level of technical complexity associated with the PLM solution. This, in turn, poses unique challenges related to interfaces to existing enterprise IT applications.

It is true that the nature and extent of these challenges would vary with the product development and organizational context. However, if PLM application implementation costs, durations, and risks are going to be reduced, then these challenges have to be addressed. And, the first step in this direction would be enhancing our awareness of the challenges. We start with the first challenge.

## 5.2 The Influential Role of the Product Engineer

Typical business process enablement projects require that the implementation team work closely with the office staff that is responsible for performing the business functions being automated. These cross-functional business teams tend to be filled with, for example, people from purchasing, order management, sales and marketing, and inventory management. The people who fill these roles are dedicated professionals who work hard and have a very proprietary company perspective. But they're not product engineers. Business representatives often drive demanding requirements into the solution design and hold the implementation team tightly to the communicated project schedule. But they're not product engineers. Business transaction experts carry a lot of clout with the executive team as they help manage the project toward the best automated process solution to execute daily operations. But they're also not product engineers.

Creating products that directly generate real revenue is extremely specialized, difficult work that carries a huge responsibility. This responsibility lies with the product engineer. Automating a company's product engineering efforts means that the PLM implementation team is injected directly into the product development processes – i.e., processes that help to differentiate a company from its competitors by successfully developing and launching compelling new products into the market place. As a result, the end user or "owner" of the PLM application and therefore the primary contributor of solution requirements and the critical PLM project team members are... product engineers.

### *5.2.1 The Product Engineer: Experienced, Senior, Touchy, ...*

A company's engineering community is a highly skilled group of individuals who are in charge of delivering the next best product into the market place. The senior executive team relies on these individuals to produce innovative, revenue-generating solutions that drive the entire business operation. Working with product engineers in a non-engineering capacity is extremely difficult, making the design, development, and implementation of a PLM solution a study in patience and "non-destructive" compromise.

#### 5.2.1.1 Senior Engineers...Too Many Cooks?

Any one who has ever watched The Discovery Channel's show called "How They Build That" knows that thc job of product engineering is a highly respected profession. Companies recognize how important these individuals are by creating special organizational structures and often career paths to encourage the product engineer to stay with the company, and just as importantly, continue working and progressing as an engineer. With titles like Engineering Fellow or Engineering Scientist it is easy to see the value that the company places on this role and on these individuals. These highly educated, complex problem solvers are critically important to the success of the PLM implementation and yet can also become one of the larger barriers to the project success – an interesting dichotomy to say the least.

The Product Engineer is the primary end user of the PLM solution and as a result is the indispensable contributor to the PLM implementation team. But including end users (such as product engineers) on IT implementation core teams is nothing new. What is unique to PLM implementations is that in many companies these senior individuals actually make up the *vast majority* of the implementation team. These engineers need to participate – with a sizable number of representatives – in the tactical requirements definition, design, and testing project activities or the delivered solution will not address the engineering needs.

Because of where the ownership of the PLM implementation resides, these projects have a significantly high number of senior project contributors as compared to a more traditional IT application implementation project. For example, compare the typical roles of senior engineers (end users) in a PLM effort against those normally found on an ERP implementation team.

As Fig. 5.1 shows, the number of senior influential people on a PLM project team tends to be much greater than that found in an ERP project team. This is primarily due to the fact that in most engineering-oriented companies (which have traditionally taken the lead in PLM implementations), there is a higher proportion of engineers in the senior management. This is a huge challenge for the PLM project's day-to-day leadership. For example, it is not unusual for the project leader to occupy a lower role in the corporate organizational hierarchy than many of the key engineer contributors. As a result, the team dynamics can be very intense and decision making can be wrought with political overtones and convoluted logic. Indeed, PLM project teams often struggle in making critical decisions, especially those requiring any sort of compromise.

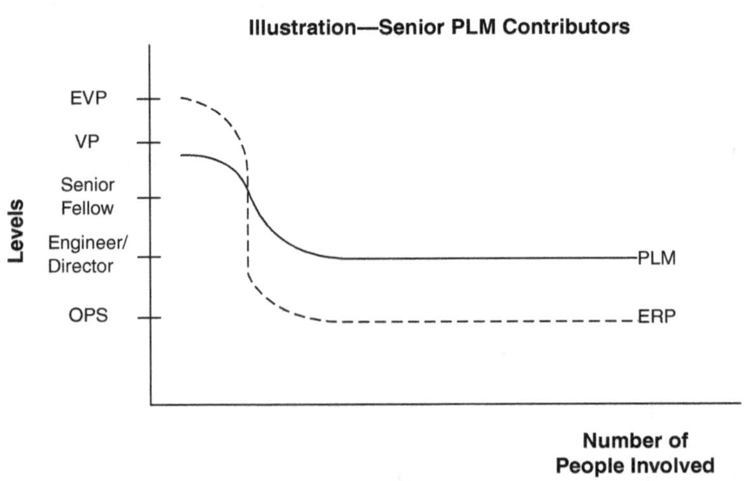


**Fig. 5.1** Role of engineers in PLM and ERP implementations

#### 5.2.1.2 Resistance to Changing the Product Development Processes...

There is a semi-conductor company in the western part of the United States that has two long hallways (that lead to and from the corporate cafeteria) lined with engineering patents awarded to individuals in the product engineering organization. It is a display of corporate pride. When that company was automating their product development processes, the non-engineer members of the PLM implementation team walked down those long hallways everyday. They would pass the patents with the names of the product engineers who had over the years made that company a leader in its market. Many of the names on those patents were the same names on the PLM implementation team roster.

Product engineers are most often the "go-to" people in a company – they are the people with the answers to the difficult, differentiating questions that companies face in this ultra-competitive place of business today. It should be no surprise to anyone that these highly esteemed, highly decorated, successfully critical people are also generally resistant to change in the product development processes.

Developing and patenting an answer to a difficult technical problem and knowing whether to change a development process to better fit a PLM solution are two different types of tasks. One thing is fairly certain, product engineers are much more comfortable in addressing a technical product design challenge than they are in representing their colleagues and defining a standard process that all engineers should follow. It is not that the engineer is incapable of contributing ideas to modify development processes to fit the PLM solution; it is just not what they are trained to do and therefore the task ends up being difficult and stressful to complete.

Product engineers often initially view being part of the PLM implementation team as a "nuisance" responsibility that can be addressed with a couple of hours or a day's attention. However, the engineer quickly learns that although the product development topics and processes are quite familiar to them, the decision-making and the tradeoffs associated with PLM implementation are very complex and conflicting. For product engineers who are used to "solving" complex problems (the patents to prove it), such a situation often leads to significant level of frustration and sometimes even embarrassment. What PLM implementation project team does not have at least one story of a senior engineer fellow who gets so mad at a project compromise that they stomp out of the room verbally threatening to never rejoin unless their feature request has been added to the project's scope? It's true.

### *5.2.2 "Not Invented Here" Attitude of the Product Engineer*

Engineers invent and develop products. Historically, engineers also developed automated solutions to help them execute product development processes. Version control, partner collaboration, and change approval management are examples of individual functions that the engineering community has addressed through small one-off programming efforts over the years. Disparate, undocumented, loosely managed "program scripts" running on an engineer's computer – located under the desk in their office – accurately describes many organization's traditional product development automation solutions. With the introduction of commercial off the shelf (COTS) PLM applications, the engineering department's necessity to develop and support its own custom functions or even an entire application suite is gone. Unfortunately, the need might be gone, but the engineer's desire to build their own PLM solution still exists. And, this creates several issues during the PLM implementation process.

#### 5.2.2.1 You Say Tomato. . .I Say Tomato

One of the worst meetings that the PLM team will have early on in the PLM implementation effort is presenting the purchased PLM application to the company's product engineering group (i.e., the primary users of the PLM). This is usually the first opportunity for the engineers to get to see the new PLM application. Typically, these engineers would not have been part of the "solution" selection committee – and as such they didn't sit through the hours and hours of vendor demos and they did not hear the perfectly reasonable sales responses to why some of the more challenging functionality does not exactly work as expected.

If you have experience with any IT application implementation you might consider this unpleasant meeting "standard fair," a rite of passage, or as one project lead likes to say "now the project can really begin!" So, why is this different for PLM implementations?

The product engineer is a "hacker at heart" and is not afraid of diving-in head first to address a technical problem. Interestingly enough, product engineers most often have a very simplified vision of a solution. Their limitations are defined by the hands-on experience that the engineer has had writing software and working with databases and the complexity of the environment (number of users, platforms, etc.) that he or she is deploying into. That being said, the difference in the product development world is that if the product engineer (user) had the time, they could probably build – or has already built – the functions the team is trying to implement. When working on the implementation of CRM or sales applications, for example, it is very unlikely that the end user would come back with a programmed, working prototype of a functionality – not so with PLM implementations. Although it is not often that the engineer community would challenge the PLM implementation team with an actual working set of functions, it has and does happen.

It is not unusual to demonstrate an application function and to have the engineer question the complexity or approach used to automate the process. This simple question can cause the team significant issues later in the project if the PLM implementation team does not thoroughly address it and resolve it with the engineer. When product engineers question the complexity, they are really thinking about the underlying function and not all of the technical complexity that actually makes individual functions work together as a PLM system. If the engineer's concerns are ignored by the PLM project team, when the project hits a snag later on (say, the deployment is delayed or the scope is reduced to stick to the schedule), the very respected, highly decorated, senior engineer will state "we could have built that ourselves, quicker, and cheaper" crushing the credibility of the project team and causing the executive sponsor to go into a tailspin.

One of the fundamental issues is that the product engineers usually do not have the same notion of "application" or automation as the PLM implementation team does. On a recent project, the PLM implementation team was working hard to plan and scope out the details of the PLM implementation. They were investigating conversion and interface requirements for the project. In one particular interview with end users, they were told about the "36 critical applications" that had been built – some that interfaced directly with the company's contract manufacturer – and how all of the data needed to be converted and the functionality of all 36 applications incorporated into the new PLM solution!

Needless to say a major warning flag was triggered. The PLM project leaders were very concerned that the initial project estimates of complexity, duration, and cost were no where near accurate; 36 data conversions and countless functional requirements unaccounted for was potentially devastating to the feasibility of the project based on current executive expectations. A meeting was quickly called between the product engineers, their boss (project sponsor), and the PLM project leader to review the 36 critical applications and discuss the feasibility of adding that much additional scope to the already tight project plan. Fortunately, what the team discovered in the meeting was that the "36 critical applications" were simply HTML pages of document links. The large number of "applications" was due to how the documents had been categorized. Since documents were already in scope and the HTML pages pointed at the same document repository that had already been analyzed by the tech team, there was no scope impact.

The key message from such examples is first not to take lightly the concerns of product engineers or end users as that could negatively impact the success of the project later on. More importantly, a thorough analysis of the issues would usually reveal easy workarounds that the project team could adopt to address the concerns.

#### 5.2.2.2 "We Can Do Better"

The "build it myself" mentality becomes very apparent as soon as the PLM implementation team starts working with the engineering team, collecting solution requirements, and reviewing vendor applications. Vendor application capabilities leave plenty of room for complaints.

The maturity and stability of the PLM applications is analogous to the ERP market 15 years ago. The functional foot print is currently being expanded through acquisitions resulting in a bit of a hodgepodge of user interface standards, process flow, and data definition. The vendors are making good progress but they are quite a distance from completion. Although this is more of a "maturity" challenge and less of a PLM unique situation, it is a significant issue for the PLM project team to manage through. Add into the mix the earlier discussion of the technically competent engineer end user and it quickly becomes apparent the incredible challenge it is to keep the team focused on a vendor-supplied PLM solution and not a new one created by the engineering department.

Flexibility issues and application performance can continue to fuel the engineers' "not invented here" attitude. In Silicon Valley there is a large company that was about to embark on a PLM implementation project. An external PLM consulting company was asked to come in and meet with the product engineering team that was leading the project to discuss how one might formulate a PLM business case and validate some of their benefit assumptions. About 20 minutes into the meeting it became obvious that they intended to build the PLM solution from scratch. Probing at the decision criteria, the external consultants soon encountered a fairly typical set of conclusions and reactions to the PLM software capabilities: medium functional fit; a focus on hardware development and not on software; ridged technical application structure; limited flexibility; and generally a poorly performing application. But ultimately, as the discussion continued, it became apparent that the real reason that this company chose to build their own solution rather than purchase from a vendor was because the application selection committee (that was led by product engineers) had convinced the company's senior management that "...we have the best engineers in the world, and therefore we can build a better PLM solution...." Rumors are that they are still working on it.

## *5.2.3 Do Engineers Really Need Help?*

Ask any product engineer if they might need help implementing a PLM application and most likely they will say "we don't"! The truth of the matter is that engineers have been implementing technical solutions for years – way before there were COTS, consultants, or IT departments focused at automating the PLM processes. The problem is, over the years, engineers have shown again and again a disregard for typical implementation best practices when leading large application implementations.

### 5.2.3.1 "Doers" Often Don't Plan

Regardless of how one defines PLM, a critical challenge that all projects face is creating a defendable "business case" for the project. IT vendors will focus their sales message on "the big numbers": total time to market (TTM) and product development productivity. The typical engineer does not think this way. As noted previously, for years, engineering has been automating parts of the product development processes around the edges of their normal responsibilities. The engineer's mentality is – if the automation is helpful then by default it is a valuable thing to do. Such a perspective is appropriate when the solution is internally directed at a contained, "local" product group and when the costs are negligible.

On the other hand, in the executive suite, there is a maniacal focus on the costs and benefits that these projects will generate. It is not that the engineering group is against a solid business case for the project. Instead, it is more of a desire to move onto what is thought to be the more valuable parts of the project. So as competent as the engineering department is at developing revenue generating products, regardless of how loudly they disagree, they need help in planning the implementation and in developing the business case for the PLM implementation.

Estimation of the project costs, the level of effort and the overall implementation complexity is another area that needs to be carefully done before the PLM implementation can be completely underway. An important problem that many PLM implementations encounter is making poor estimations of the project time and implementation costs and as a result completely mismanaging the expectations of senior executives. What is unique to PLM implementations is that most executives think that PLM projects are fairly simple, short-duration projects. Although the bravado of the engineer does not help to properly set executive expectations, the IT vendor sales team can further contribute to the confusion through the desire to be accommodating during the sales cycle.

Consider the example of PLM implementation at an electronics company that had been "spun out" from a larger organization. The leadership team identified early on that replacing the legacy product development system and the manufacturing resource planning (MRP) application could quickly drive down their escalating operating costs. They commissioned a team to select, purchase, and implement a new PLM application. The PLM team did the standard due diligence work with the PLM solution vendors and "learned" that the general rule of thumb for implementing PLM applications is 3 months per software module. Strangely enough, the quoted effort did not seem to dramatically change when they further explained some of the specifics of their particular project (e.g., complex bill of materials (BOM), re-implementing MRP on a parallel track, a very complex product data conversion from a legacy mainframe system).

Once the project team had the rough effort estimates, the rest of the business case development and planning calculations were easy. Unfortunately, experiences in implementing PLM solutions are fairly limited today and unlike ERP projects, neither the project leaders, IT departments, nor the executive sponsors think that they need to ask the tough project questions in order to ensure that the PLM estimates are correct. Fundamentally, the problem is that management inherently believes that PLM solution should be quick and easy to implement. Continuing with the example, by the time the PLM implementation team reached out for help, the project was already more than 6 months behind schedule, $1 million plus off budget with a solution that was not ready to deploy beyond the initial pilot site. On top of all of this, the executive group was furious with everyone involved in the project: engineering, IT, vendors, and consultants alike. In the end, no one associated with the project was successful.

#### 5.2.3.2 Standard Implementation Practices... Whatever

Product engineers always, *always* try to short-cut standard implementation practices. It is like they can't be labeled an engineer and follow time-tested implementation procedures! At times the process divergence and push-back can be comical but

**Table 5.1** Engineering response to PLM implementation practices

| Standard practice | Engineering response |
|---|---|
| Cross-functional teams | As engineers we know our business, why do we need to waste people's time in marketing or operations?<br>It's okay that quality department does not want to participate, we know what they need |
| As-is and to-be process modeling | We are implementing a new application, why do we need to model our current processes? |
| Application design documentation | Nobody ever looks at those documents after you deploy the system anyway |
| Minimize application customization | How hard is it to change a label on a screen? |
| Code freeze | These are just small changes that should not have any adverse impacts |
| Retire standalone systems | If this system doesn't work, I will write my own programs |
| Testing | Why can't IT look for bugs? My time is too precious to be testing the application<br>Why should we run "negative tests"? Who would normally do these things anyway? |
| Security | Product engineering resources should all be granted System Admin authority so that they can change whatever they need to change in the system |
| Metrics and measurement | We are not worried about the business case – this is an important project |
| Data cleansing | My data is fine. Why do I need to clean up the rest? |
| Training | I don't need the training. I can figure out how to use the system myself. How hard can it be? |

make no mistake, when the PLM implementation team is allowed creative license to address what should be standard practices, they significantly increase the risk of project failure.

To illustrate this point, Table 5.1 shows typical responses from product engineers (end users) when presented with standard implementation best practices in PLM implementation.

#### 5.2.3.3 A Burning Desire to (Not) Change

Collaboration, integration, global design. . .these are the standard rallying cries for taking on a costly, high risk, and complex PLM implementation – but not for the typical engineer. The globalization of business has reached the product development department it just has not necessarily reached the individual engineer.

Typically, time to market (TTM), product management, and product quality are the drivers to automate the product development processes – but product engineers just want their job to be made easier. Although it logically stands to reason that standardizing the PLM processes, integrating them with all company systems, and providing a common communication interface to partners will improve overall company-wide product development performance, at the individual product engineer's level, the impacts might be less favorable.

In large companies, it is not uncommon to have the PLM implementation initiative driven from product management. Product management is interested in finding new and faster ways to develop products, share designs, increase the quality of the designs, and design for cost. The engineers designing the products do not necessarily have the same desire to change. Time and time again it is the evolving business model through low-cost development strategies, product platforms, acquisitions, and contract manufacturing that force a management team to look at ways to scale product development. While the typical engineer would like to have the CAD software interface with the engineering BOM seamlessly, this alone is usually not enough for them to suggest a multi-million dollar PLM implementation. So essentially, the pain driving the PLM implementation effort is not the pain of the most impacted group – the product engineer!

This lack of alignment between product management and the product engineering group is one of the primary reasons why PLM implementations often deploy even when significant negative impact is identified. A couple of years ago a company that was suffering from some very public product quality issues (recalls, halted shipments, and canceled orders) embarked on a PLM implementation project. As the project neared its initial deployment, the engineering team members developed a pseudo "time and motion" analysis that illustrated how much the new system and the associated processes would negatively impact the day-to-day actions of the product engineer. The analysis also included a rough estimate of how many new engineers would need to be added to the staff in order to retain existing productivity levels due to the loss of customized legacy solutions tailored to the existing product development process. The senior executives acknowledged the good work from the team and then approved the deployment of the PLM application because the overall *corporate* benefits that the new system provided out-weighed the productivity costs to individual engineers.

## 5.3 The Elusive Standard Engineering Process

In most companies, senior executives "get" the product development process. The development process is viewed as standard across product groups, even across businesses. But once one gets into the details of how a company actually develops a product; how product development decisions are made; who is involved at the various different stages; how partner collaboration is defined and executed; etc. – the real nuances of a company's product development practices become more visible. Most companies have a product development process, even a new product introduction process (NPI). Some companies (but not all) have a retirement process as well for their products. However, the practices of the seemingly similar product development and engineering processes differ wildly across companies and even between products developed within the same company.

### 5.3.1 Standard Processes – One Size Does Not Fit All

As noted previously, the duration and cost of PLM implementation effort, often drives the executive team to a significant level of frustration. The executive perspective is that it is the products themselves that are complex, while the process of product development is straightforward. And as such, they believe PLM implementation would also be relatively easy, but they are wrong.

One of the big contributing factors is that the standard PLM process is anything but standard. Even within a company it is not uncommon to have a "lite" process for those projects that involve the development of a new product based on a common, existing product platform (or products that simply do not require a consistent amount of development rigor). The key issue is that not all the products in a company's portfolio are created equally. Often times a company's product portfolio becomes diverse, full of products that do not have the same complexity levels, testing, or even regulatory requirements. All of these factors inject a level of diversity into the product development process too.

Understanding a company's product development process variances is critical when planning a PLM implementation. It is important to know early on how the project team intends to deal with the different products and processes already deployed. Deploying more than one significant development process per project phase is not a best practice. The most common way of addressing this challenge is to analyze and configure the more complex of the process variants for the first phase of the PLM implementation and limit the deployment to development groups that use those broader processes for their new products. The goal here is to minimize the amount of "re-configuration" the project has to do during subsequent phases; having said that, this is a very tricky PLM implementation strategy to successfully execute.

Complicating the task is that the configured application cannot be the only deliverable in the overall solution. The project team must also be thinking about the necessary process changes required to effectively leverage the PLM solution. This would further increase the value addition to the product engineers and provide the right incentives for them to use the solution. If the development processes are not properly addressed and effectively aligned with the PLM application, the solution will not deliver enough value to individual engineers and they will soon find a way to work around the system.

There is a large global electronic equipment manufacturing company that has a very diverse product portfolio. They recognized a number of years ago that it did not make sense to push the "simpler" products through all of the approval and tolerance gates; change management sign-offs, etc. So they authorized a simpler product development process to be used when designing product for certain product families.

Unfortunately, the difference between the "lite" process and the standard process was dramatic and the perceived value gained from following the more comprehensive process was very low. After a number of years, the management team recognized that it was time to replace some of the aging application infrastructure – PLM was one of the areas targeted for renewal. As the PLM planning team started getting into the detail review of process metrics, phase gate deliverables, part reuse, part substitution, etc. it quickly became apparent that complex and simple development projects alike were using the same "lite" process for new product introduction and engineering change management. When the team looked into the problem, they found that it was a situation where the process names were exactly the same and the engineer incentives resulted in a behavior of presenting the product project details in such a way that the development team was often allowed to use the simpler process. Needless to say, this was "low hanging fruit" for the PLM implementation team; changes to the decision and review criteria were immediately recommended as a means to directly improve quality in certain products.

### *5.3.2 Process: A Corporate Differentiator?*

It is obvious that product development processes are similar, but not the same across product families and they are definitely not the same across companies – all of which complicates PLM implementations. Importantly, as noted previously, most senior executives use ERP as the baseline of effort for all IT application implementations because – at least until now – it was the costliest, longest project that a company had to endure. With that as a backdrop, compare the process scope and the required variant content of PLS implementations with the process focus of an ERP implementation.

ERP solutions became "commoditized" as soon as the finite sets of financial options and practices were defined and agreed too by the financial regulatory bodies. Obviously, strict government regulation and oversight of accounting practices were instrumental in finalizing these definitions. ERP implementations are not easy – no one would say that they are. But, the processes that they are automating are "standard" with-in an acceptable spectrum. No company is out there defining their own way of accounting for assets and debits. As a result, ERP projects have implementation aids like process maps, approval structures, and role-based security that is very reusable across projects. Software companies like SAP have complete implementation "templates" to help accelerate the automation effort. Oracle provides a data warehouse solution that has a direct connect to the ERP modules with predeveloped analysis cubes and reports that address the typical management views required to run a GAAP compliant business.

It is debatable whether the contributing factor to the PLM implementation challenge is the lack of a recognizable product development process within the PLM application or whether product development processes are enough of a company differentiator that they will never coalesce into standard processes unless there was a major forcing function – like government regulations or restrictions related to product intellectual property.

### *5.3.3 The Process Ripple*

Product development processes have an interesting characteristic. Since it is on the front-end of "the value chain," many of the decisions made during this stage "ripple" throughout the enterprise affecting seemingly unconnected parts of the business.

One of the more direct connections that the product development process has is with the supply chain and the manufacturing of the final product.

PLM implementations can tighten the bond between the revenue generating part of the business (product development) and the operational cost management (supply chain and manufacturing) processes that have traditionally received more attention. There is no argument that securing materials, storing, and consuming them can have a significant impact on a company's financials. But just imagine the benefits a company could receive if they not only controlled expenses well, but also selected materials and parts in such a way that the best part for the product at the right price for a given quantity at the right time was always secured!

#### 5.3.3.1 The Ever Elusive Integrated Process

A properly automated product development process could help create this nirvana – but make no mistake, driving this kind of efficiency between product development and the supply chain processes is a huge PLM implementation challenge. Many companies are aware of the obvious disconnects between the product development and supply chain process; it is an admittedly difficult area of the business to drive alignment. Some companies address the chasm by instituting groups into the organization that specifically focus on things like "product design costs." This is an expensive solution to the problem.

A great example of a process ripple is "part management." Obviously, products are made from specific parts and even the same product – for example, a computer, a mixer, or even a guitar – can be differentiated by the quality of the parts in its assembly. Sometimes the same part – say an aluminum $\frac{3}{4}$ in. Philips head screw with fine threads – can be used across multiple products even across multiple product families. However, this would require the product development engineer to recognize the opportunity to reuse such a part, easily find the reusable part, and be able to review the part specifications to ensure that the specifics for the part (e.g., tolerance limits, cost, and color) will work properly with the newly designed product. When this product development process is aligned with the company's supply chain best practices (for example, approved vendor list, demand planning, and volume purchase discounts), the actual part that the engineer picks is already accounted for in the supply chain which means the company is already getting the best negotiated price, the vendor has a successful supply history, and the necessary volumes of the part are on hand to meet the forecasted demand.

When the different enterprise processes can be integrated, products have a better chance of being delivered on-time and at an acceptable cost to the customer. The truth is that one of the primary challenges to closing this revenue and cost management chasm with the PLM implementation is team member expertise. PLM experts that can also understand supply chain issues are not easy to find, and so unfortunately, not many of today's PLM implementation address this issue. This reason alone drives many well-intentioned PLM projects to focus on "the four walls of the product development group" ultimately ignoring the potential value that could be derived from integrated processes.

### *5.3.4 The Misunderstanding of Process*

Which came first – the product or the bill of materials (BOM)? Sometimes PLM implementation teams lose sight of the fact that product engineers design and build new products – not BOM. PLM software focuses heavily on capturing and managing product data in a BOM product structure. Many product development groups – for some of the largest, most complex electronic equipment companies – still use simple solutions such as sharing Excel spreadsheets to collect product definition data. It is true that the process of experimenting, testing, collecting, verifying, and sharing product data is well understood by the engineering community. However, a funny thing happens as soon as the product data is loaded into the PLM application's structured format of levels, defined families, options, and acceptable values. Once the data is placed into the PLM application, even the most distinguished engineer fellow can be found scratching his or her head asking "where is the BOM that I developed and how can I see it?"

#### 5.3.4.1 The Chicken or the Egg

Many companies look toward PLM application vendors for complete product development solutions. Automation is important enough that PLM software selection criteria will typically include a section on process automation. The confusion with the application vendors is that although the sales brochures talk about product development processes, the applications don't automate them. This reality is often overlooked by product engineering because to them the PLM applications are either part, configuration, and document repositories (product data management); resource capability, availability, and assignment planning for projects (resource management); or products, project definitions, delivery dates, and revenue projections (portfolio management) – but they are not processes that build products.

The challenge is that although the applications don't directly automate the development process, the capture of the BOM information in the application represents the end-result of an engineer's product development efforts. Although this is not by itself a process, the creation of the BOM represents the product definition and the engineering decisions that were made "along the way." Implementation teams often don't recognize that the handful of screens used to collect a certain bit of data is not the process of product development – that actually happens outside of the application – but instead are simply the inputs to a sophisticated data repository. Typically, the engineer is confused because even though the data collected in the PLM application, it is the product data that he or she is responsible for delivering, the representation of the data is different and the process for recording the data unfamiliar.

#### 5.3.4.2 "Labradoodle" – Neither a Labrador Nor a Poodle!

The BOM implementation and data collection issues are complicated because the physical definition (structure) of the BOM – as driven by the PLM implementation team – always results in a change to the existing, known BOM definition. But this BOM structure change is important, even critical to the successful implementation and adoption of the PLM application. Without a properly designed BOM – or to be more accurate BOMs (often there are more than one BOM per product) – some of the delivered features and functions will not work in the PLM solution.

Unfortunately, the PLM implementation changes three important variables used by the product engineer: (a) the BOM definition; (b) how the data is recorded; and (c) where the data is recorded. It would be no surprise that by this point of the project, the project supporters are at best disgruntled sponsors. But even with all of this change, the PLM implementation project is not addressing the one requirement that everyone thought that they would "get" – product development process automation. So when the CTO asks whether the new PLM processes will have a direct positive impact on the quality of a product, the project lead is often unable to confidently answer the question.

## *5.3.5 Finding the Right Change Management Balance*

One of the huge benefits of standardizing an engineering development process and all of the procedures, documents, and data that go along with that effort is that it is easier to now standardize and implement an effective engineering change management process. Theoretically it should be easy: what needs to be reviewed when, by whom, and in what time frame. Also, the importance of the change process will not be doubted nor debated by anyone on the implementation team, in the product engineering department, or even in the company. As a result, one would think that this functional process area would be easy to implement – WRONG!

### 5.3.5.1 "Do as I Say. . .Not as I Do"

Product change management definitions and implementation challenges run a gauntlet of issues. On one extreme are the managers who are so excited to now, finally, have a way to get involved in the detailed development activities that they want everything (all change events) to go through a formal change approval process. At the other extreme is the truly renegade engineer who agrees that a change process is important, but thinks all of his or her changes do not fit the change management definition and therefore they do not need to follow the change process. . . except when he or she thinks that they should. Each of these groups has a defendable argument supporting their position with lots of examples of what "did not work" from past experiences.

Getting the approval process right is tough, tenacious work. One of the change management hurdles that need to be addressed in most all PLM implementations is responsiveness. Product managers and even engineering managers will often design change approval processes that "work on paper" but are cumbersome in practice.

One of the critical measures of a product development organization is time to market (TTM). In order to drive TTM consciousness deep into the engineering organization, "segments" of the product development process need to be measured.

A detailed understanding of how long it takes to perform a certain activity or complete a portion of the product design is critical for driving down a companies overall TTM. Inserting approval steps into the process can lengthen the time it takes to complete the development activities – yet these approvals might be critical to increasing product quality and reducing the level of product returns.

With the introduction of a new PLM application the approval processes are usually a big focus of the implementation team. In addition to the approval processes the project team needs to work with the identified reviewers and help them to understand the direct impact a slow response can have on the product development process and on the business. They need to analyze why certain situations might result in a slower response and look for ways to design the process and alerts to minimize such occurrences.

#### 5.3.5.2 Rubber Stamp Approvals

Another reality of many corporate engineering change management processes is the rubber stamp approval. The problem of the rubber stamp approval often works hand-in-hand with the responsiveness problem that was just discussed. It is fairly common for management to insert itself into the product development process through the engineering change management process. After all, when there is a problem (e.g., schedule slip and increasing cost) it is often traced to a decision that was made that should have had more scrutiny before it was accepted. When something bad happens, the corporate management team will get aggressive and demand to be included more in the critical decisions that cause the problems. As a result of these requirements, the implementation team builds management approval routings into the engineering change process.

On the surface, adding management approval routes to the engineering change management process seems like process improvement "low hanging fruit." But now starts the debate: can management be involved in – let alone approve – engineering changes using a PLM automated process? This is a tough issue.

Just because someone is the product manager for a product does not mean that he or she has the technical engineering capability to provide value via an approval loop. What exasperates the problem is how the approval process has been automated by the PLM applications. There is not a "wealth" of information in an engineering change notification. As a matter of fact, the whole process is really intended for a select group of people who really "know" what is going on and can provide assurances, warnings and in some cases alternatives to changes that are being suggested to the new product. The process is supposed to be a quick and easy – a way to keep engineers responsible and accountable to potentially disruptive change.

Instead, the process can cultivate a rubber stamp culture even when a solid responsible, accountable, consulted, and informed definition has been implemented. When the engineering change management process has approval routes that include people that do not have the capability to perform an informed review of a proposed change, the approvals are often delayed and usually made based on who else in the loop has already signed off on the change – in other words it is a meaningless review. Automating the engineering change process can actually dangerously and needlessly slow it down; even create a false sense of comfort that the decision is the right one by including reviewers in the process who do not have the ability to add any value to a change decision other than automatically approving the change.

The engineering change process is one of the more "standard" processes in product development. Although the PLM application vendors are not quite there yet, the engineering change process is a great candidate to develop process maps and implementation acceleration techniques similar to what is found in today's ERP implementation tool kits. Knowing this, the PLM implementation team should be sure to leverage the process experience of the vendor and the implementation partner since there should be plenty of lessons learned from other projects. Sometimes the application vendor can secure engineering change customizations that were developed and implemented at another client site. This can be a tremendous time and cost savings to the project and should not be overlooked as a valid means of expediting the PLM implementation effort.

## 5.4 The Failings of PLM Technology

There are very few really successful, truly showcase, PLM implementations so far. One can find good examples with significant results in discrete product development functional areas like resource management or portfolio management, to name two. However, in the context of truly end-to-end PLM, successes are really hard to find. Even when PLM solutions are organized into functional categories, the connections to traditional product development measures such as TTM, product profitability, and even product quality are suspiciously absent.

### *5.4.1 Lack of Maturity of PLM Solutions*

One probable answer to these questions is that PLM software suffers from a lack of maturity. As noted previously, the current PLM software market is analogous to the ERP software market 15 years ago. At that time, the ERP market was a best of breed smorgasbord of technology and capability. For example, Oracle was only a database engine and you bought an HR package from one vendor and a financial package from a different one. When a company wanted a "comprehensive" solution they purchased a number of applications from different vendors and pieced them together – often with extensive customizations and interfaces – to address their entire functional scope.

While the PLM functional footprint is improving, it is still fairly common to need two to three different vendor solutions to effectively address the company's needs, *especially* if those needs span the entire product development life cycle. As a result, the PLM solution is typically a complex collection of tools, originally developed separately and then loosely connected – sometimes by a vendor as a tool suite, but more often by the PLM implementation team.

#### 5.4.1.1 The Leg Bone Is Connected to the...

The maturity issue is not all about current application functional footprints. "Standard functionality" is another maturity related issue that most PLM solution vendors face. Even though product development has been around for many years, most of the PLM solutions deployed at company sites are home grown tools focused at automating specific steps or a particularly difficult activity in the process. Even the commercially available PLM applications were originally built to automate a particular company's way of developing products.

PLM software companies have taken those initial solutions and cleaned them up to more generically address the PLM functional area. This is one of the reasons why the different PLM software solutions have such a wide spectrum of capability and also why the quality of the software can differ so much even within modules provided by the same vendor. The company and the project that provided the original code foundation for the PLM feature function significantly impacts the software performance, stability, and usability – even today.

The PLM user interface and its general usability is a prime example of the "functional Frankenstein" that implementation teams are forced to deal with given current levels of software maturity. When project teams work to combine multiple packages from different vendors to address scope needs, the implementation challenges can include everything from the simple lack of screen flow standards, search paradigms, and inconsistent behaviors to really poor performance, software version incompatibilities, and data integrity concerns.

Once again, these issues surely are not unique to PLM software. As the flurry of consolidation slows in the industry and the PLM solution modules have a chance to gel and mature together, most of these challenges will likely disappear. To that end, many of the leading PLM vendors are working to accelerate this stabilization period by launching – and in some cases even completing – complete code rewrites to existing modules and products.

### *5.4.2 Technical Complexity of PLM*

PLM solutions are complex software packages. Just look at the configuration options and algorithms for resource utilization and capacity planning against a portfolio of diverse products, or consider the BOM substitutions and variances into the product definition of a specially configured server. The point here is not to debate which software solution is more complex than another, but instead to recognize the potential impact of the technical complexity of the PLM solution on project execution. Indeed, technical complexity is a major contributor to the implementation challenges, solution quality, and costs of a PLM implementation.

A couple of years ago, a large computer manufacturer implemented the product configuration engine from a PLM application suite. When planning for the implementation, the project team failed to recognize and communicate to management that given the complexities of the company's products and the breadth of user requirements, the implementation was going to be very complicated. After spending millions of dollars implementing the solution, the company was left with a configuration solution that took approximately two times the amount of time as their competitors to configure purchase requests. Further, sometimes configured products would not work and required an army of full-time resources to continually add product data, compatibility data, and provide manual "assists" to the configuration as it moved through the process. Needless to say, the company was not enamored with the end result of the implementation and spent the next 2 years funding a project to replace it.

#### 5.4.2.1 But, Where Is the Benefit?

The complexity of the product development process and the PLM technology used to automate that process is often reflected in the simplicity of the business cases that we have traditionally seen developed to justify these implementation efforts. Until recently, many of the companies implementing PLM and the PLM application vendors tried to rely on material scrap and productivity (headcount) alone to quantify a projects business impact. It does not require a lot of product development experience or a PLM guru to recognize that these two areas do not contribute the most benefit from product development practice automation. The problem is that the functional areas that a company wants to improve and/or automate are not simple, wholly contained subjects and they are neither easily measured nor automated.

Take for example a straightforward question like "where is this part used?" Large electronic equipment manufactures would love to get control of part use and reuse. This simple question to what should be a basic management principle desired by most all product development organizations is really, *really* difficult to effectively model in a PLM application. Yet being able to provide the engineering community parts that are already production tested and qualified would positively impact the quality, cost, and TTM for the new product.

Even though the technical complexity of PLM implementations limit the benefits that can be estimated, measured, and the functionality delivered through today's applications, managing this complexity is actually a good argument for why companies should move toward replacing home grown PLM solutions with off-the-shelf applications. Today's vendors clearly see the need to better mask the applications complexity and more directly connect the PLM solution to standard, defendable metrics. We should continue to see improvements in functional capability without an increase in complexity as the PLM solutions evolve and mature.

### *5.4.3 Customizations Encouraged – Really!*

PLM solutions typically require customizations as a critical part of the project implementation effort. There was a time in the ERP implementation business when the consultants who encouraged no customizations had a differentiating message. Today, most companies understand that ERP implementation projects should not customize the application. The leading vendors are quick to remind potential buyers how difficult and expensive it will be to redeploy a "vanilla" solution in order to re-enable the application upgrade path and re-engage the support contract. However, the PLM technology is not quite there just yet.

Although all implementation teams surely manage against needless customizations, in the end they all have made software customizations in order to address some unique user requirements. PLM solutions are simply not configurable enough or functionally capable of addressing the broad base of product development practices employed by companies across varied product markets. This reality has really caught internal IT leaders by surprise. By now, most IT departments have policies against any kind of customization made to a purchased application. Such a policy can be very challenging when implementing a PLM application especially when some companies define a customization as broadly as a simple change to an existing database call.

#### 5.4.3.1 Customizations: The New Best Practice

The question is: will the necessity of customization be an on-going characterization of PLM implementations or are customizations a necessary evil when automating the product development process? There are at least two different camps with two different answers to this issue.

Obviously, the software vendor's point of view is that the need to customize the software is simply a technology maturity factor. As more and more software releases are launched, the quality and accuracy of the PLM technology will greatly reduce – if not completely eliminate – the need to develop software customizations. Given that ERP vendors are acquiring and/or releasing their own PLM applications this point of view is easy to believe. However, some people believe that product development – the essence of the process that makes some companies more successful than their competitors – is a function that cannot be commoditized. The belief is that the development practices are differentiating and therefore a third party PLM application cannot generically model the process enough to eliminate all customizations. Regardless of which camp you align with, only time will tell which line of thinking is correct.

#### 5.4.3.2 Wanted: PLM Experienced Implementers

When looking at the technical landscape of a PLM project (e.g., best of breed application suite, complexity, and functional customizations) one can surmise that locating experienced resources that match a typical project scope is difficult. Even PLM technical consultants tend to have a narrow, targeted area of experience (e.g., change management and portfolio management) and little experience – even familiarity – with other functional areas. Throw in the project team's need to develop customizations in order to meet the scope of the user requirements and it becomes apparent how this implementation challenge quickly becomes a major project risk.

PLM application vendors do not always have the necessary skill sets internally to configure or customize a particular PLM feature function. In 2005–2006, one leading PLM vendor completely outsourced the change management functionality revisions to their India-based development partner. This must have seemed like an effective strategy until customers started requesting "experienced vendor resources" to round out project team capabilities. On one project, the team needed help customizing the approval routes required to promote an engineering BOM to a manufacturing BOM. After what appeared to the customer to be unexplained and unnecessary delays, the vendor eventually responded to the request with the local contact information for their partner's consulting services and an "aw-shucks" explanation of how they had actually outsourced the development.

## 5.4.4 *Oops! Reporting*

Reporting is the task most often left until the last minute of the project. Although not a best practice approach, many project teams wait until the period between the deployment and the testing (or even during system testing) to start working on the required reports. For some projects, it is not until this "slack period" when the implementation teams have finished their configurations and customizations and they are waiting for the rest of the application to be completed that the reporting solution is even addressed. Regardless of how the reports are approached, the problem of reports will always surprise the inexperienced PLM implementation team. But what exactly is the problem with reports? Can it be different or worse than what we are all used to from ERP or CRM implementations? Unfortunately, yes.

### 5.4.4.1 Who Forgot the Reports?!?!

Reporting on the progress of a product development effort is a very company specific requirement. Since there is no way for the PLM software company to predict the infinite number of different ways all of the different customers will layout the same data most of them don't really even try.

The reasoning aligns with some earlier points in this chapter: ERP solutions have the benefit of standardization – especially for public companies complying with the Sarbanes-Oxley regulation. This is simply not the case for product development. Escalation definitions, acceptable timeframes, approval windows, where used parts are all examples of critical management action information that is different for each company and could even be different for the same company across different product lines. Furthermore, it is not uncommon to have a lively discussion with the PLM pre-sales team regarding whether you need reports at all. The standard argument is not without some merit; the way that the PLM applications are constructed, many of the data lists that are displayed to an engineer as he/she works their way through the application contain more information than many of the real-time custom reports that most product development organizations have had.

The challenge for the implementation team is actually measuring the development process using the on-line display lists and 8–10 reports provided in the application. All of those important measure and metrics identified in the business case used to justify the cost and disruption of implementing the PLM application will most likely require custom development for the final solution – plan for it!

#### 5.4.4.2 Square Peg. . .Round Hole

The other significant PLM reporting "gotcha" is the corporate data warehouse. The corporate data warehouse contains all of the transactional data collected through the front (e.g., sales, order entry) and backend (e.g., purchasing, GL) systems. This information is then adjusted with "dimensions" (e.g., time, geography) and de-normalized to enable the kind of reporting that the executive team needs to run the business.

Needless to say, the corporate data warehouse takes a lot of work, careful management, and budget to be effective. Most PLM projects are given a directive to use the corporate data warehouse for all reporting. On the surface, this is a good idea. First, whenever existing technology investments are leveraged, that is a good thing. Second, connecting the product development cost data quickly and accurately back into the business operations makes for better business execution. Third, centralizing the data warehouse will help to contain overall support costs. So what's the challenge?

The challenge is that the PLM data is defined as an object and not as a relational structure. This does not mean that the data can't be messaged so that it too can be stored and sourced from the corporate data warehouse. The key issue is project expectations. Because of the data structure differences, executive teams are surprised by the large amount of time and effort the PLM implementation team will need to devote to "reporting" – a seemingly low-value activity. With the high cost of PLM applications and implementations, reporting budgets are one of the first items to be squeezed – hard – sometimes even cut from the initial project scope. This makes for a difficult post-deployment ROI analysis since as mentioned earlier, most of the process metrics identified in the business case justification will require custom reporting. Without those defendable metrics, convincing management that the PLM solution is delivering the value that was originally promised becomes very difficult and funding for the next phase of the project very unpredictable.

## 5.5 Conclusions and Directions for Research

Based on the PLM implementation challenges outlined in this chapter, we can identify four promising issues or topics for research in this area.

### 5.5.1 *Embracing Product Engineers as Implementation Team Members*

Many of the issues discussed earlier imply the challenges associated with partnering with product engineers in PLM implementation projects. At the same time, engineers have the potential to make crucial contributions to the success of the project. As such, a key question is how should PLM project managers engage with product engineers in implementation projects? Future studies that focus on this issue could provide valuable insights on managing the relationships with product engineers. Such studies should also consider how the engineers' culture impacts or shapes the PLM implementation project outcomes and identify the organizational mechanisms and practices that might enhance the overall success of the project.

### 5.5.2 *Business Impact of PLM Applications*

There is very limited understanding of why PLM applications are not delivering the expected business value. Have the application vendors simply automated the wrong set of functions? Is the problem that the processes are not commoditized and therefore implementation teams comprised of primarily technical resources are incapable of effectively delivering world-class process automated by technology? Should the skill composition of the teams change for PLM implementations to be 70% process and content experts and 30% IT experts? Future research that focus on identifying the factors (such as team composition, project activities, nature of process, and data standards) that would critically determine the extent of business value derived from PLM solutions would be very valuable as companies increase the level of investments made in these projects.

### 5.5.3 *Application Customization*

Although seemingly a very tactical, technical area of PLM implementation, customizations have the potential to be an early indicator for the maturity of the PLM applications and a measure of the product development process consolidation. Also, customizations have a broad and varied impact on PLM implementations. For example, a reduction in customizations will reduce implementation costs, increase solution stability, reduce internal support costs, improve software upgrade paths, and increase the frequency that the client is willing to upgrade. These are all good examples of important variables for customers and vendors alike. However, developing a deeper understanding of when customization is needed for the business is important. Studies that contribute toward such an understanding by examining the key business drivers of PLM customization and comparing those with PLM solution characteristics will be valuable. Such studies should ideally develop a framework that could guide business managers in deciding the nature and extent of PLM customization (and the associated trade-offs) in varied product development contexts.

### *5.5.4 Alignment of Executive Expectations and Costs*

As mentioned throughout this chapter, there is disbelief among executives regarding the risk, duration, and cost of PLM implementations. There are many sources for this disconnect with the executives: vendor sales pitches; insufficient executive involvement; general lack of understanding (or misunderstanding) of the complexity of PLM implementations are all good examples. Future research should examine these and other factors that shape the extent of misalignment and also identify practices that could bridge the gap between executive expectations and project manager's expectations regarding PLM project cost and time.

# Part II
# IT and Collaboration and Knowledge Management

# Chapter 6
# Virtual Customer Environments: IT-Enabled Customer Co-innovation and Value Co-creation

**Satish Nambisan**

**Abstract** In recent years, the establishment of IT-enabled customer co-innovation and value co-creation platforms or virtual customer environments (VCEs) has radically changed the nature and extent of customer involvement in product innovation and product support activities. VCEs offer facilities ranging from online customer discussion forums to virtual product design and prototyping centers and enhance the richness of customers' interactions with one another and with the company. This chapter provides an introduction to the different research themes and issues that arise from the emergence of VCEs. Specifically, four broad set of research issues are discussed. First, what are the different customer co-innovation and value co-creation roles that are enabled by IT? Second, what are the factors that motivate customer participation in innovation and value creation in VCEs? Third, what are the critical dimensions of customers' experience in VCEs? And, fourth, what are the different types of impact of customer participation in VCEs? Together, these four broad themes offer a rich and promising set of issues for future research in the area of IT-enabled customer co-innovation and value co-creation.

## 6.1 Introduction

Customers can play an important role in the development of new products and services. As early as in the 1970s itself, customer involvement was identified as a critical success factor in product development (Rothwell, Freeman, & Townsend, 1974). The potential for customers to contribute to innovation and value creation has been acknowledged in other studies as well (e.g., Lengnick-Hall, 1996; von Hippel, 1988). However, in recent years, the establishment of IT-enabled customer co-innovation and value co-creation platforms or VCEs has radically changed the nature and extent of customer involvement in product innovation and product support activities and made it more feasible and cost-effective (Nambisan, 2002). VCEs offer facilities ranging from online customer discussion forums to virtual product

S. Nambisan (✉)
Lally School of Management, Rensselaer Polytechnic Institute, Troy, NY, 12180, USA
e-mail: nambis@rpi.edu

S. Nambisan (ed.), *Information Technology and Product Development*, Annals of Information Systems 5, DOI 10.1007/978-1-4419-1081-3_6,

design and prototyping centers and enhance the richness of customers' interactions with one another and with the company (Nambisan, 2002; Sawhney, Verona, & Prandelli, 2005).

The strategic importance of such initiatives to co-opt customer competencies for value creation has become very clear (Prahalad & Ramaswamy, 2003; Thomke & von Hippel, 2002; Vargo & Lusch, 2004). Evidence from companies such as Audi, Ducati, Microsoft, Nokia, and Adidas-Salomon suggests that customer participation in VCEs offers important innovation-related benefits to the companies that host them (Fuller, Bartl, & Muhlbacher, 2006; Jeppesen & Molin, 2003; Verona, Prandelli, & Sawhney, 2006). By interacting with customers, for example, Nokia has been able to tap into innovative design concepts. Similarly, Volvo has been able to accelerate product development by involving customers in virtual product concept tests. Microsoft, meantime, has realized considerable savings by embracing "expert" customers as partners in providing product support services to other customers. Such advantages, combined with the availability of powerful and inexpensive information technologies, help explain the rapid growth of VCE initiatives in both the United States and Europe.

Given such potential to derive benefits and the increasing investments made in VCEs, it is imperative that companies develop a deeper understanding of the design and deployment of VCEs. This chapter provides an introduction to the different research themes and issues that arise from the emergence of VCEs. Specifically, four broad set of research issues assume importance and will be discussed here.

First, what are the specific ways in which customers can partner with companies in VCEs for innovation and value creation? In other words, what are the different customer co-innovation and value co-creation roles that are enabled by IT? A clear understanding of these customer co-innovation roles could help organizations deploy specific organizational mechanisms to integrate the roles with internal product-development systems and processes.

Second, while the benefits to hosting companies from VCEs are clear, another, closely related issue has received far less attention: Why do customers participate voluntarily in innovation and value-creation activities in VCEs?

Identifying the motivating factors – the actual or anticipated benefits to customers from participating in VCEs – is crucial from the point of view of designing such online forums so as to be maximally appealing to potential contributors. The broader related question of "why individuals help other individuals" through their participation in electronic networks has been examined before in the context of open source communities (e.g., Lakhani & von Hippel, 2003; Hertel, Niedner, & Hermann, 2003) and communities of practice (e.g., Constant, Sproull, & Kiesler, 1996; Wasko & Faraj, 2005). However, unlike both open source communities and communities of practice, the customer–firm relationships that underlie the VCE context raise unique issues and implications related to customer participation in VCEs.

Third, recent research has suggested the importance of understanding customers' value co-creation experience (Prahalad & Ramaswamy, 2003) as such customer experience may have implication beyond the virtual environment. Thus, another important area for research relates to the development of a coherent theoretical framework to analyze customer experience in VCEs and their impact on both online and offline customer behavior.

Finally, while customer involvement in VCEs is important, to have considerable impact on the success of product/service development it is clear that companies would need to incorporate complementary changes in its internal innovation system and processes. This forms the fourth avenue for research in this area. Specifically, what are the different types of complementary systems and processes that would need to incorporated to ensure that companies are able to benefit from VCEs?

Clearly, addressing all these questions will require drawing on concepts and insights from multiple areas including marketing, organizational behavior, IT, computer-mediated communication, and product development. This chapter emphasizes the need for such an inter-disciplinary focus in studies on VCEs and customer co-innovation.

The remainder of this chapter is organized as follows. In the following section, I examine the different customer co-innovation and value co-creation roles that VCEs can support. Following that, I describe the theoretical frameworks that could inform on the motivations for customers to participate in different innovation and value-creation activities. Section 6.4 focuses on the concept of customer experience in VCEs. The chapter concludes with a discussion of the research issues related to the impact of customer participation in VCEs is discussed.

## 6.2 Customer Roles in Virtual Customer Environments

In the strategic management and quality management literatures, studies have identified five roles for customers in value creation: as resource, as co-producer, as buyer, as user, and as product (Finch, 1999; Gersuny & Rosengren, 1973; Kaulio, 1998; Lengnick-Hall, 1996).

The first two customer roles are at the upstream or input side of organizational activity, while the other three roles cluster at the downstream or output side of the system. These roles extend to the customer co-innovation context in VCEs too. Specifically, VCEs can be designed to support five different customer roles in innovation and value co-creation: product conceptualizer, product designer, product tester, product support specialist, and product marketer (see Table 6.1).

### *6.2.1 Product Conceptualizer or Ideator*

Companies can encourage customers to interact among themselves to generate and advance product improvement and new product ideas. Customers' role in idea generation or product conceptualization has been relatively well explored in marketing and NPD literatures (e.g., Christensen, 1997; Leonard-Barton, 1995; Rothwell et al.,

**Table 6.1** Customer innovation and value co-creation roles in the VCE

| | Customer as ideator | Customer as designer | Customer as tester | Customer as marketer and support specialist |
|---|---|---|---|---|
| Primary focus | Product conceptualization | Product design and development | Product testing and prototyping | Product diffusion and after-sales support |
| Desired outcome(s) | Product improvement ideas and suggestions<br>New product ideas | Inputs on product features and design tradeoffs<br>Production and delivery of products/services | Identification of product design flaws<br>Inputs on product (prototype) performance | Delivery of product support services to peer customers<br>Diffusion of new product information<br>Product improvement suggestions |
| Examples | Microsoft, Procter & Gamble, and Ducati | Peugeot, Diesel, and Adidas-Salomon | Volvo, Ducati, and Microsoft | Microsoft, IBM, and Macromedia |
| Interaction facilities | Discussion forums<br>Messaging tools<br>Product knowledge base | Discussion forums<br>User design tool kits<br>Virtual prototyping tools and interactive games | Discussion forums<br>Virtual concept testing tools<br>Virtual product simulations | Discussion forums<br>Messaging tools<br>Product knowledge base |

1974; von Hippel, 1988). While some have argued that customers need to play a pivotal role in the generation of new product ideas, others have argued equally fervently that involving customers in idea generation will simply lead to imitative, unimaginative products. It is now relatively well established that the utility of customers as a source of innovation varies with the maturity of the technology and the alignment of product line with the current customer base (Christensen, 1997; Leonard-Barton, 1995). When both the dimensions are high (continuous innovation), customers are an excellent source of innovation, while when both the dimensions are low (i.e., evolving technologies and emerging markets), the value of current customers as resource is limited.

VCEs facilitate interactions among customer that enable the generation and gradual evolution of innovative ideas for new products and services. Consider the example of Ducati, the Italian motorcycle company. Ducati has implemented a virtual space called Tech Café where customers share design ideas (including detailed engineering drawings) for customizing and improving motorcycles; some of the suggestions have been incorporated into Ducati's next generation of products. Similar mechanisms have been employed by Hallmark and other companies to get customers to conceptualize products and channel ideas into the product-development pipeline.

### 6.2.2 Product Designer

Customers can also be product designers and design their own versions of the "ideal" product using virtual prototyping tools and design tool kits provided in the VCE.

As a co-designer of products and services, customers can contribute to a variety of product design and development activities including the validation of product architectural choices, the design and prioritization of product features, the specification of product interface requirements, and the establishment of development process priorities and metrics.

The role of customer as designer is perhaps more evident in industrial products than in consumer products (Garvin, 1988). For example, in the software industry, enterprise software developers like Microsoft and SAP often have representatives from customer organizations as members of their product-development teams (Hoch, Roeding, & Lindner, 1999). Similarly, Chaparral Steel (Chase & Garvin, 1989) and Cisco (Kambil, Friesen, & Sundaram,, 1999) rely on customers to make design choices as members of product-development teams.

In the consumer sector also, customers have played the role of product co-creator, for example, by participating in concept testing (Page & Rosenbaum, 1992), consumer idealized design (Cincianntelli & Magdison, 1993), and component selection (Kambil et al., 1999). For example, BMW has operated its Customer Innovation Lab by giving customers online design tools to develop their own ideas (particularly, related to telematics and driver-assistance systems). Similarly, both Peugeot and Swarovski, a producer of crystal, have employed such design tools to facilitate customer design efforts.

### 6.2.3 Product Tester

The role of customers in testing new products is not new. Prior studies have established the highly productive role customers can play in product and prototype testing (e.g., Dolan & Mathews, 1993; Nielsen, 1993). Customers of both industrial and consumer products have participated in product testing. For example, in the software industry, many firms have utilized their customers in beta product testing enabling them to reduce their investments in internal product testing units (Cusumano & Yoffie, 1998). Customer involvement in product testing enables firms to detect product flaws early in the development cycle and minimize costly redesign and rework. Further, by involving a diverse set of customers in product testing, firms can gain a rich understanding of how the product would behave in a variety of user contexts.

The application of virtual product technologies enables a greater level of involvement of customers in the testing of new products and services. For example, both Volvo and Audi have implemented virtual reality tools to involve customers in product concept testing. The inputs from customers enable the firms to minimize the number of early design flaws in the product concept and thereby accelerate the product development and enhance its potential market effectiveness.

### 6.2.4 Product Support Specialist

Perhaps the most common role for customers is supporting other customers as product support specialists. Customers are also uniquely qualified to provide product support to other users. Customers often acquire significant knowledge or expertise on various aspects of product usage, which then becomes the basis for providing product support to peer users. The homophily (i.e., the degree to which pairs of individuals are alike in terms of certain attributes) between peer customers contribute to their effectiveness in understanding and appreciating the concerns of product users and their particular usage problems, a critical success factor in product support (Brown & Reingen, 1987; Kay, 1999). Additionally, over a period of time, expert users may discover new ways of product usage as well as shortcuts and other methods to enhance the overall value of the product.

Technology companies such as HP, Novell, Cisco, and Microsoft have been at the forefront of this area. Further, industry organizations, such as the California-based Consortium for Service Innovation, have been pursuing projects focused on enhancing customer's role in product support through the innovative application of knowledge-based tools and technologies in VCEs.

### 6.2.5 Product Marketer

Finally, customers can also play a critical role in product marketing. Some companies have leveraged the expertise of customers in product marketing activities carried out in VCEs. Customers can diffuse information about new products to peer customers and shape their perceptions about the new product or service through dialogue and discussions. Further, VCEs provide an effective venue for customers to learn about new products.

Both Samsung and Suzuki, for example, have experimented with virtual product launch centers employing interactive product simulation technologies that incorporate customers as active participants in product marketing. Customers' role in product/service marketing is likely to evolve over the years as newer technologies facilitate diverse types of interactions, thereby enhancing the diffusion rate.

Each of the above customer co-innovation and value co-creation roles has a lot to offer to companies. Depending on the market and organizational context, some roles are likely to have more relevance to certain companies than others. For example, while Microsoft's Most Valuable Professional (MVP) program concentrates primarily on product support activities, Ducati's Tech Café focuses mainly on developing product concepts.

Two broad research issues related to customer roles are worth mentioning. First, what are the specific customer capabilities and expertise that facilitate each of the above roles? Few studies have focused on this issue and future research may consider the roles vis-à-vis customer knowledge and identify mechanisms for organizations to select or identify potential customer innovators. Research may also focus on the mechanisms that companies can deploy to prepare customers to contribute to the various innovation and value-creation activities.

The second research issue relates to the incentives for customer to play the different roles. It is evident that there are different types of incentives that could be established to promote customer involvement in innovation. However, depending on the customer innovation role, the nature of these incentives might differ. The following section expands on this issue.

## 6.3 Customer Motivations for Value Co-creation in VCEs

Many different theoretical frameworks could potentially offer clues concerning the nature of customer motivations for co-innovation and value co-creation. One of the more relevant ones relates to the "uses and gratifications" (U&G) approach (Katz, Blumler, & Gurevitch, 1974), a framework widely used in the field of communication. The U&G model has been employed in media studies to identify the different types of benefits that can be obtained from media usage and to examine how those benefits shape such media-usage behavior (Palmgreen, 1984; Parker & Plank, 2000; Stafford, Stafford, & Schkade, 2004).

The U&G framework (Katz et al., 1974) identifies four broad types of benefits that individuals can derive from media usage (in this case, from participation in VCEs): (a) cognitive benefits that relate to information acquisition and strengthening of the understanding of the environment; (b) social integrative benefits that relate to strengthening consumer's ties with relevant others; (c) personal integrative benefits that relate to strengthening the credibility, status, and confidence of the individual; and (d) hedonic or affective benefits such as those that strengthen aesthetic or pleasurable experiences. The four benefit categories can be interpreted in the context of the VCE as follows.

### *6.3.1 Cognitive or Learning Benefits*

In the current context, cognitive benefits reflect product-related learning – i.e., better understanding and knowledge about the products, their underlying technologies, and their usage. Like offline-product communities, VCEs also hold valuable collective knowledge on the product and its usage that is generated and shared through continued customer interactions (Rothaermel & Sugiyama, 2001; Wasko & Faraj, 2000). The greater the extent of product-related content in the interactions (in terms of both the diversity and depth of product-related knowledge), the greater would be the opportunities to acquire information and to learn about the product, the associated technologies/features, and the usage (Hertel et al., 2003; Jeppesen & Molin, 2003). While the diverse nature of the topics discussed provides opportunities for customers to learn about various aspects of a product, the depth of topics discussed enables them to gain a more fundamental understanding of the product – learning that may lead to more effective product usage.

### *6.3.2 Social Integrative Benefits*

In a VCE, the social context is defined by the participating customers and members of the host firm. Social integrative benefits reflect the benefits deriving from the social and relational ties that develop over time among the participating entities in the VCE (Nambisan, 2002). Such social relationships provide a range of benefits to the customer, including enhancement of a sense of belongingness or social identity (Kollock, 1999). Studies on brand communities (McAlexander, Schouten, & Koening, 2002; Muniz & O'Guinn, 2001) have documented the considerable value customers place on such social identity and relationships.

Interactions in VCEs that involve identity persistence enhance the probability of deriving gains from the social ties in the future (Kollock, 1999). Such identity persistence enhances customers' expectations regarding future interactions with peer customers. Prior studies (e.g., Walther, 1994) have shown that anticipation of future interactions in a community lead members to invest more in mutual understanding and facilitate the creation of the social identity. This has also been evidenced in the case of brand communities (Muniz & O'Guinn, 2001). Thus, it is expected that the extent of stable identity afforded by the VCE will be related to customer perceptions about social integrative benefits.

### *6.3.3 Personal Integrative Benefits*

Personal integrative benefits relate to gains in reputation or status and the achievement of a sense of self-efficacy (Katz et al., 1974). VCEs serve as a venue for individual customers to exhibit their product-related knowledge and problem-solving skills.

By contributing to product support, customers can enhance their expertise-related status and reputation among peer customers as well as with the product vendor (Wasko & Faraj, 2000; Harhoff, Henkel, & von Hippel, 2003). The more in-depth and diverse the product-related issues that are discussed in the VCE, the better would be the opportunity for individual customers to demonstrate their unique knowledge and/or breadth of expertise (Jeppesen & Molin, 2003) – and hence, the greater the potential to enhance their product-related status in the community. Kollock (1999), drawing on social exchange theories (e.g., Blau, 1964), has emphasized the power and sense of self-worth or self-efficacy that individual customers may feel by exercising such influence in online customer forums. Discussions that relate to complex product-usage problems provide the context for customers to suggest innovative ways of product usage (thereby influencing peer customers' product usage) as well as innovative product improvement ideas (thereby influencing the host-firm's product-development plans). By exercising such influence, they may realize a sense of self-efficacy.

### *6.3.4 Hedonic Benefits*

Customers' interactions in the VCE could also be a source of highly interesting/pleasurable as well as mentally stimulating experiences. First, studies on brand communities show that customers derive considerable pleasure from conversing with one another about the product, features, and the idiosyncrasies of the usage context (Muniz & O'Guinn, 2001). Such positive reactions and enjoyment, rooted in the product context, are equally applicable in VCEs too (Jeppesen & Molin, 2003). Second, the problem solving that underlies much of the interactions in a product-support-focused VCE can also be a source of mental or intellectual stimulation that forms another aspect of hedonic benefits.

Thus, by leveraging the U&G framework, we can identify a cogent set of four benefit categories that can potentially inform on customer participation in innovation and value creation, and are also theoretically rooted in the interactions occurring in the VCEs. Recent empirical works (Nambisan & Baron, 2007; Nambisan & Baron, 2009) have shown that these different potential benefits all have strong positive impact on customer participation in innovation and value creation.

A dominant perspective in the online community literature is the one relating to "citizenship" behavior. It has been widely acknowledged and empirically shown (e.g., Constant et al., 1996) that individuals assist others (often strangers) with little or no expectation of direct or immediate recompense (the "kindness of strangers"). The empirical work in the area of VCEs indicates that customers do not participate in these online forums purely on the basis of such "altruistic" or "citizenship" motives. On the other hand, they expect to attain considerable benefits from their participation in innovation and value creation – benefits such as enhanced product knowledge, communication with other knowledgeable customers, enhanced reputation, cognitive stimulation, and enjoyment.

This has important directly implications for managerial practice. Most organizations seem to assume that customers' citizenship or "altruistic" feelings drive their value co-creation and innovation activities in VCEs. Recent studies on open source and other such "communities of creation" (Sawhney & Prandelli, 2000) have only further emboldened such assumptions. This has resulted in many organizations adopting a "when we build it, they will come" approach toward VCEs – in other words, if the technological infrastructure is put together for an online forum, customers will come and support one another endlessly. The implication is that companies do not need to invest additional resources in such initiatives (other than the basic technological infrastructure). However, the empirical work in the VCE indicates the opposite. Specifically, they suggest that customers' active participation in VCEs is strongly influenced by their beliefs concerning benefits they will receive from engaging in such activities. Thus, companies that are interested in having their customers participate in innovation and value co-creation activities must take proactive measures to create and sustain online environments that would contribute toward such benefits.

Some of the empirical work on the VCE (e.g., Nambisan & Baron, 2009) have also identified the key antecedents of these interaction-based customer benefits. Specifically, the empirical work shows that the extent of product-related content in customer interactions in the VCE impact – three of the four benefits – learning benefits, social integrative benefits, and hedonic benefits. Similarly, the customer's identity as a member in the community hosted by the VCE is also found to shape both social integrative benefits and hedonic benefits. Finally, the degree of human interactivity facilitated by the virtual environment (or the IT-based facilities in the VCE) is found to impact social integrative benefits and hedonic benefits.

Thus, as shown in Fig. 6.1, attributes or characteristics related to customers' interactions in the VCE shape the extent of the four types of benefits they derive from such interactions and they in turn drive future participation and contribution.

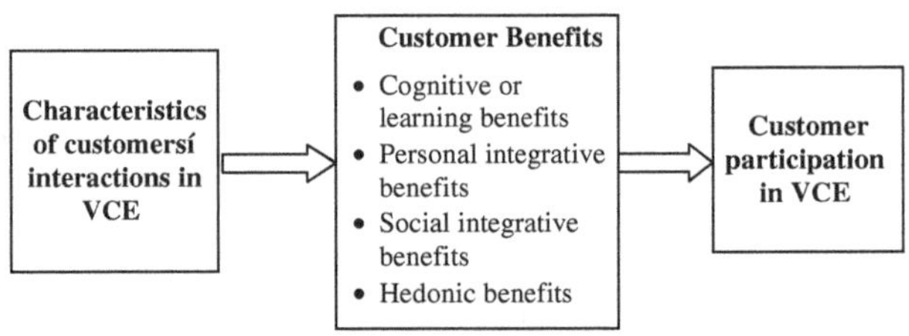


**Fig. 6.1** Customer Interactions, Benefits, and Participation in VCEs

It is important to note here that much of the empirical work on VCEs so far has involved customer participation in technology-based product and service contexts. Thus, future research may need to go beyond and validate the relevance and impact of these different benefits in other types of product/service and industry contexts.

The different benefits that customers derive are based on their interactions in the VCEs. Closely related to these are then the nature of customer's co-innovation and value co-creation experience in VCEs. As Prahalad and Ramaswamy (2003) note, such customer experience in virtual environments can have potentially significant implications for not just continued customer involvement but also customer loyalty and satisfaction. Next, we consider the theoretical dimensions of customers' interactions experience in VCEs.

## 6.4 Customers' Interaction Experience in VCEs

Three fundamental contextual factors frame customers' interaction experience in the VCE: product context, community context, and technology mediation (Nambisan, 2002). First, customer interactions in the VCE are primarily rooted in the context of the firm's product, i.e., interactions related to knowledge that underlies the different aspects of the product life cycle. Second, customer interactions in the VCE occur in a social or community context, a community that consists of peer customers as well as members of the host firm. Third, interactions occur in a computer-mediated environment, i.e., interactions are mediated (supported/constrained) by the technological infrastructure of the VCE.

Customer interactions in the VCE vary in the nature and the level/intensity of product-related knowledge that is transacted (Franke & Shah, 2003; Fuller et al., 2006; Hertel et al., 2003; Wasko & Faraj, 2000). For example, interactions may relate to different types of product knowledge – product-technology knowledge, product-market knowledge, or product-use knowledge. The information exchanged may also vary in terms of complexity – high-level interactions that assume much prior knowledge about the product or low-level interactions that don't presume such prior understanding.

The second dimension emphasizes the extent to which customer interactions are situated in the community context. Prior studies on brand communities and virtual groups (e.g., Fischer, Bristor, & Gainer, 1996; Muniz & O'Guinn, 2001; McAlexander et al., 2002; Burgoon, Bonito, Bengtsson, Ramirez, & Dunbar, 2000) have identified two characteristics as constituting the community context – the extent to which the interaction *involves* the community and the extent to which the interaction entities reveal their *identity* to others. Given that interactions in a product-support-focused VCE will in general always be visible to (or involve) the community, the interaction characteristic of interest in the current study context is the extent to which members reveal their *identity.* As prior studies in computer-mediated communication (e.g., Walther, 1994) have shown, the salient type of identity in an online environment is not necessarily the "real-world" identity of the participating members, but their "online" identity (which may or may not be their real world identity). The more important issue is how consistently members maintain and reveal such an identity in their interactions (Walther, 1994) – and this is the perspective that is adopted here to conceptualize member *identity* in the VCE.

The third dimension underlines the nature of technology mediation of the interactions in the VCE. Te'eni (2001) developed a meta-model of communication in computer-mediated environments that emphasized three characteristics – interactivity, channel capacity, and adaptiveness. Interactivity is the responsiveness (Rafaeli, 1988) or "the potential for immediate feedback from the receiver" (Te'eni, 2001, p. 271). It can be conceptualized as human interactivity (between customers) and machine interactivity (between a customer and the computer) (Hoffman and Novak, 1996). Channel capacity relates to the potential to transmit a high level of cues (Daft & Lengel, 1984) and adaptiveness reflects the ability to adapt a message to a particular receiver (Te'eni, 2001). In this study context, channel capacity, adaptiveness, and machine interactivity hold limited relevance since the interactions in the online product support forums are largely text based and require minimal computer navigation. However, the extent of *human interactivity* forms an important consideration here as product-related discussions and debates among the community members form the primary activity in the VCE.

The above three contextual factors in turn imply four components for customer's co-innovation and value co-creation experience in VCEs: pragmatic experience, sociability experience, usability experience, and hedonic experience (Nambisan & Nambisan, 2008).

### 6.4.1 Pragmatic Experience

Most customers who visit or participate in VCEs do so to acquire information about a product, its underlying technologies, or its usage. The pragmatic component relates to customer's experience in realizing such product-related informational goals in the VCE (for example, their perception of the quality of information acquisition processes). Note that there are multiple ways for customers to achieve such goals – interacting with peer customers and company representatives, searching product knowledge centers, or experimenting with product prototyping tools – and depending on this, their pragmatic experience would vary.

### 6.4.2 Sociability Experience

Interactions in a VCE often enable customers to perceive themselves as members of a group or community, and the underlying social and relational aspects of such interactions form the sociability experience of the customer. Thus, the sociability component emphasizes the importance of community dialog and the social policies (or, rules of engagement) that frame such dialog. The promotion of a shared social or community identity in VCEs has been shown to contribute to positive sociability experience. As one customer commented, "I really like the camaraderie and the shared understanding that has evolved over here [in the VCE] and the constant give-and-take with these folks have led to some very interesting experiences for me."

### 6.4.3 Usability Experience

In a VCE, information technology mediates customer interactions. The quality of the human–computer interactions defines the usability. Regardless of whether the technologies used are simple (for example, online discussion boards) or more complex (for example, 3D product simulation tools), the ease with which customers can interact and perform tasks shapes their overall experience. Thus, it is important to consider the learning curve to customers.

### 6.4.4 Hedonic Experience

Customers' interactions in the virtual environment can also be mentally stimulating or entertaining, and be a source of pleasure and enjoyment. The hedonic component captures this dimension. It can encompass both the interaction with other customers and with tools and technologies. Consider the following comment from a customer: "I have always enjoyed solving technical puzzles and my interactions [in the VCE] have given me numerous opportunities to indulge in such pursuits that are very satisfying."

Together, the four components offer a holistic view of the experience a customer participating in a VCE can have. Preliminary evidence (Nambisan & Nambisan, 2008) indicates that based on the nature of the customer's interactions and value co-creation activities, some components are likely to be more important than others.

For example, it was found that VCEs oriented toward product support activities tend to feature lively discussions and debates that leverage the expertise of the entire community and make them better able to address individual customer's product-related problems. As such, the customer experience profiles tend to be skewed toward pragmatic and sociability experience components. By contrast, virtual environments that focus on helping customers become product conceptualizers tend to be more stimulating for participants as product improvement ideas are developed, shared, and improved upon. Thus, in these VCEs, the emphasis tends to be on pragmatic and hedonic components.

Future studies may examine these in more detail and develop a deeper understanding of how customer experience profile is tied with the nature of their innovation and value-creation activities in the VCE.

Another valuable research avenue relates to the organizational mechanisms that companies can deploy to enhance customer experience in VCEs. It is evident that each company would need to examine its own circumstances and weigh the unique product and customer context in order to decide which customer experience profile is most appropriate. A clear understanding of this – specifically, the relative importance of the different experience components – could help companies tailor their VCE strategies and practices.

## 6.5 Impact of Customer Participation in VCEs

There is a vast literature on the impact of customer involvement in innovation and value creation. This literature has identified two broad sets of outcomes – customer relationship management (CRM) related outcomes and innovation-related outcomes (see Fig. 6.2).

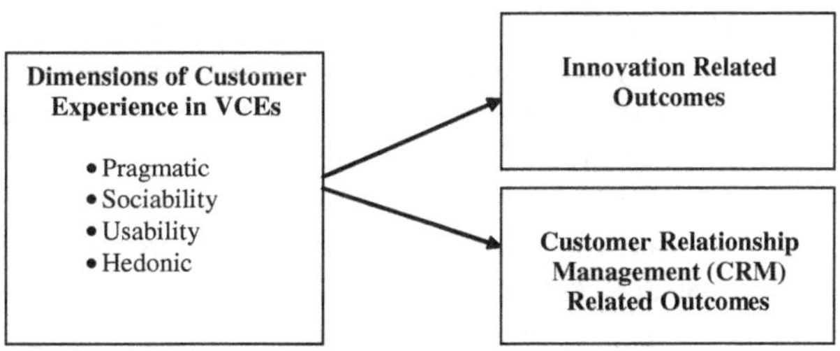


**Fig. 6.2** Customer Experience in VCEs and their Impact

First, consider the outcomes related to CRM. Prior studies have shown that customer involvement in production activities (customer co-production of products and services) may lead to different types of psychological outcomes – for example, on customer loyalty and on customer satisfaction (Bendapudi & Leone, 2003). These findings can be extended to the VCE context too.

Customers may attribute their VCE experience (good or bad) directly to the company connected with that initiative. And, as such, this experience may shape their perceptions about the company as well as the affiliated product or service (Nambisan & Nambisan, 2008). In other words, customers who have a highly pragmatic experience in the VCE may feel that the related product is valuable or useful. Similarly, a high degree of sociability experience in the VCE may lead the customer to conclude that the product (or service) embody similar social or community attribute which they identify with. Thus, in general, it can be concluded that positive (negative) customer experiences lead to positive (negative) psychological outcomes with significant implications for the company's CRM strategies and practices.

Importantly, it should also be noted that customers' experience may also shape their product/service purchase intentions and decisions. Thus, beyond just attitudes toward the company (or even the product/service), the experience in the VCE may actually impact their future actions related to the product, with important implications for product marketing.

The second set of outcomes relates to the innovation itself. It is likely that customer participation in innovation activities may impact the three important outcomes variables related to innovation – namely, innovation cost, time-to-market, and product/service quality (or market effectiveness). For example, customers who perceive positive interaction experience in the VCE may continue or even enhance their level of participation or make more valuable contributions to the innovation process, thereby affecting the cost, the time, and the quality of the innovation.

In addition to the above two sets of outcomes, managers will also need to carefully consider and manage the varied risks that the deployment of VCEs might entail. While a VCE may accelerate the product-development process, it could also lead to delays if the development process is not able to accommodate and manage the additional process uncertainties. Similarly, inappropriate use of data gathered from a VCE may lead to the development of a product based on the needs of a highly vocal and visible set of online customers, but not necessarily representative of the customer majority. Finally, inappropriate or excessive innovation process transparency may be detrimental to the firm's market competitiveness as it may forewarn competitors about new product developments. Hence, managers have to carefully define the level of transparency and security needed in a VCE as well as the type of customers they would like to share information with. Thus, all of these indicate the potential for negative outcomes related to customer participation in innovation and value creation in VCE and the need for companies to be aware of such outcomes and manage the related risks.

Future studies should focus on empirically validating these and other potential impacts of customer experience in VCEs in diverse industry and product/market contexts. It is evident that the nature and degree of customer experience will vary with the characteristics of the product/service. As such, care should be taken in conducting such studies to clearly identify and control for the important product (or service) characteristics.

## 6.6 Organizational Strategies to Enhance Customer Participation in VCEs

The most important implication of research on VCEs relates to the strategies and practices that companies can adopt to enhance value-adding customer participation in VCEs. Studies on the issues outlined in this chapter so far, from the nature of customer role to customer motivations to customer experience, could provide valuable directions for companies in identifying a portfolio of VCE strategies. Broadly, these managerial implications fall into three categories: design elements of VCEs; integration of VCEs with other parts of the innovation system; and customer relationship management.

### *6.6.1 Designing VCEs to Promote Customer Participation*

Evidently, companies can create richer innovating environments by incorporating key design features into their VCEs. For example, having enough product-related content in the VCE is important not only to advance customer innovation capabilities but also to enhance learning. Companies such as Microsoft are experimenting with product content rating systems – for example, peer ratings and other social metrics that help customers gauge the depth and accuracy of product-related knowledge in the interactions. Similarly, new semantic visualization tools have been created that allow customers to identify patterns in customer conversations and navigate toward the content-rich part of those conversations (Donath, 2002; Erickson, Halveson, Kellogg, &Wolf, 2002; Smith, 2002). Companies can also create product knowledge centers that can feed customers the right knowledge at the right time. Such centers can also offer virtual product simulation tools that allow customers to acquire deeper product knowledge.

Companies including IBM, HP, and Microsoft have instituted programs that confer titles and awards to customers taking part in VCEs. For example, every year Microsoft selects "Most Valuable Professionals," or MVPs from customers who contribute to the product support activities through its VCE. Customers value these titles because they come from a customer community they identify with. Similarly, design features that provide customers with better social cues – that is, add to the social translucence – offer richer social experiences and permit richer customer discussions. Companies can also create gated customer forums within their VCE that give members a sense of exclusiveness and add to the sociability experience. Such exclusive forums not only permit companies to have deeper customer engagement with but also provide customers a stronger sense of social identity, which in turn leads to more positive experiences.

### *6.6.2 Integrating VCEs with Internal Innovation Teams*

Companies that want to benefit from their customers' creativity need to adopt strategies that link their external customer innovating environments with internal product-development teams.

This might involve establishing new organizational roles to connect the VCE with the internal product teams. For example, Microsoft has specially-designated employees called "buddies" who play such a bridging role. Buddies interact directly with customer contributors in the VCE and ensure that their inputs are fed to the appropriate people within the organization. This also allows the company to participate in the conversations that occur in the external innovation forums and contribute to the customers' hedonic experience.

Similarly, companies could also establish new communication mechanisms – both formal as well as informal communication avenues. Some of the companies have used formal communication methods such as white papers to provide vision and direction to customers' innovation and value co-creation activities. Informal mechanisms can be equally important. Some companies have started using blogs and wikis to facilitate informal conversations between internal experts and customers (for example, Microsoft's Channel 9 that promotes open conversations between customers and Microsoft employees).

Finally, new processes may need to be established that tie together the activities in the VCE with those in the internal innovation teams (for example, processes related to managing risks, coordinating tasks across organizational boundaries, and information sharing). Instituting appropriate processes to accommodate the VCE activities and their outcomes can go a long way toward enhancing the customer experience and ensuring returns to the company.

### *6.6.3 Managing Customer Relationships and Expectations*

The third type of managerial implications relates to managing customer expectations and minimizing potential negative outcomes.

Clarity about customer roles, innovation and value-creation processes, and the outcomes can reduce the potential for misplaced customer expectations regarding their participation in innovation and value creation and lead to a more positive customer experience. Strategies to enhance transparency vary according to the VCE context. For example, some companies have tried to enhance clarity by making customer roles and processes explicit through published policies and guidelines. Open discussions with the customer community about their involvement may also help clarify perceptions and expectations. Similarly, explicit recognition of the issues related to intellectual property rights in co-innovation value co-creation is critical for enhancing outcome transparency. Practices that bring clarity to "who owns what intellectual asset" and communicate that effectively to the customer community will be of utmost importance.

Strategies and practices that help the company integrate VCE initiatives with other CRM initiatives are also of particular importance. This lets the company enhance the customer experience by finding synergies with a customer's other product-related interactions (for example, offline product events). For example, product-marketing activities may be initiated in the VCE and be continued in offline settings. Such an approach may enable finding and leveraging synergies between VCE activities and the company's overall approach to brand management.

In conclusion, VCEs portend a new era in customer involvement in innovation and value creation. As the number of companies deploying different forms of VCEs to embrace customers as partners in innovation continue to increase, the importance of research on issues related to the successful design and deployment of such virtual environment also increase. This chapter has provided an introduction to the concept of VCEs and outlined several issues for future research. It is hoped that future studies will explore these and other issues and contribute toward a better understanding of the deployment and management of VCEs in varied innovation contexts.

## References


Bendapudi, N., & Leone, R. (2003). Psychological implications of customer participation in co-production. *Journal of Marketing, 67*, 14–28.

Blau, P. (1964). *Exchange and Power in Social Life*. New York: Wiley.

Brown, J., & Reingen, P. H. (1987). Social ties and word-of-mouth referral behavior. *Journal of Consumer Research, 14*(3), 350–363.

Burgoon, J. K., Bonito, J. A., Bengtsson, B., Ramirez, A., & Dunbar, N. (2000). Testing the interactivity model: communication processes, partner assessments, and the quality of collaborative work. *Journal of Management and Information Systems, 16*(3), 33–56.

Chase, R. B., & Garvin, D. (1989). The service factory. *Harvard Business Review, 57*(4), 61–69.

Christensen, C. M. (1997). *The innovator's dilemma*. Boston, MA: HBS Press.

Ciccianntelli, S., & Magdison, J. (1993). Consumer idealized design: Involving customers in the product development process. *Journal of Product Innovation Management, 20*, 318–330.

Constant, D., Sproull, L., & Kiesler, S. (1996). The kindness of strangers: The usefulness of electronic weak ties for technical advice. *Organization Science, 7*(2), 119–135.

Cusumano, M., & Yoffie, D. (1998). *Competing on internet time*. New York: The Free Press.

Daft, R., & Lengel, R. H. (1984). Information richness: A new approach to managerial behavior and organization design. *Research in Organizational Behavior, 6*, 191–233.

Dolan, R. J., & Mathews, J. M. (1993). Maximizing the utility of customer product testing: beta test design and management. *Journal of Product Innovation Management, 10*(4), 318–330.

Donath, J. (2002). A semantic approach to visualizing conversation. *Communications of the ACM, 45* (4), 45–49.

Erickson, T., Halveson, C., Kellogg, W., & Wolf, T. (2002). Social translucence: Designing social infrastructures that make collective activity visible. *Communications of the ACM, 45*(4), 40–44.

Finch, B. J. (1999). Internet discussions as a source for consumer product customer involvement and quality information. *Journal of Operations Management, 17*(5), 535–556.

Fischer, E., Bristor, J., & Gainer, B. (1996). Creating or escaping community? An exploratory study of internet consumers' behavior. *Advances in Consumer Research, 23*, 178–182.

Franke, N., & Shah, S. (2003). How communities support innovative activities: An exploration of assistance among users of sporting equipment. *Research Policy, 32*(1), 157–178.

Fuller, J., Bartl, M., & Muhlbacher, H. (2006). Community based innovation: How to integrate members of virtual communities into new product development. *Electronic Commerce Research, 6*, 57–73.

Garvin, D. A. (1988). *Managing quality*. New York: The Free Press.

Gersuny, C., & Rosengren, W. R. (1973). *The service society*. MA: Schenkman Press.

Harhoff, D., Henkel J., & von Hippel E. (2003). Profiting from voluntary information spillovers: How users benefit from freely revealing their innovations. *Research Policy, 32*(10), 1753–1769

Hertel, G., Niedner, S., & Hermann, S. (2003). Motivation of software developers in open source projects. *Research Policy, 32*(7), 1159–1177.

Hoch, D., Roeding, C., & Lindner, S. (1999). *Secrets of software success*. Boston: HBS Press.

Hoffman, D. L., & Novak. T. P. (1996). Marketing in hypermedia computer-mediated environments: conceptual foundations. *Journal of Marketing, 60*, 50–68.

Jeppesen, L., & Molin, M. (2003). Consumers as co-developers: Learning and innovation outside the firm. *Technology Analysis & Strategic Management, 15*(3), 363–383.

Kambil, A., Friesen, G., & Sundaram, A. (1999). Co-creation: A new source of value. *Outlook Magazine, June*, 23–29.

Katz, E., Blumler, J. G., & Gurevitch, M. (1974). Utilization of mass communication by the individual. In J. G. Blumler & E. Katz (Eds.), *The uses of mass communications: current perspectives on gratifications research* (pp. 19–32). Beverly Hills: Sage.

Kaulio, M. A. (1998). Customer, consumer, and user involvement in product development: A framework and a review of selected methods. *Total Quality Management, 9*, 141–149.

Kay, A. (1999). *Reaching out for help*. CIO Magazine, October, 23–25.

Kollock, P. (1999). The economies of online cooperation. In M. Smith & P. Kollock (Eds.), *Communities in cyberspace* (pp. 220–242). London, UK: Rutledge.

Lakhani, K., & von Hippel, E. (2003). How open source software works: Free user-to-user assistance, *Research Policy, 32*(6), 923–943.

Lengnick-Hall, C. A. (1996). Customer contributions to quality: A different view of the customer-oriented firm. *Academy of Management Review, 21*, 791–810.

Leonard-Barton, D. (1995). *Wellsprings of knowledge*. Boston, MA: HBS Press.

McAlexander, J., Schouten, J., & Koening, H. F. (2002). Building brand community. *Journal of Marketing, 66*(1), 38–49.

Muniz, A., & O'Guinn, T. (2001). Brand Community. *Journal of Consumer Research, 27*, 412–432.

Nambisan, S. (2002). Designing virtual customer environments for new product development: Toward a theory. *Academy of Management Review, 27*(3), 392–413.

Nambisan, S., & Baron, R. (2007). Interactions in virtual customer environments: Implications for product support and customer relationship management. *Journal of Interactive Marketing, 21*(2), 42–62.

Nambisan, S., & Nambisan, P. (2008, Spring). How to profit from a better virtual customer environment. *MIT Sloan Management Review*, 53–61.

Nambisan, S., & Baron, R. (2009). Virtual customer environments: Testing a model of voluntary participation in value co-creation activities. *Journal of Product Innovation Management, 26*(4), 388–406.

Nielsen, J. (1993). *Usability engineering*. San Diego, CA: Academic Press.

Page, A., & Rosenbaum, H. (1992). Developing an effective concept testing program for consumer durables. *Journal of Product Innovation Management, 9*, 267–277.

Palmgreen, P. (1984) Uses and gratifications: A theoretical perspective. In R. N. Bostrom (Ed.), *Communication yearbook 8* (61–72). Beverly Hills, CA: Sage Publications.

Parker, B. J., & Plank. R. (2000). A uses and gratifications perspective on the Internet as a new information source. *American Business Review, June*, 43–49.

Prahalad, C. K., & Ramaswamy. V. (2003). *The future of competition: Co-creating value with customers*. Boston: HBS Press.

Rafaeli, S. (1988). Interactivity. *Annual Review of Communication Research, 16*, 110–134.

Rothaermel, F. T., & Sugiyama, S. (2001). Virtual Internet communities and commercial success. *Journal of Management, 27*(3), 297–312.

Rothwell, R., Freeman, C., & Townsend, J. (1974). SAPPHO updated: Project SAPPHO, Phase II. *Research Policy, 3*, 258–291.

Sawhney, M., & Prandelli, E. (2000, Summer). Communities of creation: Managing distributed innovation in turbulent markets. *California Management Review, 42*, 24–54.

Sawhney, M., Verona, G., & Prandelli, E. (2005). Collaborating to create: The Internet as a platform for customer engagement in product innovation. *Journal of Interactive Marketing, 19*(4), 4–17.

Smith, M. (2002). Tools for navigating large social cyberspaces. *Communications of the ACM, 45*(4), 51–55.

Stafford, T. F., Stafford, M. R., & Schkade, L. L. (2004). Determining the uses and gratifications for the internet. *Decision Sciences, 35*(2), 259–288.

Te'eni, D. (2001). A cognitive-affective model of organizational communication for designing IT. *MIS Quarterly, 25*(2), 251–312.

Thomke, S., & von Hippel, E. (2002). Customers as innovators: A new way to create value. *Harvard Business Review, 80*(4), 74–80.

Vargo, S., & Lusch, R. (2004). Evolving to a new dominant logic for marketing. *Journal of Marketing, 68*, 1–17.

Verona, G., Prandelli, E., & Sawhney, M. (2006). Innovation and virtual environments: Towards virtual knowledge brokering. *Organization Studies, 27*(6), 765–788.

von Hippel, E. (1988). *The sources of innovation.* New York: Oxford University Press.

Walther, J. (1994). Anticipated ongoing interaction versus channel effects on relational communication in CMC. *Human Communication Research, 20*(4), 473–501.

Wasko, M. M., & Faraj, S. (2000). Why people participate and help others in electronic communities of practice. *Journal of Strategic Information Systems, 9*, 155–173.

Wasko, M. M., & Faraj, S. (2005). Why should I share? Examining social capital and knowledge contribution in electronic networks of practice. *MIS Quarterly, 29*(1), 1–23.

# Chapter 7
# From Closed to Open Innovation: The Evolving Nature of Teams and the Use of Information Technology

**Elisa Fredericks and Dawn R. Schneider**

**Abstract** Innovation is both rewarding and risky. However, external environmental pressures resulting from increasing globalization, rapid technological advancements, increasing competitive pressure, and a fluctuating marketplace force firms to continually rethink their innovation models. Newer models suggest more open collaboration, increased interdependence between firms, shared resources, and network-centric practices. As firms adapt to more openness, boundaries blur between intra- and inter-organizational teams. Challenges surface regarding how to manage new relationships within the firm as well as those with customers, suppliers, and even competitors. Firms must now reassess their capabilities and the associated risks and rewards of moving to more open forms of innovation. In this chapter, we characterize closed and more open innovation models and compare and contrast factors facilitating the use of each one. We explore the role of the team, a pivotal force spearheading innovation, and the role of information technology (IT) in supporting both teams and teamwork. While IT makes it possible to structure, facilitate, and manage open innovation, increasing demand for alternative and more adaptive innovation models will spur an increased demand for new forms of technology that can make it all possible. We provide in-depth case study analysis with several large multinational firms and an extensive review of the literature to enhance our understanding of innovation success. The chapter concludes with several suggestions for future research on this topic.

## 7.1 Introduction

Innovation has always been at the forefront of organizational initiatives, with firms often adhering to the "innovate or die" mantra. Product innovation activities have frequently been shown as the cornerstone for increasing market share and customer value, and have been the primary long-term survival mechanism for most firms. Many firms find that new product development (NPD) efforts contribute to

---

E. Fredericks (✉)
College of Business, Northern Illinois University, DeKalb, IL 60115-2897, USA
e-mail: elisa@niu.edu

S. Nambisan (ed.), *Information Technology and Product Development*, Annals of Information Systems 5, DOI 10.1007/978-1-4419-1081-3_7,

35–45% of firm sales (Page & Yu, 2003) and therefore represent the lifeline for sustained organizational success. However, innovation is also risky, as decisions made throughout the process cannot be reversed once the product is introduced, and there could be considerable uncertainty regarding future rewards. By the time a product moves through the innovation process and funnels through the distribution pipeline, 90% of associated development costs have already been spent (Kahn, 2001).

Firms are forced to seek less risky and cost-intensive modes of innovation as they face rising costs, shortened product life cycles, and significant market and technology risks. The pressure of innovation combined with its challenges and frequent, if not expected, failure rate has created what some have referred to as a "period of disillusionment" or "innovation fatigue" (McGregor, McConnon, Weintraub, & Holmes, 2007). According to a recent Boston Consulting Group Survey, only 52% of senior executives were satisfied with their return on innovation spending (Andrew, Haanaes, Michael, Sirkin, & Taylor, 2009). While this is an improvement over the previous year (43%), the numbers are still alarming. Executives have also admitted to a decreasing emphasis on innovation, as the number that consider it a top priority falls. Sixty-four percent of respondents ranked innovation as a top-three priority, the lowest percentage in the six year history of this report (72% peak in 2006).

External environmental pressures resulting from increasing globalization and rapid technological advancements, increasing competitive pressure, shrinking product life cycles, and fluctuating marketplace and customer demands are forcing firms to continually rethink their innovation models. Many organizations are finding it difficult to respond to new technologies, fast-changing consumer demands, and the impact of globalization given their current innovation structure. In addition, rapid and constant changes in these factors further complicate innovation activities (Ozer, 2003). Many firms are reaching the conclusion that *innovating without any external help* may not be a good strategy. Succeeding at innovation today often demands new insights, new viewpoints, and new roles. Many CEOs believe that competitive advantage requires new business models in addition to well-developed products. This realization has led to a dramatic shift – and for some, the redefinition of innovation as we have come to know it.

Current models of innovation can be limiting as they frequently restrict the firm's ability to innovative quickly, responsively, and creatively. A critical realization in this regard is that companies should not go it alone (McGregor et al., 2007). The response is a shift toward more open models of innovation as firms attempt to adapt to the new business environment. Through these open models, companies increasingly draw external partners and suppliers into their innovation networks, bringing diverse expertise together and often speeding up product development. "Once seen as novel and risky, such external collaborations are now accepted as necessary and even routine ways of doing business" (McGregor et al., 2007).

With an open innovation model, distributed knowledge, and increasing levels of virtuality, the traditional product development team as we know it may become a thing of the past. Today's product development team are quite different from the teams of yesterday and new perspectives on team structure, function, and team management are necessary. Regardless of the changing nature of teams, they are still, and will remain, a fundamental organizational mechanism for driving innovation. It is important for both researchers and practitioners alike to understand the nature and characteristics of the product development team of today, and even more importantly, that of the team of tomorrow. By looking at the evolution of teams as we move toward more open innovation models, and the role that information technology (IT) plays in this evolution, we can better understand how some of the challenges of open innovation can be met.

In this chapter, we look at the movement from closed to open innovation, a paradigm shift that is creating new opportunities and challenges for both theory and practice. We address crucial research issues that arise as companies increasingly adopt more open forms of innovation.

The focus is twofold: on the product development team and on the role of IT in supporting both teams and teamwork. While the organization itself embraces new innovative practices, it is the team that must act upon these new philosophies and carry them out in a tactical nature. Thus, we look to address the nature of teams and teamwork in an open innovation context. This type of research is crucial during this point of transition from closed to more open models of innovation, as it is likely that standard theories of organization and teamwork may no longer apply in this new innovation context.

The chapter is organized based on three key elements that define and shape product development teams: team structure, team function, and team management. We discuss each aspect as it relates to both a traditional organization in addition to one that embraces more open forms of innovation practices. Information technology, often the foundation in shaping each one of these elements, is addressed throughout the chapter as it pertains to the structure, function, and management of innovation teams. In addition, we highlight research questions within each one of these elements that offer focus and direction as we begin to further investigate this emerging phenomenon.

## 7.2 Closed Innovation and the Traditional Organization

Closed innovation models are characterized by internally focused firms that generate innovative product ideas, invest heavily in R&D, and manufacture, distribute, and service their own innovations. Essentially, both the development and marketing of new products take place within the boundaries of the firm. In addition to being supported by large R&D organizations, these firms make effective use of a highly educated and savvy workforce.

The traditional team is central to this process. While suppliers, distributors, customers, and competitors may contribute on an as-needed basis, they take a backseat and witness as the innovation process unfolds. As a strategy, closed innovation firms may also use intellectual property defensively by not letting other firms have access to extended uses and thereby miss out on potential revenue streams (Chesbrough, 2003).

In many firms today, innovation is "still largely confined to specific, select departments, which have a monopoly on new ideas" (Tucker, 2002). While functional, bureaucratic approaches have been the traditional dominant management paradigm, there is common agreement that new organizational forms are needed in order to respond to the increasing complexity of production, communications, and technology (Gann & Salter, 2000).

In a recent study, CEOs placed internal R&D labs eighth out of nine important sources of innovation, far behind the general employee population, business partners and customers (Koch, 2007). Despite this fact, only half of respondents felt their organizations were collaborating beyond a moderate level. R&D still plays a role, but on a global basis more CEOs now believe that competitive advantage will be achieved through new business models (54%) compared to new products and services (46%) (Rowell, 2006). The traditional organization often cannot respond to new technologies, fast-changing consumers, and globalization, all of which now require companies to react by transforming the way they innovate (Chesbrough, 2003a; Dodgson, Gann, & Salter, 2006; Margulius, 2006). The team is at the helm of innovation, and therefore its importance cannot be overlooked.

### *7.2.1 Team Structure*

What we refer to as a "traditional NPD team," in this chapter, is not automatically synonymous with the origin of the work team concept. The bureaucratic-hierarchical pattern that characterizes almost all organizations today was developed in the industrial age of the nineteenth century. The Industrial Era called for a stronger form of organization and new forms of bureaucracies emerged (Lipnack & Stamps, 1999). The earliest NPD teams were functional and hierarchically based, originating from the bureaucratic and hierarchical organization. This is not necessarily the team we refer to when we discuss the traditional NPD team.

In the mid-1980s, bureaucratic structures were deemed stagnant by many organizational theorists, unable to adapt to international competition and demographic pressures (Ashkenas, Ulrich, Jick, & Kerr, 1995; Fukuyama, 1999; Fulk & Desanctis, 1995). The resulting network-like alternative, sometimes known as the "virtual organization," was derived from the application of IT, which facilitated greater interaction, agility, and flexibility (Byrne, 1993; Metes, Gundry, & Bradish, 1998; Palmer, 1998). This was also the time when we first began to hear the cross-functionalism buzz. Both researchers and practitioners agreed – cross-functional teams were the wave of the future. Best practices research confirmed this fact and firms moved to multidisciplinary teams – using them for projects regardless of the level of innovation involved (Page, 1993; Griffin, 1997). While not all companies immediately responded to this trend, the multidisciplinary team became acknowledged as a standard practice.

Teams are generally representative of their organizational structure, which can be viewed along a continuum from the classic pure functional organization to the project-based organization (Galbraith, 1971) (see Table 7.1). The pure functional organization divides a development project into segments by relevant functional group, with the head of each functional group responsible for that specific segment

**Table 7.1** Team organization structure

| | Functional | Project based | Matrix | Virtual |
|---|---|---|---|---|
| **Nature of the team organization** | Hierarchal-based structure with functional department heads responsible for coordination of a core set of activities | Project manager leads a team of specialists that work outside traditional organizational boundaries to complete a project | Combination of functional and project-based structures in which managers report to two individuals in order to achieve project goals | Networked organization, highly dependent on IT to manage and coordinate geographically distributed project activities |
| **Key governance issues** | Departments often work as silos resulting in less communication, coordination, and cooperation | Suited for long-term projects with manager/VP coordinating activities across departments with greater focus and project control versus functional or matrix structures | A manager or team leader coordinates activities with a set of core cross-functional members | Developed to address changes emanating from globalization, competition, and technology |

(Larson & Gobeli, 1989). In the project-based structure, a project manager manages a team of specialists that often work outside traditional organizational boundaries to complete a project. These specialists form the core project team, conduct the majority of project work internally, and may defer to their functional departments for information or other resources (Larson & Gobeli, 1989).

In between these two spectrum ends lie different forms of the matrix organization, in which benefits of both the functional and project structures are sought. Matrix organizations frequently have two chains of command – one functional and one project, and participants are often assigned to multiple projects simultaneously (Larson & Gobeli, 1989). While team structures tend to mimic organizational structures, most organizations today embrace more than one team format. "Even a fundamentally functional organization may create a special project team to handle a critical project" (Hyväri, 2006).

As a result of the factors discussed above, combined with increasing globalization and technological advancements, we have seen an increase in the presence of virtual structures in many organizations. Advances in IT can enable firms to work across geographic and organizational boundaries, supporting the "shift toward more open, collaborative, and network-centered innovation practices" (Dodgson et al., 2006).

Technology has created new opportunities by increasing communication both within and between teams, and between teams and suppliers and/or customers (Hauser, Tellis, & Griffin, 2006). Demand and competition has moved to a global level, and in order to address this, organizational structures are becoming more flexible. These flexible organizational structures are being reflected in the nature of the team. Recent research has indicated a growth in the use of global teams, in addition to the expectation that this growth will continue (McDonough, 2000). Often whether a team is collocated or distributed, and or working in a face-to-face or virtual environment have been portrayed as dichotomous choices. The decision to use global and/or virtual teams is not a strategy that firms choose, but an operational reality mandated by necessity (Gassmann & Zedtwitz, 2003).

### *7.2.2 Team Function*

As noted previously, teams in a closed organization may operate in a variety of formats ranging from purely functional organization to project based. While some still function under a strict hierarchy, many have flattened, as virtual and global teams increase in both popularity and necessity. Although many organizations have adopted the networked concept, a limit to the flow of communication and knowledge in these organizations continues to exist.

Chesbrough (2003) likens this type of structure to "a series of fortified castles located in an otherwise impoverished landscape." While each one of these "castles" is "relatively self-sufficient, receiving occasional visits from outsiders, and its inhabitants ventured out occasionally into the surrounding landscape to visit universities or scientific expositions," he notes that "most of the action occurred within the castle walls, and those outside the castle could only marvel at the wonders produced from within." This is the origin of departmental silos and the "not invented here" philosophy. These organizations continue to rely on internal development and believe external knowledge opportunities are both limited and not worthy of pursuit (see Table 7.2).

The traditional NPD team often operates in some form of hierarchy, yet portrays a network-like structure. These teams are cross-functional, manage decisions in a decentralized manner, and share information between levels of the organization. The use of cross-functional teams is one of the cornerstones of a closed innovation process. In many instances, the structure emphasizes integration between marketing and R&D and is touted as the mostly frequently used configuration for developing and commercializing an innovation.

Research has shown that innovation outcomes are highly dependent upon the interface between cross-functional team members (Maltz & Kohli, 2000; Sethi, 2000; Maltz, Souder, & Kumar, 2001), as communication, cooperation, and coordination are critical to innovation success. The literature is rich with research espousing the importance of R&D/marketing integration (Griffin & Hauser, 1995; Rein, 2004), manufacturing/marketing relationship (Kahn & McDonough, 1997), design influence (Nussbaum, 2003; Veryzer, 2005), and engineering prominence in innovation (Michalek, Finberg, & Papalambros, 2005). Top management support, along with vision and resources, stimulate the team to achieve project success.

**Table 7.2** Characteristics and implications of "closed innovation" teams

| Characteristics of product development teams | Implications |
|---|---|
| • Internal idea generation, development, testing, commercialization, distribution, and servicing of an innovation.<br>• High R&D focus with heavy investment in research facilities.<br>• One firm dominates and controls the innovation process.<br>• Reliance of cross-functional innovation with strong integration between marketing, research and development, and manufacturing.<br>• May have high levels of conflict among them due to interdepartmental differences arising from varying goals, objectives, "language," and timeframes.<br>• Defensive and very tight control of intellectual property designed to prevent extended use by others. | • Continued spiraling development costs and high risks borne by a sole firm. Long innovation cycle time.<br>• Limited application of knowledge to innovation as the value chain is limited or excluded from the process.<br>• Limited knowledge creation and creative solutions to innovation. Restricted view of customer needs and wants.<br>• Limited idea generation and development as "outsiders" are not utilized as potential collaborators.<br>• Limited IP application and restricted revenue streams. |

These cross-functional team members are generally collocated, and are consistent from development through manufacture and commercialization. Through the network aspect to this structure, teams can communicate internally, between each other, and even across organizational boundaries. Partners are occasionally involved, but participation in the process is limited. After a specific task or period of involvement, the partner within a closed innovation framework merely steps back to watch as the rest of the process takes place within specified organizational boundaries.

### *7.2.3 Team Management*

Closed innovation teams follow the NPD process and hold regularly scheduled meetings in which cross-functional team members discuss team and project particulars. The Product Development and Management Association (PDMA) reports that over 60% of firms follow a formalized development process with steps including idea generation, screening and selection, testing, business analysis, development, and commercialization. The innovation process includes gates signaling go/no go project decision points, and senior managers determine whether the project moves further along in the process (Griffin & Somermeyer, 2007).

Studies indicate that communication between cross-functional collaborators is fraught with conflicts due to discipline-specific language differences, varying reward systems, dissimilar time horizons, and varying functional priorities. Managers may not exchange information at the appropriate time or may not even know who needs what information, where it is located, or its timely and best use (Zahay, Griffin, & Fredericks, 2003) – all of which cause delays during the innovation process.

At the project level, innovation teams are challenged by meeting budget parameters, integrating knowledge, communicating with each other, and finding ways of decreasing time-to-market. Joint reward systems, collocation of team members, and job rotation have been espoused as alternatives for alleviating cross-functional conflict. Further, closed innovation teams' success in product development is often limited by the extent of internal expertise they possess.

## 7.3 The Open Innovation Paradigm

In open models of innovation, the boundary between a firm and its environment is permeable, as companies work both individually and collectively throughout the innovation process. According to Simard and West (2006), "a crucial goal of open innovation is to capture external knowledge that flows between organizations, allowing firms to be more successful at innovation than firms that close off such flows." Open models often induce collaboration, co-development, strategic and informal alliances, innovation networks, and joint ventures.

Many firms acknowledge the benefits of linking internal investments with external resources and are moving from a R&D model toward a connect and develop model (Huston & Sakkab, 2006). Chesbrough (2003) conceptualizes this trend as open innovation with access to and exploitation of external knowledge. This approach reflects the increasing availability of outside expertise from universities, research consortia, lead users, producers, entrepreneurs, specialized suppliers, and a host of other externals willing to accept the risks and rewards of innovation as they collaborate with each other.

Such a movement is fuelled by increasing competitive pressures from substantial investments in innovation projects, a growing number of international competitors, and technological opportunities residing outside firms' traditional fields of expertise. This impetus is forcing firms to search for outside opportunities to increase effectiveness and efficiency. This openness materializes as a heightened demand for external knowledge, the release of internal resources, and other external inputs key to innovation success (Fagerberg & Mowery, 2005; Monjon & Waelbroeck, 2003; Peters, 2003).

Instead of developing a new technology, open innovators may acquire or merge with externals to achieve innovation success. These collaborative environments with seamless boundaries are not just a way to enhance or improve innovation. This mindset unleashes vast reservoirs of skills, knowledge, and abilities housed in collective sets of innovators and materialize as more creative, customer-oriented products. The firm capitalizes on its strengths and seeks external partners with complementary assets and resources. The result is shared risks, costs, and rewards as collaborators engage in knowledge creation and application. Firms produce stronger and enhanced internally developed capabilities, form new alliances and partnerships, and commercialize more timely and customer-focused innovations. A shortened development cycle and time-to-market have firms reconsidering the benefits of open innovation models.

### *7.3.1 Guiding Principles and Characteristics*

Nambisan and Sawhney (2007) synthesize four complementary guiding principles practiced by network-centric (or open) innovation collaborators as they move through the development process (see Table 7.3). These include shared goals, shared world views, engagement in knowledge creation, and architecture of participation, all of which set the stage for more effective open innovation.

**Table 7.3** Guiding principles of network-centric innovation (adapted from Nambisan & Sawhney, 2007)

| Guiding principles | Explanation |
|---|---|
| Shared goals | Complimentary goals, norms, and values facilitating communication and coordination. A tacit principle which channels co-developers' skills, knowledge, abilities, and resources. |
| Shared world view | Common assumptions and mental frameworks regarding how the world operates and internal firm functioning in relationship to the development of innovation. |
| Social knowledge creation | Places emphasis on interaction and forms the basis for value creation through the synergistic effects of knowledge acquisition, processing, integration, and application. |
| Architecture of participation | Includes roles, responsibilities, task, and communication vehicles which act as the conduit through which participants will contribute and be rewarded in a coherent and synchronized manner. |

When collaborating organizations embrace shared goals, this facilitates communication and coordination among external developers. Shared goals form the basis for the development of shared norms and values and enhance coordination of tasks and activities. With complementing norms and values, firms engage in more seamless communication, engage in a common understanding of how to achieve targeted goals, and determine mutually agreeable ways of solving conflicts. In open innovation models, firms also have a common understanding of "how the world works" in terms of industry practices, competitor hierarchy, and competing and supporting technologies, and thus are able to respond to external environmental shifts more rapidly than collaborators without such world views. Accumulated knowledge developed from a common set of experiences forms a shared world outlook of views and assumptions on how things get done around the world as well as how things are done within firms. Legitimacy is imbedded in conversations as dialogue is reduced from why things are done and moves in the direction of how to get things done rapidly and efficiently. Although information is open to interpretation, it is very much conditioned by these world views.

When firms embrace shared goals and a shared world outlook regarding practices and procedures, information is more easily transformed into knowledge that can now be processed and integrated into an innovation. Without engagement in the co-development of knowledge creation, firms may miss important customer needs. In more closed models of innovation, lack of technological, market, and/or customer knowledge may inhibit an individual firm from obtaining sufficient knowledge to develop a more customer-centered innovation. Furthermore, a firm may be trapped by its own way of doing things. Previous success may have engrained firm-specific processes and procedures in its organizational memory and may now limit an expanded interpretation and application of knowledge to current business projects.

An architecture of participation overrides previously held firms-specific views and assumptions by detailing avenues for communication and coordination of project roles, responsibilities, and tasks. More importantly, co-developers synchronize key resources, determine the extent of open innovation participation, and define how members will be rewarded. Thus, the guiding principles of shared goals, shared world views, knowledge creation, and architecture of participation work in tandem for successful open innovation.

Dell Computers represent a case in point. Although the firm has begun to experiment with more new products, Dell's failure to incorporate new business models early on may have contributed to its lack of success. It seems the firm relied on current business models to implement new strategies, making the shift to more open business models difficult and unsuccessful. Thus this limited world view and closed approach have cost the firm dearly. However, Dell is now rebounding by testing new methods and processes which capture more openness during the innovation process (Nambisan & Sawhney, 2007).

On the other hand, when faced with falling sales, Kraft adopted a more open innovation policy by soliciting new product ideas from visitors to its web site. Previously, this practice was shunned by company managers and the firm operated in a more closed knowledge creation environment, shut off potential new ideas, and missed important customer-centered input. By embracing a more expanded form of knowledge creation, Kraft now enjoys many outlets from which new ideas emanate and is ready to move on those that seem to be most promising.

Both Dell and Kraft recognize that within open innovation models, knowledge may exist across functions, hierarchies, and organizations. The unique characteristics of open innovation (see Table 7.4) enable firms to tap into a new reservoir of knowledge and collectively share, integrate, and apply new applications in the development of a new product.

In open innovation models, firms may also form alliances to pursue new businesses, expand into new geographic regions, or enter new market segments. Strategic research alliances in particular, enable two or more firms to pursue joint research by pooling complementary resources and capabilities. Such alliances help firms share resources, share risks, and may even facilitate competitive repositioning. Many such alliances result in new product design and development, improved production methods, innovative marketing, and distribution systems.

According to a survey conducted by Coopers and Lybrand, more than half of the fastest growing companies in the US are involved in strategic alliances both within and across industries (WSJ, 1995 in Chan, Kensinger, Keown, & Martin, 1997).

Star Alliance and One World represent two cases in the airline industry where cooperative alliances between major airlines and foreign carriers allow for expanded capabilities and sales (Beamish, Morrison, Inkpen, & Rosenzweig, 2003). Joint ventures allow collaborators to pool resources and to coordinate innovation activities to achieve results not easily attainable if either acted as a solo developer. As a source of increased innovation sales, firms may enter new markets, market their products in new territories, or diversify into new categories or new markets.

IKEA, the world renowned Swedish furniture retailer, collaborates intensively with a network of global suppliers. For some component suppliers, IKEA provides designs, technical support, leased equipment, and may even provide much needed financial assistance. Suppliers are accorded with enhanced capabilities, continued access to one of the world's largest retailers, and more balanced sales while IKEA enjoys low-cost, high-quality furniture. International giants Toyota and General Motors are engaged in a joint venture in California – vehicles produced from this locale are clearly branded GM or Toyota, and then are sold on a competitive basis through each one's distribution network. Brands maintain their unique identity as these cooperating competitors increase market share in their respective vehicle categories (Beamish et al., 2003).

Several studies have identified positive performance effects from incorporating external knowledge at various levels. Such effects range from innovation success, to increased novelty of innovations and higher returns on R&D investments (Grimpe & Hussinger, 2008). For instance, many firms may use an offensive approach to intellectual property by licensing to outside parties, and some may even be their own competitors. Qualcomm Inc., the maker of cellular technology, makes chips and sells licenses to its technology. Genzyme licenses technology from the outside, further develops it in-house, and transforms external ideas into an array of new cures for rare diseases (Chesbrough, 2007).

Open innovation models are changing the project type mix of many firms' portfolios. From 1982 to 2004, PDMA members reported more incremental new product introductions versus new-to-the-firm and new-to-the-world introductions. A composite view of projects showed repositioning at 8%, cost reductions at 11%, improvement at 38%, additions to existing lines at 24% with new-to-the-firm projects and new-to-the-world projects at 18% and 8%, respectively (Adams-Bigelow, 2004). On a continuum of project innovativeness, new-to-the-firm and new-to-the-world projects are more risky and are characterized by higher levels of know-how, longer lead times, and higher development costs. With more risky new product introductions, prevailing technologies are transformed, whereas with incremental innovations prevailing technologies are refined. Incremental innovations tend to reinforce existing market structures and competitive positions and strengthen existing barriers to entry and so more stable industries or product categories seem to follow an incremental innovation strategy.

**Table 7.4** Characteristics of open innovation

| Characteristics | Results |
| --- | --- |
| Firm capitalizes on its strengths by utilizing external developers with complementary assets and resources. | • Shared risks, costs, and rewards.<br>• More timely and more customer focused innovation brought to the market. Enhanced knowledge creation and internal capabilities and development. |
| Collaboration with others for enhanced idea generation, sources of new technology, design, development, commercialization, and servicing. | • New knowledge acquisition, processing, sharing, integration, and application to innovation.<br>• Suppliers, lead users, universities, research consortia, producers, and outside organizations may partake in and become a vital part of the innovation process. |
| Shared goals and objectives, world views, knowledge creation, and architecture of participation. | • Expanded innovation team with coevolving capabilities, roles, and responsibilities engaging in more timely and customer-centered innovation. |
| Offensively uses IP with emphasis on licensing to outside parties. | • New and extended IP applications.<br>• Additional revenue streams. |

However, it seems the project mix is now changing as new avenues for knowledge creation propel firms to venture into areas previously perceived as risky. Ettlie and Subramaniam (2004) find support for internal and external sources of knowledge creation and application during innovation. In their study of manufacturing firms, they found firms developing new-to-the-firm, new-to-the-industry, and new-to-the-world innovations. This means these firms were venturing outside of their existing expertise, venturing into more risky innovations, and finding success in doing so as they collaborate with external partners.

According to Navi Radjou, principal analyst and vice president at Forrester Research, "75% of CEOs across industries now view external collaboration as indispensable to innovation (Rowell, 2006)." Nick Donofrio, EVP of innovation and technology at IBM Corporation, believes that "one of the most profound shifts transforming business and society in the early twenty-first century is the rapid emergence of open, collaborative innovation models" (Tapscott & Williams, 2006).

## *7.3.2 Team Structure*

In both closed and open innovation models, teams continue to be representative of their organizational structure. Closed models of innovation utilize collocated teams with members situated within close proximity to each other, often within the same building, office complex, or city. At times members may be scattered throughout a state or a country. While organizational and team structure are often viewed along a continuum from purely functional to project based, we have seen a shift toward the use of projects and project management approaches throughout the innovation process as firms react to advances in technology and fluctuating customer and marketplace demands (Acha, Gann, & Salter 2005; Gann & Salter, 2000; Hobday, 2000; Turner & Keegan, 1999). This movement toward the use of the project-based structure is an important one to be aware of, as team structures impact a variety of organizational outcomes, including the style of interaction and strategies used for information processing (Saunders & Ahuja, 2006).

Project-based teams increasingly span more organizational boundaries as innovation transitions to dispersed collaborators who may be located between sites, at other companies, and even headquartered at competitors (Smulders, Boer, Hansen, Gubi, & Dorst, 2002). To integrate diverse forms of specialized knowledge from around the world, firms embrace a network structure (Heckman et al., 2006; Suchan & Hayzak, 2001) as it opens up the innovation practices.

Networked members have become increasingly dispersed as organizations strive to capture knowledge potential available at multiple locations (Gassmann & Zedtwitz, 2003; Hoegl, Ernst, & Proserpio, 2007). The open innovation team in a network-connected organization often finds members geographically, culturally, and organizationally dispersed (McDonough, Kahn, & Barczak, 1998). In these decentralized organizations, networked teams are often assembled on a project-by-project basis. In addition, as team member dispersion continues across multiple locations and time zones, the innovation process itself is transforming to one that is diverse and global (Dahan & Hauser, 2002).

In a benchmarking study of 26 firms with 54 successful virtual teams, results portrayed an enhanced snapshot into team dynamics. Researchers found both global and regional teams. Half the teams were long-term and half had been set up just for a single project. Fewer than 4% of the 293 participants reported ever meeting fellow team members face-to-face, and less than 7% reported ever meeting with any other member in person. Almost two-thirds of teams included people from at least three time zones, and slightly more than three-quarters had members from more than one country. Fifty-seven percent of teams performed different functions and 48% originated from more than one company (Majchrzak, Malhatra, Stamps, Lipnack, 2004). Thus, we find individuals are frequently assigned to multiple concurrent teams, have multiple responsibilities, and experience variability in the amount of time that can be spent on any one project.

### *7.3.3 Team Member Roles*

Participants in product development projects often are from external organizations including co-development partners, suppliers, and even customers (Rafii, 1995). As teams work to manage increased distribution and virtuality, the role of these new partners must also be addressed. The case examples provided later in this chapter frequently portray a core–periphery structure.

Typically, in this type of structure there exists a dense, cohesive "core" of innovators and a sparse, unconnected "periphery" (Crowston, Wei, Li, & Howison, 2006; Cummings & Cross, 2003). The core is generally small, consists of tightly interconnected team members and exhibits a high level of interaction, while the periphery is disconnected, larger, and displays a much lower level of interaction (Crowston, Annabi, Howison, & Masango, 2005). The idea that some groups or organizations have core/periphery structures is not a new one. The core–periphery model has been used for models of employment (Felstead & Gallie, 2004), and most recently dominates the discussion of open-source software development (Crowston et al., 2005, 2006) in which communities of software developers actively participate and contribute to the development of an innovation.

The differentiation between core and periphery members is important, as the processes of norm development, conflict resolution, etc. are likely to involve core members differently compared to peripheral members (Crowston et al., 2006). Partners may change roles over the life of a project, but the level of knowledge and understanding that must be maintained by core members creates a significant barrier to entry (Crowston et al., 2005). Crowston et al. (2005) also notes that "shared mental models," akin to group identity, are likely to be more important for a core than peripheral model. As Nambisan and Sawhney (2007) note, shared norms and shared world views are two important antecedents to successful open innovation.

## *7.3.4 Team Function*

The processes and operation of an open innovation team becomes increasingly complex due to the nature and structure of these teams. With members spread across boundaries and the often short-term, project-based nature of the team, it can be a challenge to both create and facilitate such teams. Three particular issues – multiteaming, boundary spanning, and connectiveness – appear to be at the center of this challenge.

### 7.3.4.1 Multiteaming

To address the demands of today's environment, individuals are frequently assigned to multiple concurrent teams, have multiple responsibilities, and experience variability in the amount of time that can be spent on any one project (Ancona & Caldwell, 1990). For example, at Intel over 60% of the employees report participation in three or more teams concurrently, while 28% are on five or more teams (Chudoba, Wynn, Lu, & Watson-Manheim, 2005). As employees spread their time between multiple teams both within their organization, and across organizational boundaries, issues may arise. There may be consequences due to the fact that a limited number of experts are often in demand for multiple projects. While many organizations believe that efficiency is increased when development staff works simultaneously on multiple projects, some believe the opposite to be true (e.g., Khurana & Rosenthal, 1997). Multiteaming is likely to be on the rise as organizations move toward open models.

#### 7.3.4.2 Boundary Spanning

As organizations adapt their innovation business models to meet demands, boundaries blur between teams, organizations, and industries. Communication is no longer simply intra-organizational but has expanded to capture both at the intra- and inter-organizational levels with permeability among them (Smulders et al., 2002; Yan & Loius, 1999). As innovation models become more open, the role of boundaries and the interfaces between them become increasingly important. Organizations, once defined by their boundaries, will be defined by their connectivity, or "the range and number of connections to the outside environment" (Mulgan & Briscoe, 2003). Individuals operating at the periphery or boundary of a permeable organization, or "boundary spanners" will be responsible for relating the organization with elements outside it.

#### 7.3.4.3 Connecting Team Members

The common denominator among collocated, virtual, or global teams is how knowledge is applied to an innovation and how IT is used to enhance innovation success. Both core and peripheral members of a team must be connected, though the level and amount of required connectedness may vary per individual, role, and circumstance.

As the open innovation team becomes increasingly physically distributed, members rely more on IT to bring them together using a bundle of technologies to achieve project goals. Interconnectedness in an open innovation team is often achieved through digital technology. Members may never actually meet face-to-face and are often together only once, for the length of a project. Advances in technology increase the ability of firms to work across geographic and organizational boundaries, supporting the "shift toward more open, collaborative, and network-centered innovation practices" (Dodgson et al., 2006). This makes IT an important and integral part of the open innovation team and its relevance and importance are worth noting.

### *7.3.5 Team Management*

The shift to open innovation is one that occurs throughout the organization. While we have discussed many of the benefits that can take place through permeable organizational boundaries, challenges also arise. Fundamentally, open innovation is about operating in a world of abundant knowledge in which a firm must recognize that "not all the smart people work for you" (Callahan, 2003). This creates a need for management to find those with the needed resources, to connect to them, and to build upon what they can do. But bringing in outsiders is not always easy, as corporate cultures can clash and some outsiders just simply do not conform well to working in a business environment (Vaitheeswaran, 2007). In addition, management must find ways to leverage and build upon external knowledge, fill in gaps internally, and integrate both internal and external knowledge usefully.

As team members become increasingly distributed, dispersed members use different tools and possess different worldviews (Hauser et al., 2006), creating challenges in coordination. As a result, the quality of teamwork may suffer (Hoegl & Parboteeah, 2006). In addition, leadership effectiveness often suffers as members of the same team are located in different geographical areas and time zones (Hoegl et al., 2007). Boundaries between individuals, teams, and organizations create additional management complications. It is likely that the strategies for managing boundary interfaces will differ between large corporations, other businesses in supply and distribution networks, small specialist firms, and independent individual experts (Dodgson et al., 2006). It will be increasingly necessary to understand how organizations are managing these interfaces as boundaries become more permeable.

## 7.4 The Role of Information Technology

It can be easily recognized that without recent technological advances the concept of open innovation would not be feasible. Yet, the relationship between IT and open innovation models is complex and circular in nature. While IT makes it possible to structure, facilitate, and manage open innovation, the continued demand for alternative and more adaptive innovation models has spurred an increased demand for new forms of technology that can make it all possible. As firms continue to open their boundaries they will increasingly adopt IT to enable this way of organizing. Not only will firms adopt new technologies, but they will also demand new technological advances to create efficiencies in a world where boundaries are erasing and competitors are becoming co-operators.

### *7.4.1 IT in Closed Versus Open Innovation Models*

IT in closed innovation models is primarily used to automate existing operations and to increase the speed of communication. The replacement of paper, and sometimes people, often occurs as information collection and storage tasks are absorbed by IT. Despite advances in IT, little change in the way work was done and discussions shifted to the "productivity paradox," suggesting that IT investments were not generally reflected in outcomes. Collaboration tools used by closed innovation teams are generally limited to face-to-face exchanges and e-mail or audio conferencing, all rich communication media because of their ability to impart multiple cues between sender and receiver. However, these media may impair companies' ability to successfully use more open innovation models (Malhotra & Majchrzak, 2005), as they limit the knowledge creation and application which are both vital to successful innovation.

With the open innovation model, new forms of teams adopt new technologies in order to derive competitive advantage through the circulation and pooling of global expertise. New types of IT offer a variety of opportunities, including the ability to visualize the entire work process, create products in a flexible and real-time environment, collaborate virtually, and conduct what-if scenarios (Zammuto, Griffith, Majchrzak, Dougherty, & Faraj, 2007). Advances like these in networking and communication technologies make information more widely and readily available, reduce the use of a hierarchy to manage information flows, and coordinate activities more easily and swiftly. As a result, newer technologies decrease the need to move information through a hierarchical process and instead allow collaborators to organize around work and determine what can be done with the information obtained (Zammuto et al., 2007). While new technologies increase knowledge capacity and provide more opportunities for knowledge application, they may also decrease reliance on closed innovation teams and propel the shift to newer, more open forms of organizing.

### *7.4.2 Intra- and Inter-firm IT Applications and Benefits*

Competitive advantage does not emerge from technology itself but rather through the adoption of new business paradigms that harness the capabilities these technologies seek to provide. IT enables networked members to process, share, and transform information and has the added potential of increasing the timeliness, accuracy, and comprehensiveness of information obtained. However, these IT-related capabilities and the knowledge created are not the single source of innovation. It is the swiftness with which information is distributed and the repositioning of resources that provide the best use for networked collaborative members.

The Internet and related technologies provide companies with the ability to harvest the talents of individuals working outside organizational boundaries. For example, P&G uses a secure IT platform to link its R&D professionals with top suppliers who employ over 15,000 scientists from all over the world. These networked individuals then discuss technology briefs, project particulars, and transform information into successful innovations. As a result of such collaborative efforts supported by IT, P&G now boasts a 30% increase in innovation projects shared with its network of suppliers (Huston & Sakkab, 2006).

In addition to its effect on shaping team communication, IT now has the ability to facilitate co-creation. By delegating portions of control to outsiders, firms may take advantage of cost efficiencies, minimized risk, and shortened time-to-market by eliminating bottlenecks that often come with total control (Manyika, Roberts, & Sprague, 2008).

Some firms have developed and perfected savvy IT development practices, such as joint application development and rapid application development and are significantly able to reduce both costs and time-to-market. Majchrzak and Rice (2000) determined that collaborative technologies were responsible for improvements in quality ratings, fewer parts utilized, lower costs, and reduced time-to-market when compared to previous design efforts. Hewlett Packard attributes its ability to reach across inter- and intra-organizational networks to its strong IT human and technical infrastructure, infrastructures that are integrated with its innovation strategy.

As both intra- and inter-firm communication increases, "new technologies are providing the means for dispersed (different place), asynchronous (different time), and virtual work" (Massey, Montoya-Weiss, & Hung, 2003). Advances in technology continue to enhance collaborative environments – making networked workspaces increasingly comparable to face-to-face experiences (see Table 7.5 for more technology benefits). McAfee (2006) notes that newer technologies "can potentially knit together an enterprise and facilitate knowledge work in ways that were simply not possible previously." While it is debatable whether networked environments can replace face-to-face interaction, companies are increasingly adopting newer technologies and providing virtual collaborative environments for their development teams.

Thus, we see IT as a dynamic collaborative vehicle through which internal and external firm innovators funnel project information. In this digitally created environment, projects move seamlessly from concept generation, screening, design, analysis, prototyping, and manufacturing, while incorporating customer and market-based information. This dynamic integration system utilizes intranet and the Internet to integrate tasks, synchronize project design changes, and capture evolving customer information. IT affords firms the ability to integrate knowledge across networks of organizations by building alliances with third party developers, to engage in joint development projects, and to foster an open product architecture and modular design. The goal is to capture a rich understanding of customer needs and develop alternative solutions as the project progresses and integrate knowledge from markets and technologies. The shift to open innovation provides an opportunity for IT tools to increasingly become the "glue for a new, more distributed innovation process" (Koch, 2007). This opportunity does not come without its disadvantages. As a firm opens its boundaries, it increasingly invites customers, suppliers, and even competitors into the innovation process and collaboration becomes an increasingly crucial aspect of success. New business models involving these diverse individuals can be less productive than old ones without effective communication, collaboration, and sharing of information (Koch, 2007).

### 7.4.3 Open Innovation: Redefining the Role of IT

Not only do firms adopt new forms of IT as they move toward more open forms of innovation, but they also continue to use existing IT infrastructure. Firms use intranets and the Internet to support more open forms of innovation and often transform the way work is done. An intranet represents a depository of a firm's intellectual capital, industry benchmarking data, and competitive intelligence, all useful for successful innovation. In addition, intranets may also facilitate the location of industry experts with relevant skills and past experience and allow developers to apply information to current projects. Intranets allow for integration of tasks, synchronize design changes, and capture customer information as the project evolves. The project team is able to keep track of relationships, schedules, and design changes in a dynamic and time-efficient way.

For example, Silicon Graphics, a leading manufacturer of workstations and servers, makes extensive use of the company's intranet to coordinate development activities. Lead users in target application segments, who are also known as "lighthouse" customers, are linked directly to internal development teams. This feedback mechanism allows teams to get fast and effective guidance on critical decisions as the project evolves (Iansiti & MacCormack, 1997). This combination of people and technology provide for easy and rapid flow of information (Nambisan & Sawhney, 2007). Cambrian House, a software development firm housed in Calgary, Alberta, hosts an online suggestion board in which interested parties can post potentially successful and in demand ideas. In this way, ideas are generated and screened, and winning ones are tested. If an idea is commercialized by Cambrian, then winners partake in some portion of future profits.

In addition to using existing IT applications, firms also continue to search for new technologies to meet the demands of the open innovation model. Communication technologies integrate an organization and facilitate knowledge generation, sharing, and application. The newest generation of communication tools and networking technologies often fall under what many refer to as Web 2.0, the second generation of the Web which is perceived as a participation platform versus a statistic information-only resource.

Web 2.0 technologies such as wikis, blogs, and peer-to-peer and social networking represent a new internet-based digital platform. The movement to adopt Web 2.0 technologies by organizations is frequently referred to as Enterprise 2.0 (McAfee, 2006). By fostering creativity, enhancing collaboration, facilitating coordination, and smoothing out the process of information sharing and application, these tools can be key to implementing and enhancing open innovation models. More importantly, Web 2.0 technologies provide an architecture of participation in which systems, mechanisms, and processes allow participants to engage in knowledge creation, value-added innovation, and value appropriation. The resultant impact is more focused and enriched innovation leading to increases in revenues. Firms may also create internal Web 2.0 infrastructures by purchasing platforms and including add-on features. The toolkit usually includes technologies like messaging software, blogs, and wikis, which are used to create a more transparent vehicle for viewing firm practices and output of knowledge workers.

Dresdner Kleinwork Wasserstein (DrKW), an investment bank headquartered in London and Frankfurt, implemented a Socialtext wiki organization-wide in 2004 (Socialtext, 2006). The tool thus far has had a significant impact on idea generation and exchange, problem resolution, and the strengthening of interpersonal relationships. DrKW has noted that since adoption, "meetings run more smoothly and are more productive; unnecessary barriers between teams are being broken down; the quality of product specifications and documentation is improving; presentations are written faster and more effectively; and the risks posed by staff leaving are reduced" (Socialtext, 2006).

Workers at companies like Walt Disney, Eastman Kodak, Yahoo!, and even the US military are ditching traditional technologies in favor of software tools that function as real-time virtual workspaces (Conlin, 2005). Intel is an example of an organization that has embraced virtual workspace technologies. A team of nine from Israel, the Philippines, and the US, with members crossing both human resource and IT functions, routed all information through a virtual workspace versus using e-mail. The workspace included functionalities ranging from links, search features, and discussion threads, to document annotation capabilities. The team also made extensive use of synchronous tools, using an electronic whiteboard for real-time brainstorming and synchronous application sharing for collaboratively editing documents on screen. They also used technology-based meeting aids, such as a raise-hands function when someone had questions during a virtual presentation, a silent-voting function to determine if there was consensus among meeting participants, and a feature to end discussions and progress to the next topic (Malhotra & Majcrzak, 2005).

### *7.4.4 IT Enhancements to the Value Chain*

Open innovation models emphasize internal as well as external collaboration, and firms are cashing in on the rewards of knowledge creation and application. The movement from closed to open innovation is not apparent in one specific area or process; shifts take place across the entire value chain as companies are increasing inflows and outflows from concept to commercialization with partners ranging from consumers to competitors. Chesbrough (2003) identified the biggest weakness of closed innovation as the ignorance of the wealth of knowledge that can be found on the other side of the wall. Many companies appear to be listening and are breaking down borders to increase communication flow both internally and externally.

The concept of an "idea marketplace" is one of the more recent ways technology has been incorporated to foster open innovation. This forum provides a reservoir for idea generation and exchange. Companies such as Whirlpool, Estee Lauder, and Royal Dutch/Shell have created internal idea markets to harvest and evaluate ideas for new processes, products, services, and markets (Yamada, 2001). Companies seeking to collaborate with the outside can go to a variety of third-party idea markets, including NineSigma, YourEncore, and InnoCentive (Tapscott & Williams, 2006) and tap into a rich source of information.

Likewise, companies seeking solutions to R&D challenges can access the 95,000 plus scientists from 175 countries who have registered with InnoCentive (InnoCentive, 2006). Registered companies such as Boeing, Dow, DuPont, Novartis, and Proctor & Gamble (Tapscott & Williams, 2006) anonymously post problems on the InnoCentive website. "Solvers" submit solutions via a bidding process. Once selected, solution winners are provided with a cash reward.

Dell is actively using Salesforce.com's Ideas product to gather and filter ideas and comments from customers. On Dell's Ideastorm, customers tell the company what new products or services they would like to see. Through Ideastorm, Dell has a two-way communication with its customers by responding to comments and suggestions. Customer submitted ideas receive responses indicating "under review,"

Table 7.5 Information technology functionalities and benefits

| Open innovation | IT functionality | IT benefits |
|---|---|---|
| Intra-firm | • Firm repository of intellectual capital, competitive intelligence, and industry protocol<br>• Integration and synchronization of innovation processes, activities, scheduling, design parameters, and collaborator efforts | • Rapid information flow<br>• Enhances knowledge generation, sharing, and application<br>• Enhances creativity, collaboration, and coordination<br>• Creation of value-added innovation |
| Inter-firm | • Flexible innovation creation<br>• Asynchronous and synchronous collaboration<br>• Distribution and pooling of global expertise<br>• Knowledge integration | • More and better information flow and knowledge application<br>• Minimizes the use of hierarchical pathways to information access<br>• Enhances information timeliness, accuracy, and comprehensiveness<br>• More seamless value chain collaboration, capability utilization, and contribution<br>• Enhanced design efforts |

"reviewed," "partially implemented," or "implemented." This bi-directional communication flow enhances Dell's idea generation, screening, and selection phases of the innovation process.

The ability to integrate knowledge across networks of organizations is most important, and yet it is difficult for a single organization to research, manufacture, market, and service their product alone. This requires a heightened awareness of people, technology, and capabilities and a commitment to open innovation such that the organization and the technologies are seamlessly integrated into the innovation process. IT as an enhancer to open innovation provides a host of collaborative benefits (see Table 7.5 for detailed functionalities and benefits).

Several firms seem to have captured the essence of open innovation and have experienced tremendous growth and success. We present a snapshot of the efforts.

## 7.5 Exemplary Examples of Open Innovation and the Use of IT

The success of The BBC, Toyota, Proctor and Gamble, and Boeing serves as a backdrop to understand the many options available to firms implementing open innovation models, and using IT effectively to support such product development initiatives. To various degrees, these companies have enabled their boundaries to become more porous by increasing the flow of internal and external knowledge, increasing the amount and type of partners, and by changing the way they manage relationships throughout the innovation process.

### *7.5.1 The BBC*

In order to spur creative new ideas, the BBC invites independent new media companies, individuals, and/or freelancers to respond to a set of briefs (BBC). Selected teams are invited to a 5-day long "Innovation Lab" in which they work together with BBC commissioners and other mentors to develop the idea and prepare to deliver a final pitch for further development funding. The labs are aimed at independent media companies with a track record of producing innovative new media products. The BBC aims to commission further development of prototypes selected for the labs, but for those projects not selected, any IPR will remain the property of the company that brought it to the lab (BBC).

### *7.5.2 Toyota Motor Corp*

Toyota, the world renowned auto manufacturer, looked to the role of suppliers in its innovation process in order to achieve design improvements while simultaneously raising quality and reducing costs (Green & Toyama, 2005). The "value innovation" strategy integrates suppliers "further back in the design process to find savings spanning the entire vehicle systems" (McGregor et al., 2006). By involving suppliers early in the innovation process, both parties can work together to identify and solve potential problems (Teresko, 2006). In an environment where competitors such as Ford and GM have separated from long-term supplier relationships, Toyota has not only continued to closely collaborate with suppliers, but has actually increased its equity position with key suppliers in its network (Teresko, 2006).

### *7.5.3 Procter & Gamble Co. (P&G)*

P&G acknowledged a changing landscape and realized that in order to meet its growth objectives and to retain its position as the premier consumer products company, it would need to reinvent the company's innovation business model (Huston & Sakkab, 2006). The new model includes a portfolio of open innovation approaches, including external idea sourcing, enabling idea outflows, and increased collaboration with suppliers, partners, and even competitors. Suppliers and partners have assumed an increasingly important role in P&G's innovation process and the company is working on additional initiatives to induce more supplier-to-supplier collaboration (Tapscott & Williams, 2006). With the objective of obtaining 50% of its innovations from outside of P&G labs (Huston & Sakkab, 2006; McGregor et al., 2006), the "Connect & Develop" open innovation model identifies promising new ideas throughout the world and then develops them internally (Sakkab, 2002). In addition to incorporating external ideas, the company has enabled outflows of knowledge and technology. If a patent has been active for 3 years or dormant for 5 years, P&G now makes it available for licensing to any outsider, including competing firms (Tapscott & Williams, 2006).

### 7.5.4 Boeing

Boeing has taken innovation to a new level through mass collaboration in the development and manufacture of aircrafts. Partners from around the world are engaged in every aspect of development – including the sharing of knowledge, cost, and risk (Gates, 2007; Nambisan & Sawhney, 2007; Tapscott & Williams, 2006). Working off a single digital copy of the new 787 Dreamliner, high-level, real-time collaboration between globally distributed partners takes place through the support of state-of-the-art technologies (Gates, 2007). While Boeing is not new to co-development, previous partners were not part of development until the last stage of design (Tapscott & Williams, 2006), at which point they produced from a common blueprint and sent them to Seattle for assembly. With the 787 and more open innovation, partners are involved in creating entire sections of the plane, from concept and design to production and participate in assembly via online modeling (Cone, 2006; Nambisan & Sawhney, 2007).

## 7.6 Future Research Directions

For those firms considering open innovation models and for those firms who have already adopted such a model, many questions continue to surface with respect to assessing firm capabilities, relationships with external innovators, division of labor, and associated risks and rewards. More importantly, issues related to supporting open innovation practices through IT. Researchers might ponder some of the following questions as they investigate the dynamics and implementation of more open forms of innovation.

### 7.6.1 Team Structure

Firms thinking of moving toward more open forms of innovation have many questions. Many of these questions remain unanswered and are often still unaddressed in the literature. In order to make this paradigm shift more feasible, researchers and practitioners need to better understand how a firm and its teams should organize under the open innovation model. Putting the right structures, processes, and people in place cannot occur until we better understand what these structures look like.

Researchers will need to do more than simply look at this new model of innovation. While open innovation may be exciting, the "old" closed model will not just disappear. Instead traditional forms of innovation will continue to be adapted as closed innovators will learn from open models, and hybrid mixes of the models will become popular. This research agenda represents a beginning point, and we hope, sparks interest for those willing to learn more about the evolving nature of organizational structures, teams, and technology.

First, we need to better understand how to describe the various models of innovation, ranging from the closed, traditional organization, to the open organization and possible hybrid models in-between. How does a firm access it capabilities and determine which of these models is the best for its use? What structure will be most suitable for effective collaboration and successful innovation? How should companies devise their IT infrastructure to support these varied forms of innovation that may co-exist? How do we get firms to continue moving along the continuum and share outwardly? Which models are appropriate for a particular project or firm?

What models might address the continuum for closed to open innovation? Researchers might be interested in applying social network analysis (SNA), a tool often used in conjunction with the core–periphery model (Boyd, Fitzgerald, & Beck, 2006). Through SNA, actors and their interactions are studied to better understand patterns of ties between team members (Crowston & Howison, 2006). This type of analysis can identify core and peripheral individuals, and provide insight into the relationships that exist between members. The application of the core–periphery model may be quite useful in understanding management of product development teams in open innovation contexts. It appears that the use of peripheral team members on teams is becoming more common in real practice, as teams become increasingly distributed and individuals play roles in multiple teams within their organizations (Chudoba et al., 2005). In addition, the core–periphery model appears to be quite complementary to the open innovation concept. Together with SNA, this model may be a useful framework in understanding team structures and the interaction and communication processes that take place between team members. And, in turn, this may be valuable insights on deploying appropriate IT applications to support team member's interactions in open innovation contexts.

### *7.6.2 Team Function*

Individuals operating at the periphery or boundary of an open model, or "boundary spanners," will be responsible for relating the organization with elements outside it. As boundaries become increasingly permeable, this role and the individuals that occupy it will become increasingly important to address (Ancona, Bresman, & Kaeufer, 2002; Reid & de Brentani, 2004). In addition to understanding the boundary spanning role and its corresponding activities, we need to better understand other roles that team members may undertake. Do new roles develop as a boundary becomes more permeable? What types of roles do individuals outside of the organization hold? What is the impact of multiteaming on innovation project success? How can IT support these new roles in product development teams?

We might also consider the extent to which firms that open up their boundaries to enjoy innovation success. What types of internal ideas and technologies do they receive? What do they share and with whom? What types of IT applications are required to support such sharing of information across organizational boundaries?

Another important research question relates to the nature of open innovation projects firms can pursue and the impact on speed-to-market. Earlier, we noted that open innovation models which allow for more external collaboration enable firms to participate in more riskier projects (since risks are shared in open innovation projects) and to potentially introduce the innovations to the market more quickly.

Thus, the relationship between the level of innovativeness and the speed-to-market in open innovation require additional investigation.

Next, questions exist as to whether or not existing technology is sufficient for new collaboration settings and new working structures. Researchers need to better understand the role of IT – both how it works in the open innovation context and where the gaps are likely to be in terms of technology-based capabilities. What is the impact of different types of IT-based collaboration tools on innovation productivity, extent of creativity or innovativeness, and other innovation outcomes? How should companies select and deploy IT-based tools to maximize open innovation outcomes? Researchers continue to investigate the ability of virtual workspaces to replace or complement face-to-face meetings in innovation projects. Researchers also need to focus on the usage behaviors (e.g., communication mode repertoires), productivity outcomes, and collaboration challenges associated with such virtual environments.

### *7.6.3 Team Management*

While the concept of open innovation may be appealing, this model also has its perils. Costs of open innovation, such as management distraction and lost intellectual-property rights, are not nearly as well studied as its benefits (Vaitheeswaran, 2007). It still remains unclear what capabilities companies will need, or how they will organize those capabilities in order to take advantage of the benefits that this model offers.

The role of the CEO and CIO appears to be crucial to both the adoption and long-term success of this innovation model. Moving to open innovation requires managing a cultural change and retooling a company's approach to innovation with full support from upper management (McGregor et al., 2007)

Knowledge flow barriers exist in an organization regardless of its level of openness, and these barriers will not be broken by technology alone. In addition, organizations unable to move past their closed innovation practices cannot blame the absence of participative technologies (Enterprise 2.0 technologies such as wikis and blogs), as simply embracing this type of technology will not dissolve an existing organizational hierarchy. In the event, knowledge does flow fluidly among all innovation partners; there remains the risk and complication of an overwhelming amount of data requiring proper storage, distribution, and analysis.

Incentives and innovation metrics form another valuable research area. Few companies today link incentives and success metrics together. Managers will need to understand how to incentivize external partners to contribute to the innovation project and also how to keep both core and peripheral members engaged throughout the innovation process. Questions remain as to how managers measure the contributions of collaborators and how project success will be determined. What metrics will be employed and how will organizations know which ones to use given the various types of innovation projects? How will tasks, risks, and rewards be equitably divided and what supporting rules, guidelines, and processes are required? Most importantly, technology can play in making such incentive system more transparent.

This indicates additional issues for future research. Specifically, how should companies design their IT infrastructure so as to enhance the transparency of the innovation interactions and the associated reward structure?

With respect to collaboration with external partners in open innovation models, several additional research questions can be identified. For example, how should a firm access the capabilities of its external collaborators? What type of innovation collaborator would complement firm capabilities? What are the roles and responsibilities of the various partners as well as the depth and range of their associated relationships? How, when, and by whom will those roles and responsibilities be determined? What type of IT applications will help facilitate or support those roles and relationships? Who should invest in establishing such IT infrastructure?

The research agenda described here address the evolving nature of organizations, innovation teams, and the use of IT in open innovation contexts. We hope the research issues raised here will be pursued rigorously in the future. The findings from such studies could provide valuable insights to companies as they expand their innovation boundaries through appropriate use of IT.

## 7.7 Conclusion

The movement from closed to open innovation is a paradigm shift, and one that creates new opportunities and challenges in both theory and practice. The definition of innovation itself may be changing, and our acknowledgement of this is vital as we press forward toward a better understanding of the changes and adaptations in the marketplace. Transitioning to an open innovation business model will not simply happen overnight. Yet, while transition may take time, firms slow to accept such a change may find significant retardation in their ability to compete in the future. A 2006 Innovation Networks Report indicates that when compared to their peers, early adopters of collaborative networks aggressively grew their top lines while also boosting customer satisfaction (Radjou, 2006).

A critical component of such an approach to open innovation would be the identification and the deployment of an appropriate portfolio of IT applications. Through a new perspective on product development teams and information technologies as described in this chapter, both researchers and practitioners can work together to better understand, anticipate, and react to shifts in innovation business models.

## References

Acha, V., Gann, D. M., & Salter A. J. (2005). Episodic innovation: R&D strategies for project-based environments. *Industry & Innovation, 12*(2), 255–281.

Adams-Bigelow, M. E. (2004). PDMA foundation new product development report of initial findings. *PDMA Foundation*. Mount Laurel, NJ.

Ancona, D., Bresman, H., & Kaeufer, K. (2002). The comparative advantage of X-Teams. *MIT Sloan Management Review, 43* (3 Spring), 33–39.

Ancona, D., & Caldwell, D. (1990). Beyond boundary spanning: Managing external dependence in product development teams. *The Journal of High Technology Management Research, 1*, 119–135.

Andrew, J., Haanaes, K., Michael, D., Sirkin, H. L. & Taylor, A. (2009). Innovation 2009: Making Hard Decisions in the Downturn. Retrieved September 22, 2009, from http://www.bcg.com/documents/file15481.pdf.

Ashkenas, R. N., Ulrich, D., Jick, T., & Kerr, S. K. (1995). *The boundaryless organization: Breaking the chains of organizational structure*. Jossey-Bass.

Beamish, P. W., Morrison, A. J., Inkpen, A. C., & Rosenzweig, P. M. (2003). *International management* (5th ed.). New York: MCGraw-Hill/Irwin.

Boyd, J. P., Fitzgerald, W. J., & Beck, R. J. (2006). Computing core/periphery structures and permutation tests for social relations data. *Social Networks, 28*(2 May), 165–178.

Byrne, J. (1993). The virtual corporation: The company of the future will be the ultimate in adaptability. *Business Week, February 8*, 98–103.

Callahan, R. H. (2003). *Open innovation: Interview with Henry Chesbrough* (http://ideaflow.corante.com/archives/2003/04/16/open_innovation_interview_with_henry_chesbrough_part_1.php ed.).

Chan, S. H., Kensinger, J. W., Keown, A. J., & Martin, J. D. (1997). Do strategic alliances create value? *Journal of Financial Economics, 46*(2), 199–221. (http://www.sciencedirect.com/science/article/B6VBX-4227VF0-4/2/60ae27facc2dbe758edd7a77e5b4f4b8).

Chesbrough, H. W. (2003). *Open innovation: The new imperative for creating and profiting from technology*. Boston, MA: Harvard Business School Press.

Chesbrough, H. W. (2007). Why companies should have open business models. *MIT Sloan Management Review, 48*(Winter), 22–28.

Chudoba, K. M., Wynn, E., Lu, M., & Watson-Manheim, M. (2005). How virtual are we? Measuring virtuality and understanding its impact in a global organization. *Information Systems Journal, 15*(4), 279–306.

Companies Seek Innovation — Not Gimmicks. (2007). Available at http://www.msnbc.msn.com/id/18490291/

Cone, E. (2006). Boeing: new jet, new way of doing business. *CIO Insight, CASE STUDIES*.

Conlin, M. (2005). E-mail is so five minutes ago. *Business Week, 3961*, 111–112.

Crowston, K., Annabi, H., Howison, J., & Masango, C. (2005). Work practices for FLOSS development: A model and propositions. *38th Annual Hawaii International Conference on Systems Sciences* (HICSS '05).

Crowston, K., & Howison, J. (2006). Hierarchy and centralization in free and open source software team communications. *Knowledge, Technology, and Policy, 18*(4), 65–85.

Crowston, K., Wei, K., Li, Q., & Howison, J. (2006). Core and periphery in free/libre and open source software team communications. *Proceedings of the 39th Annual Hawaii International Conference on System Sciences (HICSS'06) Track 6*, 118a.

Cummings, J. N., & Cross, R. (2003). Structural properties of work groups and their consequences for performance. *Social Networks, 25*(3), 197–210.

Dahan, E., & Hauser, J. (2002). The virtual customer. *Journal of Product Innovation Management, 19*(5), 332–353.

Dodgson, M., Gann, D., & Salter, A. (2006). The role of technology in the shift towards open innovation: The case of Procter & Gamble. *R&D Management, 36*, 333.

Ettlie, J. E., & Subramaniam, M. (2004). Changing strategies and tactics for new product development. *Journal of Product Innovation Management, 21*(2), 95–109.

Fagerberg, J., & Mowery, D. C. (2005). *The oxford handbook of innovation*.

Felstead, A., & Gallie, D. (2004). For better or worse? Non-standard Jobs and high involvement work systems. *International Journal of Human Resource Management, 15*(7), 1293–1316.

Fukuyama, F. (1999). *The great disruption; Human nature and the reconstitution of social order*. New York: Free Press.

Fulk, J., & DeSanctis, G. (1998). Electronic communication and changing organizational forms. *Organization Science, 6*, 337–349.

Galbraith, J. R. (1971). Matrix organization designs how to combine functional and project forms. *Business Horizons, 14*, 29–40.

Gann, D., & Salter, A. (2000). Innovation in project-based, service-enhanced firms: The construction of complex products and systems. *Research Policy, 29*(7, 8), 955–972.

Gassmann, O., & Zedtwitz, M. (2003). Trends and determinants of managing virtual R&D teams. *R & D Management, 33*(3), 243–262.

Gates, D. (2007). Boeing Shares Work, but Guards its Secrets; Building the Dreamliner – 787 Project: Some Worry about Partners′ Access to 'Crown Jewels. *The Seattle Times*. Seattle.

Green, W., & Toyama, M. (2005). 10 Questions for Katsuaki Watanabe. Available from http://www.time.com/time/magazine/article/0,9171,1086192,00.html

Griffin, A. (1997). PDMA research on new product development practices: Updating trends and benchmarking best practices. *Journal of Product Innovation Management, 14*(6), 429–458.

Griffin, A., & Hauser, J. (1995). How to boost marketing and R&D teamwork. *Institute for the Study of Business Market Insights, 5*, 1–2.

Griffin, A., & Somermeyer, S. (2007). *The PDMA toolbook for new product development*. Hoboken, NJ: John Wiley & Sons, Inc.

Grimpe, C., & Hussinger, K (2008). Formal and informal technology transfer from academia to industry: Complementarity effects and innovation performance. *ZEW – Centre for European Economic Research*, Discussion Paper No. 08-080

Hauser, J., Tellis, G. J., & Griffin, A. (2006). Research on innovation: A review and agenda for marketing science. *Marketing Science, (November 1)*, 687–717.

Heckman, R., Crowston, K., Li, Q., Allen, E., Eseryel, U.Y., & Howison, J. (2006). Emergent decision-making practices in technology-supported self-organizing distributed teams. *International Conference on Information Systems* (ICIS), Milwaukee, WI.

Hobday, M. (2000). The project-based organization: An ideal form for managing complex products and systems? *Research Policy, 29*(7, 8), 871–893.

Hoegl, M., Ernst, H., & Proserpio, L. (2007). How teamwork matters more as team member dispersion increases. *Journal of Product Innovation Management, 24*(2), 156–165.

Hoegl, M., & Parboteeah, K. P. (2006). Team reflexivity in innovative projects. *R&D Management, 36*(2), 113–125.

Huston, L., & Sakkab, N. (2006). Connect and develop: Inside Procter & Gamble's new model for innovation. *Harvard Business Review, 84*(3), 58–66.

Hyväri, I. (2006). Project management effectiveness in project-oriented business organizations. *International Journal of Project Management, 24*, 216–225.

Iansiti, M., & MacCormack, A. (1997). Developing product on internet time. *Harvard Business Review, 75*(5), 108–117.

InnoCentive, Inc. (2006). *Seeker brochure*, 1–4.

Intel Corporation. *People and practices research group*. Available at http://www.intel.com/research/exploratory/papr/#Overview

Kahn, K. B. (2001). *Product planning essentials*. Sage Publications, Inc.

Kahn, K. B., & McDonough, E. F. (1997). Marketing integration with R&D and manufacturing: a cross-regional analysis. *Journal of International Marketing, 5*(1), 51–76.

Koch, C. (2007). IT builds a better idea. *CIO, 20*, 1.

Khurana, A., & Rosenthal, S. R. (1997). Integrating the fuzzy front end of new product development. *Sloan Management Review, 38*(2), 103–120.

Larson, E. W., & Gobeli, D. H. (1989). Organizing for product development projects. *Journal of Product Innovation Management, 5*, 180–190.

Lipnack, J., & Stamps, J. (1999). Virtual teams: The new way to work. *Strategy and Leadership, 27*(1), 14–19.

Majchrzak, A., Malhotra, A., Stamps, J., & Lipnack, J. (2004). Can absence make a team grow stronger? *Harvard Business Review, 83*(5), 131–137.

Majchrzak, A., & Rice, R. E. (2000). Technology adaptation: The case of a computer-supported inter-organizational virtual team. *MIS Quarterly*, *24*(4), 569–600.

Malhotra, A., & Majchrzak, A. (2005). Virtual workspace technologies: Emerging technologies enable virtual and distributed teams to communicate – and innovate – more effectively. *MIT Sloan Management Review, Winter* (1).

Maltz, E., & Kohli, A. J. (2000). Reducing marketing's conflict with other functions: The differential effects of integrating mechanisms. *Journal of the Academy of Marketing Science*, *28*(4), 479–492.

Maltz, E., Souder, W. E., & Kumar, K. (2001). Influencing R&D/marketing integration and the use of market information by R&D managers: Intended and unintended effects of managerial action. *Journal of Business Research*, *52*, 69–82.

Manyika, J. M., Roberts, R. P., & Sprague, K. L. (2008). Eight business technology trends to watch. *McKinsey Quarterly*, 60–71.

Margulius, D. L. (2006). The uncertain future of R&D. From http://www.infoworld.com/article/06///Opanalysis_1.html

Massey, A. P., Montoya-Weiss, M. M., & Hung, Y.-T. (2003). Because time matters: Temporal coordination in global virtual project teams. *Journal of Management Information Systems*, *19*(4), 129–155.

Metes, G., Gundry, J., & Bradish, P. (1998). *Agile networking: Competing through the internet and intranets*. New York: Prentice-Hall.

McAfee, A.P. (2006). Enterprise 2.0: The dawn of emergent collaboration. *MIT Sloan Management Review, 47*(3), 19–28.

McDonough, E. F., III (2000). Investigation of factors contributing to the success of cross-functional teams. *Journal of Product Innovation Management*, *17*(3), 221–235.

McDonough, E. F., III, & Kahn, K. B. (1998). Effectively managing global new product development teams. *International Product Development and Management Association Proceedings*.

McGregor, J., Arndt, M., Berner, R., Rowley, I., Hall, K., Edmonson, G., et al., (2006). The world's most innovative companies. *Business Week*, 4/24/2006, 63–74.

McGregor, J., McConnon, A., Weintraub, A., & Holmes, S. (2007). The 25 most innovative companies. *Business Week, 52*.

Michalek, J., Finberg, F. M., & Papalambros, P. Y. (2005). Linking marketing and engineering product design decisions via analysis target cascading. *Journal of Product Innovation Management*, *22*(1), 42–62.

Monjon, S., & Waelbroeck, P. (2003). Assessing spillovers from universities to firms: Evidence from French firm-level data. *International Journal of Industrial Organization*, *21*(9), 1255–1270.

Mulgan, G., & Briscoe, I. (2003). The society of networks. *Managing Innovation and Change*. J. Henry and D. Mayle, Sage Publications Inc, 276–280.

Nambisan, S., & Sawhney, M. S. (2007). *The global brain: Your roadmap for innovating faster and smarter in a networked world*. Upper Saddle River, NJ: Wharton School Publishing.

Nussbaum, B. (2003). WINNERS 2003 the best product designs of the year. *Business Week* (3840), 68–71.

Ozer, M. (2003). Process implications of the use of the internet in new product development: A conceptual analysis. *Industrial Marketing Management*, *32*(6), 517–530.

Page, A. L. (1993). Assessing new product development practices and performance: Establishing crucial norms. *Journal of Product Innovation Management*, *10*, 273–290.

Page, A. L., & Yu, J. (2003). *Benchmarking the sales impact of new products*. International Product Development and Management Association, Boston, MA.

Palmer, J. W. (1998). In M. Igbaria, M. Tan (Eds.), *The use of information technology in virtual organizations*, Idea Group Inc (IGI).

Peters, M. A. (2003). Education policy in the age of knowledge capitalism. *Policy Futures in Education*, *1*(2), 361–380.

Radjou, N. (2006). *Innovation networks*. Global Progress Report, 1–26.

Rafi, F. (1995). How important is physical collocation to product development success? *Business Horizons, 38*(1), 78–84.
Reid, S. E., & de Brentani, U. (2004). The fuzzy front end of new product development for discontinuous innovations: A theoretical model. *Journal of Product Innovation Management, 21*(3), 170–184.
Rein, G. L. (2004). FROM EXPERIENCE: Creating synergy between marketing and research and development. *Journal of Product Innovation Management, 21*(1), 33–43.
Rowell, A. (2006). Interview with Navi Radjou, Forrester Research.
Sakkab, N. Y. (2002). Connect & develop complements research & develop at P&G. *Research Technology Management, 45*(2), 38–45.
Saunders, C., & Ahuja, M. (2006). Are all distributed teams the same? Differentiating between temporary and ongoing distributed teams. *Small Group Research, 37*(6), 662–700.
Sethi, R. (2000). Superordinate identify in cross-functional product development teams: Its antecedents and effect on new product performance. *Journal of the Academy of Marketing Science, 28*(3), 330–344.
Simard, C., & West, J. (2006). Knowledge networks and the geographic locus of innovation. In H. W. Chesbrough, W. Vanhaverbeke, & J. West (Eds.), *Open Innovation* (pp. 220–240). New York: Oxford University Press
Smulders, F. E., Boer, H., Hansen, P. H. K., Gubi, E., & Dorst, K. (2002). Configurations of NPD – production interfaces and interface integration mechanisms. *Creativity and Innovation Management, 11*, 62–73.
Socialtext (2006). *Dresdner Kleinwort Wasserstein case study.*
Suchan, J., & Hayzak, G. (2001). The communication characteristics of virtual teams. *IEEE Transactions on Professional Communication, 44*(3), 174.
Tapscott, D., & Williams, A. D. (2006). *Wikinomics: How mass collaboration changes everything.* New York: Portfolio.
Teresko, J. (2006). Learning from Toyota – again. *Industry Week, 255*(2), 34–41.
Tucker, R. B. (2002). *Driving growth through innovation: How leading firms are transforming their futures.* San Francisco, CA: Berrett-Koehler.
Turner, J. R., & Keegan, A. (1999). The versatile project-based organization: Governance and operational control. *European Management Journal, 17*(3): 296–309.
Vaitheeswaran, V. (2007). Something new under the Sun: A special report on innovation. Available at http://www.economist.com/surveys/displaystory.cfm?story_id=9928227 (Ed.) *Economist.com.*
Veryzer, R. W. (2005). The roles of marketing and industrial design in discontinuous new product development. *Journal of Product Innovation Management, 22*(1), 22–41.
Yamada, K. (2001). Trends: Idea markets. *CIO Insight.*
Yan, A., & Louis, M. R. (1999). The migration of organizational functions to the work unit level: Buffering, spanning, and bringing up boundaries. *Human Relations, 52*(1), 25–47.
Zahay, D., Griffin, A., & Fredericks, E. (2004). Sources, uses, and forms of data in the new product development process. *Industrial Marketing Management, 33*, 657–666.
Zammuto, R. F., Griffith, T. L., Majchrzak, A., Dougherty, D. J., & Faraj, S. (2007). Information technology and the changing fabric of organization. *Organization Science, 18*, 749–762.

# Chapter 8
# Enabling Consumer-Driven Service Innovation in Health Care: The Role of Online Health Information Technologies (HIT)

**Priya Nambisan**

**Abstract** In the past few years, consumer participation in health care has increased significantly with the ready availability of medical information on health websites and the ability to interact in disease-focused online health communities. Importantly, such consumer participation also involves creating new knowledge based on consumers' direct experiences with particular diseases and treatments – new knowledge that could lead to new or improved services. Such consumer-driven service innovation has assumed critical importance as most healthcare organizations come under considerable pressure to enhance the value they offer to their consumers (or patients). In this chapter, we argue that an important task for value-driven healthcare organizations is to facilitate consumer driven service innovation in health care through appropriate use of online health information technologies. We adopt a knowledge creation perspective and propose a theoretical framework that explains how health websites and online health communities together can facilitate creation of innovative service ideas through knowledge socialization, combination, externalization, and internalization. Implications for future research on the role of IT in service innovation in health care are discussed. The implications for strategies and practices adopted by healthcare organizations are also examined.

**Keywords** Consumer participation · Service innovation · Health care · Knowledge creation

## 8.1 Introduction

Consumer participation in health care – self-care – has increased significantly in the past few years or so with the ready availability of medical information on the Internet. In addition, consumers' ability to connect with people with the same

---

P. Nambisan (✉)
Department of Health Policy, Management and Behavior, School of Public Health, University at Albany, SUNY, One University Place, Rm 185, Rensselaer, NY 12144, USA
e-mail: pnambisan@albany.edu

S. Nambisan (ed.), *Information Technology and Product Development*, Annals of Information Systems 5, DOI 10.1007/978-1-4419-1081-3_8,

disease or health condition and form disease-focused support groups has led another type of active participation – namely, collective consumer knowledge creation.

For example, consider the case of Gleevec, an experimental drug that showed some evidence to shrink tumors in patients affected by chronic myelogenous leukemia, a potentially deadly disease. Patients with this disease formed a group called "Life Raft," a listserv, where they shared their knowledge about the drug itself, the benefits, and the side effects as well as their experiences at the clinical trial. This in turn led hundreds of similar patients to sign up for the clinical trials, eventually forcing the FDA to fast track the drug approval process. In October 2001, this group that did not have any formal medical education published a review of Gleevec's side effects in a medical journal (Solowitch, 2001).

The increasing number of such examples in consumer-driven collective knowledge creation (Solowitch, 2001) attests to the fact that consumer participation in online health communities has gone beyond merely extending support to one another. The collective pooling of resources and information by consumer groups can lead to different types of innovation – for example, generating ideas for innovative healthcare services or improving the quality of existing services; advancing medical research on particular diseases; or developing extensive experiential knowledge on specific treatments. The potential for consumer to take active part in such service innovation holds important implications for healthcare organizations and the healthcare industry in general, and forms the primary focus of this chapter.

Most healthcare organizations are under considerable pressure to enhance the value they offer to their consumers (or patients). The notion of value-driven healthcare organization (Addleman, 1995) and value-based competition is gaining increasing importance (Porter & Teisberg, 2006) as consumers are increasingly voicing their discontentment with existing quality of healthcare services. Porter and Teisberg (2006) in their book on "Redefining Healthcare" call for competition based on value and results.

Partnership with customers to enhance their ability to innovate and co-create disease-focused knowledge implies another significant opportunity to enhance the agenda of such value-driven health organizations. Such a partnership would acknowledge the increasing ability of customers to engage in collective knowledge co-creation as well as the availability of sophisticated information-technology-based infrastructure to support that process. However, pursuing such a partnership with consumers would require a deeper understanding of the knowledge creation process as well as the contextual factors that would shape the success of such efforts.

Thus, this chapter aims to contribute toward developing such a theoretical understanding of IT-enabled consumer knowledge co-creation and co-innovation in health care. We first introduce the notion of value-driven healthcare organization and discuss the relevance of consumer participation in service innovation in this context. Following that, we describe the notion of service innovation and discuss the relationship between service innovation and healthcare quality. We argue that an important task for value-driven healthcare organizations is to facilitate consumer driven service innovation in health care through appropriate use of online health information technologies (HIT).

We adopt a knowledge creation perspective (Nonaka, 1994, Nonaka, von Krogh, & Voelpel, 2007; Nonaka, 1998) and propose a theoretical framework that explains how health websites and online health communities together can facilitate creation of innovative service ideas through knowledge socialization, combination, externalization, and internalization. We use the case study of CHESS, a healthcare center affiliated with the University of Wisconsin-Madison, to illustrate some of our propositions. We conclude the chapter by discussing some of the important implications for future research on the role of IT in service innovation in health care. The implications for strategies and practices adopted by healthcare organizations are also examined. We start by describing the concept of value-driven healthcare organization.

## 8.2 Value-Driven Healthcare Organization

The value-driven healthcare initiative was launched in early 2007 by the Health and Human Services Department of the US Federal Government for the betterment of healthcare quality and to empower people to derive better value from the healthcare system (HHS, 2007). It is directed at healthcare organizations to increase transparency, improve quality, and provide value for money to health consumers. This would empower consumers with better choices and allow better comparisons based on cost and quality (HHS, 2007; Feder, 2008; Seicean & Neuhauser, 2007).

Value-driven health care is premised on four cornerstones, all of which focus on enhancing the value offered to consumers (HHS, 2007).

1. Improve the extent of standardization in HIT to make them more interoperable: Prior studies have shown the importance of HIT adoption to improve transparency, quality, and efficiency, but still most healthcare organizations are well behind in adopting these IT systems, particularly when it comes to adopting HIT systems that are interoperable.
2. Improve quality standards, so that consumers can compare the quality of care information from different providers: Quality standards need to be developed with the consensus of different types of stakeholders. Without commonly accepted quality standards, consumers are unlikely to be able to compare services across different healthcare organizations. Healthcare organizations will then need to make available data based on these quality standards or metrics.
3. Improving price standards, so that consumers can compare service fees across providers: Some healthcare organizations have started providing the price of their different services through their websites, but in general, this is not a standard practice in most parts of the healthcare industry. This information is crucial for consumers to compare prices as well as to evaluate whether they are getting the value for the money they are giving for the various services.
4. Improving the incentive structure for all the network participants: This is a call for designing appropriate incentives that reward all the parties in the healthcare network – those who provide healthcare services as well as those that avail

them. Currently, a few such arrangements are outlined such as incentives for pay-for-performance methods of reimbursement. However, this remains an area where healthcare organizations can be innovative and develop and implement new arrangements that bring in value to everybody including the consumer.

What are the implications of the above value-driven healthcare framework for individual healthcare organizations? A common theme that runs across the above four cornerstones of value-driven health care is the need for transparency. As such, perhaps the most critical task for health organizations intending to pursue value-driven health care will be to develop strategies and practices that increase transparency at all levels, particularly by deploying and using appropriate types of HIT.

It is from such a perspective that IT-enabled consumer-driven service innovation assumes importance in health care. To better understand this, first let us examine the concept of service innovation in more detail.

## 8.3 Service Innovation in Health Care

The term "service innovation" is a relatively new entrant in management. Much of the focus of both management practitioners and researchers so far has been on product innovation. However, over the past 10 years or so, the proportion of the service sector in the global economy has increased significantly to a state where now the service sector dominates over the manufacturing sector.

The concept of service innovation includes innovation in service products (the development of new or improved service products); innovation in service processes (new or improved ways of designing and producing services); and innovation in service firms (new or improved business models). Given that many of the most successful companies in the contemporary world are service companies – for example, Google, Amazon, e-Bay, Walt-Disney, etc. – it is not surprising that the concept of and the practices associated with service innovation have started to attract considerable attention in the management research community (e.g., Bitner, Ostrom, & Morgan, 2008; Möller, Rajala, & Westerlund, 2008; Windrum & García-Goñi, 2008).

With the change in global economy and the emergence of technology-based service companies such as Amazon and e-Bay, it has become quite critical that companies develop business practices that promote both innovative service outcome as well as innovative processes of service delivery, and most importantly, focus on creating meaningful and valuable experiences for customers as part of the service (Prahalad & Ramaswamy, 2004).

Service innovation calls for the adoption of innovative models and practices that are beneficial to both the company and its customers and as such a need for company–customer (or client–provider) collaboration to co-create long-term meaningful relationships and bonds that will result in better quality goods and services (Bitner et al., 2008; Moller et al., 2008). This is more so in the case of a service-oriented industry such as healthcare.

In the healthcare industry, much of the focus in the past couple of decades has been on innovation in medical technologies that can be deployed in the clinical diagnosis, intervention, and the treatment of diseases. This has brought about tremendous advances in surgical equipments, non-invasive treatment methods, and radiological instruments as well as advancements in the pharmaceutical innovation (i.e., drug discovery) processes.

However, such a focus on medical technologies has been at the expense of a focus on innovation in the customer-facing services in the healthcare sector. Customer satisfaction and customer approval rates of many of our hospitals are at an all time low. Concerns regarding cost and quality have dominated much of the news in the past several years. The concept of value-driven healthcare organization described earlier reflects this desire to bring the focus on healthcare quality and the innovations that would help enhance the level of customer satisfaction in healthcare services.

An important factor that companies in many industries have realized, but perhaps not the ones in the healthcare arena, is that "quality" is often defined by customer perceptions of value. As such the ability to "listen to customers" to understand their needs (Urban & Hauser, 2004) and to embrace them as active participants in service innovation – creation and delivery of innovative healthcare services – have become critical success factors for many healthcare organizations (Mills, Chase, & Margulies, 1983; Mills & Morris, 1986; Berry, 1995; Nambisan & Nambisan, 2009).

Studies done in other industries have also found that customer participation in services delivery can significantly improve customers' perceptions about the organization and its services (Claycomb, Lengnick-Hall, & Inks, 2001; Bowen, 1986; Wang, Wang, & Zhao, 2007; Kelley, Donnelly, & Skinner, 1990). Such participation would also allow customers to understand organization's offerings and operations and increase the perceived transparency – and help move toward the goals outlined by the value-driven healthcare initiative. In addition, such collaborative arrangements with customers will also bring rewards based on the new incentive structure that is being proposed in the value-driven healthcare initiative.

More importantly, advances in information technologies has helped to provide promising opportunities for healthcare organizations to engage their customers (or patients) in service innovation – creating knowledge that lead to new or improved services or new ways of disease treatments. In particular, online IT applications – for example, online health communities, health information websites, etc. – could support such patient-driven service innovation activities. In sum, IT-enabled customer participation in service innovation has the potential to become an important element of value-driven health care, and as such implies the need for healthcare organizations to take a careful look at how they can embrace and support such an approach.

In the following section, we provide some examples to illustrate the specific nature of consumer participation, namely, consumer knowledge sharing and creation. This helps to set the context for presenting our theoretical framework in the following section.

## 8.4 Customer Knowledge Co-creation and Service Innovation in Healthcare Organizations

As noted previously, today's medical consumers are more knowledgeable and they are becoming increasingly vocal about not only their needs but also their dissatisfaction with services offered by healthcare organizations. In addition, as mentioned previously, through the Internet, they have gained access to more diverse and advanced healthcare information, which allows them to actively participate in their own health care as well as voice their discontentment by forming activist online groups.

According to the Pew Internet & American life project, 80% of American Internet users (some 113 million adults) have searched for information on at least one of 17 health topics (2006 Pew Report). More than 70,000 websites disseminate health information (Cline & Haynes, 2001; Grandinetti, 2000). While healthcare websites do offer a rich mine of health information for consumers, their participation is stoked more by the rapid increase in health-focused online communities and discussion forums. Prior studies have examined the phenomenon of online health consumer communities in order to understand why consumers are attracted to these online health communities (Walther & Boyd, 2002), how these communities are being utilized (Gustafson, Hawkins, et al., 1999; Gustafson, McTavish, et al., 1999), the benefits consumers are deriving from their interactions there (Shaw, McTavish, Hawkins, Gustafson, & Pingree, 2000).

The dominant perspective in research on online health communities has been that such online groups function mainly as support groups. However, as several recent examples indicate these online groups are more than just support groups and instead have become a platform for consumers to share as well as co-create knowledge (i.e., innovate). Indeed in many respects such online communities become "centers of research" driven by consumers.

For example, consumers with rare diseases such as 18 q- (a partial deletion of the 18th chromosome) and pseudoxanthoma elasticum (PXE) (a rare genetic disorder) discovered that there was very limited focus on their diseases in the scientific community, partly due to the small number of affected patients (Solowitch, 2001). In the late 1990s and early 2000s, some of these consumers came together to organize research-focused online health communities, i.e., online communities focused on researching specific diseases. These communities allowed them to not only share knowledge and experiences related to the disease with one another but also to play the role of "citizen scientist" and collaborate in finding cures. Their activities involved establishing blood and tissue banks, building vast genetic databases, raising millions of dollars for research, and getting researchers in traditional research centers to collaborate with them on specific research initiatives. The early success of some of these activities implies that consumers (patients) "often know more about the diseases than health care providers" (Solowitch, 2001, p. 2) and the collective pooling of resources and information by online consumer groups focused on advancing medical research on particular diseases hold particular promise (Ferguson, 2002).

In the case of Gleevec described previously, consumers also used the online communities to recruit people to participate in clinical trials in ways that bypass the "lethal lag time." These and other such examples indicate consumer participation in health care can range from sharing knowledge (e.g., about providers' service quality and pricing, about specific diseases and treatments, etc.) to creating new knowledge (e.g., research-oriented disease databases, clinical trial experiences, etc.). Such trends in consumer participation have the potential to radically change the medical market place and the very way in which healthcare organization create value for consumers. Organizations able to incorporate and support such consumer participation as part of their service infrastructures would likely succeed in creating truly value-driven healthcare organizations (Liu & Yuh – Yun Lin, 2007).

The discussion so far indicates that healthcare organizations need to adopt a knowledge management perspective in order to understand IT-enabled consumer participation in service innovation and knowledge creation in health care and to adopt appropriate set of support strategies and practices (Fottler, Ford, Roberts, & Ford, 2000). We take the initial step toward this by presenting a theoretical framework that draws on contemporary knowledge management theories to explain how HIT – specifically, online health communities and health websites – can enable consumer-driven service innovation in health care. We start by describing the knowledge management perspectives relevant in this context.

## 8.5 Knowledge Management Perspectives

Despite all the evidence regarding consumers-driven service innovation in health care, there hasn't been much theoretical effort expended to understand this phenomenon or to identify the factors that may facilitate such participation. Two related research streams in the area of knowledge management offer the foundation to develop such a theoretical understanding of consumer participation in health care. The first relates to the two modes of knowledge management while the second offers a dynamic theory of knowledge creation. We now describe these knowledge management research areas in more detail and then apply them to the context of consumer participation in service innovation in health care.

### *8.5.1 Repository and Network Models of Knowledge Management*

Two primary models of knowledge management have been identified in the literature: the *repository model* and the *network model* (Alavi, 2000; Fahey & Prusak, 1998; Hansen, Nohira, & Tierney, 1999). The former relates to static knowledge or knowledge that resides in inanimate objects (databases, reports, etc.) while the latter relates to knowledge that resides in human beings and is accessible through interactions.

While much of the early research on knowledge management adopted the repository model perspective and focused on managing knowledge embedded in documents, organizational routines, processes, practices, and norms (Davenport & Prusak, 1997; Huber, 1991), more recent research have adopted the network model perspective and started focusing on managing knowledge resident in individuals by deploying new types of information technologies and creating richer and more effective communication channels.

The network model attempts to capture the information that is resident in individuals by facilitating interactions among these individuals. Rather than extracting information from these individuals and storing it as in the case of repository model, the network model facilitates communication channels among individuals, so that knowledge can be developed and transferred.

The network model also emphasizes the emerging *sociological perspective* of knowledge management (Sawhney & Prandelli, 2000). Social relationships are increasingly becoming the foundation for knowledge creation. Also, the relationships between the different types of knowledge reflect the social relationships that exist among the entities that create and store such knowledge. Thus, from the sociological perspective, the interactions between individuals and groups assume importance in the context of knowledge management.

Recent studies in knowledge management have focused on such social processes and ties that underline knowledge and value creation in organizations. For example, the concept of "ba" introduced by Nonaka and Konno (1998) reflects the need to create environments that nurture and promote social relationships that in turn would fuel the knowledge creation process. Information technology has a critical role to play in establishing and maintaining such knowledge creation social environments.

### 8.5.2 The Dynamic Theory of Knowledge Creation

The other major perspective of knowledge management was offered by Nonaka in 1994. He posited a dynamic theory of organizational knowledge creation, which describes four patterns of interactions in the knowledge creation process: socialization, combination, internalization, and externalization.

The fundamental thesis behind this model is that knowledge is created by individuals and that knowledge creation occurs through a continuous exchange of two types of knowledge – tacit knowledge and explicit knowledge. Polanyi (1962) described tacit knowledge as knowledge that is highly personalized, hard to formalize and communicate. This type of knowledge resides within the individual and is deeply rooted in action and involvement in that particular context. On the other hand, explicit knowledge is codified knowledge and can be formalized and communicated in a systematic language. This type of knowledge is easily accessible and available and can be expressed in words or numbers.

Nonaka's conceptualization drew on the four possible modes of conversion possible between these two types of knowledge. First is the tacit to tacit conversion: the process of creating knowledge through this mode is called "socialization" as this requires people with tacit knowledge to interact with one another and also be involved in some form of shared experiences so that they can derive tacit knowledge from one another through learning. The second is the explicit to explicit conversion: this process is called "combination" as it is a process where explicit knowledge held by different individuals are brought together and combined to form new knowledge. This type of knowledge creation is fairly common in many kinds of collaborative work and sometimes, even computers can combine two existing information and create a new body of information. The third and fourth modes involve the transformation of tacit knowledge to explicit knowledge or "externalization" and that of explicit knowledge to tacit knowledge or "internalization." While the former mode (externalization) requires interactions among individuals to bring forth the tacit knowledge and externalize it so that other people can acquire such knowledge, the latter mode (internalization) focuses on individuals receiving explicit knowledge and integrating it with their own particular experiences, thereby internalizing it (or converting it into tacit knowledge). These four modes of knowledge conversion are complementary and together they enable new knowledge creation. As such companies that facilitate all the four knowledge conversions by providing appropriate technological and organizational infrastructure are more likely to derive the benefits of such new knowledge creation (Nonaka, 1994).

## 8.6 A Theoretical Framework of Consumer-Driven Service Innovation in Health Care

We now apply these two related knowledge management theories in the context of consumer-driven service innovation (i.e., knowledge sharing and knowledge creation) in healthcare. Figure 8.1 provides an overview of the theoretical framework.

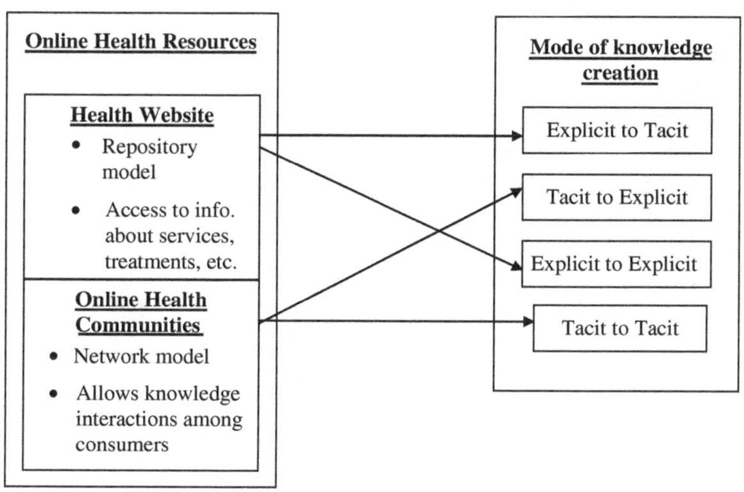


**Fig. 8.1** Modes of consumer knowledge co-creation in health care

The objective here is to describe customer participation from a knowledge management perspective and to derive a few important research propositions that would inform on the strategies and practices that healthcare organizations would need to adopt to facilitate it and enhance the value offered to consumers.

The real world manifestation of knowledge management activities in the healthcare context occurs in the form of *health information websites* maintained by different healthcare organizations as well as *online health communities* and discussion forums. Broadly, we posit that these two types of online consumer health resources or facilities together offer opportunities for new knowledge creation by consumers – specifically opportunities to socialize, combine, internalize, and externalize knowledge. We start with the role of online health communities in facilitating knowledge socialization and knowledge externalization.

### *8.6.1 Online Health Communities and Knowledge Socialization/Externalization*

Traditionally, for knowledge socialization and knowledge externalization to occur, members would need to be at physical proximity so that they can be involved in shared experiences that would allow conversion of tacit knowledge into tacit or explicit knowledge. In the healthcare context, an example would be that of a medical resident learning from an attending physician. Such tacit knowledge resides within experts and if opportunities for knowledge socialization do not exist, such knowledge is typically lost when the expert leaves the organization.

Knowledge socialization also occurs in the consumer context. For example, a patient may gain additional tacit knowledge about a disease if any of the other family members are also dealing or have dealt with the same disease. Through storytelling and the sharing of experiences, patients may learn unique aspects of the particular disease (or associated treatments) that are not available as explicit knowledge anywhere else. However, typically such knowledge resides only within that particular family unit and hence opportunities to share with other people are often limited.

A radical change is occurring in both these types of knowledge conversions with the easy access to online discussion forums and communities that connect people and help implement the network model. First, consider online physician communities – such communities enable experts to converse with one another and share tacit knowledge derived from their unique experiences.

A good example of this is the online physician community called "Sermo." Sermo is an online community that is accessible only to physicians – it allows them to post their medical observations, discuss new clinical findings, report unusual medical experiences, and work together to improve patient care. The connections made between physicians working in the same area and their continued conversations become the vehicle for both knowledge socialization and knowledge externalization (Halperin, 2007)

The same applies in the consumer context. The earlier-mentioned example of "Life Raft" community is a good illustration of this potential for supporting knowledge conversions. In that community, the consumers (or patients) ended up publishing an article on the side effects of Gleevec. In other words, tacit knowledge regarding the treatment and its side effects were collectively converted into explicit knowledge in the form of a research paper written by the consumers. These and similar such examples show that healthcare organizations that provide such online communities and discussion forums for their patients and medical experts can support shared or collective knowledge creation through both socialization and externalization. More importantly, the new knowledge that is created can lead to improvements in existing healthcare services (or development of new services) that healthcare organizations can further develop and deploy.

Thus, based on the above discussion, we can conclude that the network model of knowledge management that manifest in the form of online health communities and forums would enhance the opportunities for consumer knowledge creation through knowledge socialization and knowledge externalization. Hence, the following proposition:

**Proposition P1:** *The network model of knowledge management implemented in the form of online health communities will enhance the extent of consumer knowledge creation through knowledge socialization and knowledge externalization.*

## 8.6.2 Health Websites and Knowledge Combination/ Internalization

Most healthcare organizations also possess several static repositories of knowledge (e.g., patient medical records, treatment and medical procedure details, physician expertise details, etc.). Depending on the type of the healthcare organization (e.g., academic/research institution, HMO, profit/non-profit hospitals, community centers), it could also be a repository for other types of explicit knowledge, such as the latest medical research findings related to a disease, insurance information, treatment quality and pricing information, patient education literature, etc.

We argue that a Web-based implementation of the repository model of knowledge management will facilitate consumer service innovation through knowledge combination and knowledge internalization.

As noted previously, there are several consumer health information websites such as WebMD and Mayo clinic that provide comprehensive information on diseases A–Z. These types of databases clearly support explicit–explicit knowledge conversion (or combination). Consumers can acquire information from multiple or separate database and combine them to create new knowledge that help them in dealing with specific diseases or creating/improving service aimed at specific healthcare issues.

The Web-based health databases also support internalization as consumers can acquire specific explicit knowledge and contextualize such information – i.e., situate and reinterpret the information in their unique context – thereby creating tacit knowledge or internalizing it. This could create promising opportunities for consumers to make suggestions that relate to implementing valuable services that they have encountered elsewhere.

The key challenge here is to provide consumers with access to varied types of information in ways that would facilitate knowledge conversion and thereby generation of innovative ideas. Many healthcare organizations are reluctant to share explicit knowledge for various reasons and further many organizations do not have well-developed health websites with information that would be relevant (or in a usable form) to consumers. Another constraint is the lack of information standards that make sharing and combining such information across organizations difficult. The availability of such standards would help implementing interoperable HIT applications, one of the cornerstones of value-driven healthcare. This would enable consumer to access and connect relevant explicit knowledge (from different sources) enhancing the possibilities of knowledge creation through knowledge combination and internalization.

Based on the above discussion, we can conclude that the repository model of knowledge management, characterized by health information websites, will support consumer-driven service innovation through knowledge combination and internalization.

**Proposition P2:** *The repository model of knowledge management implemented in the form of online health websites will enhance the extent of consumer knowledge creation through knowledge combination and knowledge internalization.*

### *8.6.3 Supporting the Four Modes of Knowledge Conversion*

As discussed previously, all the four modes of knowledge conversion are equally important. Moreover, as Nonaka has showed, they complement one another and form the spiral of knowledge creation (Nonaka, 1998). Healthcare organizations have a concrete role to play in supporting these four modes of knowledge conversion and thereby consumer-driven service innovation.

Apart from overcoming the challenges related to information standards and IT infrastructure, healthcare organization can also provide meaningful connections between online health communities and health information websites, thereby further supporting the "spiral of knowledge creation." This requires identifying appropriate information sources, categorizing such information, and building bridges between health websites and online health communities based on specific diseases, treatments, type of consumers, etc.

Early efforts in this area by healthcare organizations such as Kaiser Permanente demonstrate this potential. Kaiser has established well-developed consumer-oriented health information websites, where patients can have access to not only relevant disease-specific information and services but also identify appropriate online communities where they could connect with disease experts or peer patients. Such efforts will accelerate consumer knowledge creation and lead to better consumer perceptions of healthcare quality thereby favoring the healthcare organization itself.

Based on the above discussion, we propose that adopting a holistic view of the four modes of knowledge conversion will enhance opportunities for consumer knowledge creation. Hence, the following proposition:

**Proposition P3:** *The extent and effectiveness of consumer-driven service innovation and knowledge creation in health care will be dependent on the quality of support provided for all the four modes of knowledge creation (i.e., combination, internalization, externalization, and socialization) by the value-driven health care organization.*

From the above set of propositions, it is clear that value-driven healthcare organizations will need to support both the network and the repository model of knowledge management. In other words, they need to offer IT-based solutions that bring together a variety of health information sources and knowledge sharing facilities.

As prior technology implementation studies have informed us (Orlikowski, 1992), customers' actual usage and usage preferences is critical for effectively carrying out the above task. We now use a real world case study of a healthcare provider namely, the Wisconsin-based Comprehensive Health Enhancement Support System (CHESS) run by the Center for Health Enhancement Systems Studies that offers both websites and online communities, to understand the pattern of consumer usage of these facilities. Our objective is to offer some preliminary guidance on how healthcare organizations should proceed in offering the above knowledge creation facilities.

## 8.7 Consumer Participation in CHESS: An Exploratory Study

CHESS is an online health information system run by the Center for Health Enhancement Systems Studies at the University of Wisconsin–Madison for patients with certain types of health crisis or medical concern, primarily, cancer.

In this exploratory study, we look at the services provided specifically for breast cancer patients. CHESS provides a highly sophisticated website with reliable, up-to-date, well-organized, and accessible information for patients diagnosed with breast cancer. In addition to providing general information, it also tailors and personalizes the information, provides decision-making tools, provides an extensive resource directory as well as tools for tracking and monitoring the services related to their treatments.

Unlike many websites that are static, CHESS website provides a more interactive environment by incorporating features such as "Ask an expert" that allows consumers to interact with experts in an anonymous manner. Patients can also post their stories on the website. Along with all this, CHESS also provides an online discussion board where patients can share information and experiences related to dealing with the specific disease or make suggestions for improving the quality of services. The website and the discussion board have been utilized by several patients for the last 15 years or so and the project has been funded by several organizations including NIH, Department of Defense (DOD), and National Library of Medicine (NLM).

### 8.7.1 Exploratory Research Questions and Study Findings

With respect to the framework discussed earlier, the Web site component of CHESS represents the repository model and the online discussion board component of CHESS represents the network model of knowledge management. To better understand the pattern of usage of these two IT-based facilities, we formulated a set of exploratory research questions. These questions do not directly relate to the propositions discussed earlier; however, they provide some preliminary evidence on how consumers use these facilities, and thereby, throw some light on the role of IT in consumer-driven service innovation. We examined three issues:

a) Does the time spent by consumers in the online discussion board and in the website differs?
b) Do the time spent in the online discussion board and in the website vary with the user's cancer stage? What are the demographic (and other patient-specific) factors that moderate the above relationship?

In formulating these questions, we were limited by the type of information that was available for analysis. We used log data related to the usage by the subjects who were given access to both breast cancer website as well as discussion boards. The subjects were all women who were diagnosed with breast cancer and were at varying stages of cancer ($n = 394$). The log statistics for the first 16 weeks were collected on an individual keystroke level as the participants used the system.

The key variables are the extent of website usage and discussion board usage. These variables are operationalized as total time spent (in minutes). The data was analyzed using paired sample *t* tests to see if there was any significant difference between the total time spent on the website and the total time spent on the online discussion board. An independent sample test was also conducted to see if time spent in website versus discussion boards varied with cancer stage (75% of the participants had early stage and 25% of participants had late stage). Mean age of the participants was 51 years; 73% were Caucasians; 25.1% were African Americans, and 1.9% other minorities.

The results from the paired sample *t* tests showed that there was statistically significant differences between the usage of the website and that of the discussion board ($t = -7.025$; $p < 0.001$) (see also Figs. 8.2 and 8.3). The stage of breast cancer however was not found to have any moderating effect, although a significantly higher amount of time was spent by early stage breast cancer patients on the website and the discussion boards, compared to late stage breast cancer patients.

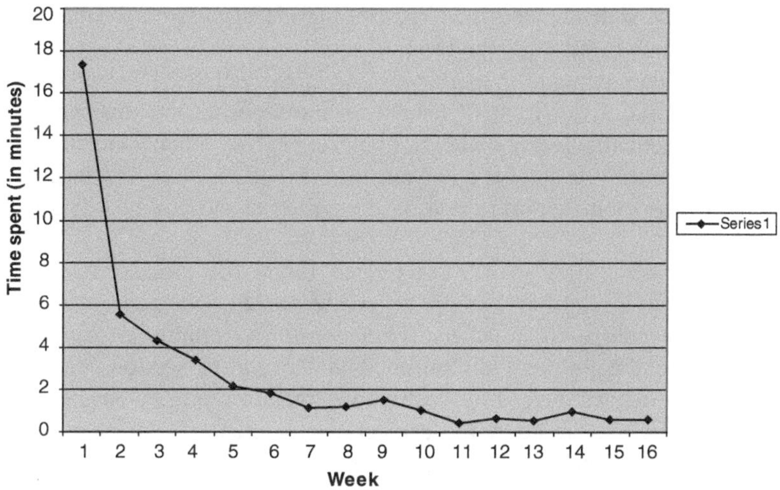


**Fig. 8.2** Time spent by the patients on the CHESS website

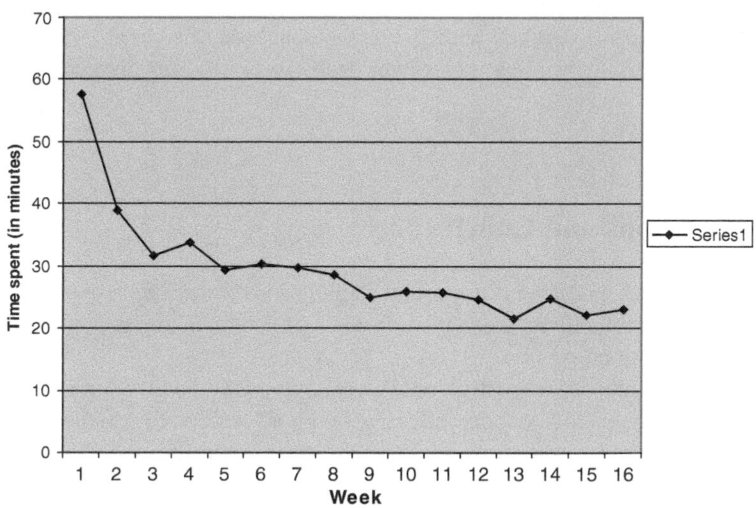


**Fig. 8.3** Time spent by the patients on the CHESS online discussion board

Demographic variables such as income, education, and age also did not have any statistically significant moderating effect on the difference between the time spent on the website and the time spent on the online discussion boards.

Overall, the results of this exploratory study show a preference by health consumers for online discussion boards compared to websites. Results from other CHESS-based studies (Shaw, Han, et al., 2007; Shaw, McTavish, et al., 2000) that used qualitative methods (interviews, focus groups, etc.) show that consumers acquire data from websites and then visit the online discussion forums to collectively interpret such information and to find additional meanings from such explicit data based on other patients' experiences. As is evident from the above figures, following the initial acquisition of data from the website, the time spent on the website falls drastically in the following weeks. On the other hand, much of the knowledge co-creation based on other patients' experiences occurs in the following weeks, and as such the time spent on the online discussion boards tends to be greater.

One study (Shaw, Han, et al., 2007) also found that breast cancer patients who used online discussion boards to greater extent showed more information competence compared to others. Thus, while our empirical study does not directly relate to the propositions outlined in the earlier section, they do indicate the added emphasis placed by health consumers on online discussion boards. More importantly, they indicate the critical complementary role that online discussion boards could potentially play in enhancing the usefulness of healthcare websites.

In sum, this brief exploratory study indicate the promise for future research to validate the propositions outlined here and to ascertain the complementary nature of health websites and online health communities that is evident from the knowledge perspective adopted here. Next, we conclude this chapter by discussing some of the important implications of the framework offered here for healthcare organizations.

## 8.8 Implications and Conclusions

The research model has several important implications for future research and management practice related to the application of IT systems for promoting service innovation in health care.

As previously noted, a critical challenge that most healthcare organizations currently face relates to the poor effectiveness and efficiency of the delivery of healthcare services to customers. Further, the healthcare industry has also fallen behind in adopting new technologies, compared to many other industries. At the outset, the presence of more empowered consumers (who actively seek health information on the Internet and hence are well informed about their healthcare options) may seem to pose another major challenge for physicians and healthcare organizations. However, as our framework indicates it can also offer numerous opportunities for healthcare organizations to embrace consumers as active participants in the creation and delivery of healthcare services in ways that add real value to consumers, thereby truly becoming value-driven healthcare organizations.

The first implication relates to the role of online communities as a complementary resource for patients. The high cost of physicians has led to significant deficiencies in providing patients who are chronically ill with the necessary support. While it is evident that online health communities can be utilized to provide consumers with the needed social or emotional support, the emerging examples discussed here implies a more powerful role for online communities. It can empower consumers to create collective knowledge about diseases, treatments, provider services, etc. that not only help them to deal with their particular health situations more effectively but also evaluate and identify those services that deliver value.

Healthcare organizations can facilitate this by providing the associated technological infrastructure (for example, establish online health communities as part of their service offering). Such a strategy would enhance the overall quality and value of their services portfolio and at the same time achieve it in a cost-effective manner. The involvement of health experts in such online communities can further enhance their positive impact. However, all of this would call for cultural changes in healthcare organizations as it would involve bringing transparency in the processes, sharing knowledge with consumers, etc. Overall, the study framework implies the critical need for healthcare organizations to incorporate online resources (including online communities) as an important element of their service portfolio.

The second implication relates to the need to integrate such online health communities with existing health information websites that the healthcare organization may already be maintaining. As the application of the knowledge creation perspective showed there are important synergies between such websites and online communities in facilitating different types of knowledge creation activities. The ability of healthcare organizations to identify appropriate linkages between these two IT-based solutions and to enable consumers to leverage such linkages effectively will go a long way in determining the overall value consumer perceive in such facilities. Related to this is the important need for healthcare organizations to arrive at appropriate HIT information standards that would facilitate such integration. As such, the framework presented in this chapter also has important implications for government and non-governmental agencies that are playing a supportive role in steering the healthcare industry toward such information standards.

It would also be important to note that consumers' interactions in the online health community could redefine their perceptions regarding the healthcare organization in ways that are not always within the control of the organization. Thus, healthcare organizations will need to deploy new and innovative mechanisms so as to facilitate those knowledge interactions that are likely to lead to positive attitudes and perceptions. Future research may focus on identifying and validating the effectiveness of such organizational mechanisms.

Finally, while not directly evident from the discussion so far, the framework also implies the need for healthcare organizations to adopt a holistic perspective in deploying their online and offline patient relationship and support strategies. It is evident that patients' offline interactions and experiences (say, with their physicians) will complement their interactions and experiences in the online health community. Strategies and practices to find potential synergies between offline healthcare facilities and the online facilities will also be very beneficial. Future studies may also focus on the manner in which the different experiences are integrated and how it affects the value derived by consumers as well as their overall service-related perceptions and attitudes.

## References


Addleman, R. B. (1995). Value-driven healthcare. *The Healthcare Forum Journal, 38*(6), 46–50.

Alavi, M. (2000). Managing organizational knowledge. In R. W. Zmud (Ed.), *Framing the domains of IT management projecting the future. Through the past*(pp. 15–28). Cincinnati, OH: Pinnaflex Education Resources, Inc.

Berry, L. L. (1995). Relationship marketing of services – growing interest, emerging perspectives. *Journal of the Academy of Marketing Science, 23*(4), 236–245.

Bitner, M. J., Ostrom, A. L., & Morgan, F. N. (2008). Service blueprinting: A practical technique for service innovation. *California Management Review, 50(3),* 66–94, 29.

Bowen, D. E. (1986). Managing customers as human resources in service organizations. *Human Resource Management, 25*(3), 371–383.

Mills, P. K., Chase, R. B., & Margulies, N. (1983). Motivating the client/employee system as a service production strategy. *Academy of Management Review, 8*(2), 301–310.

Mills, P. K., & Morris, J. H. (1986). Clients as "partial" employees of service organizations: Role development in client participation. *Academy of Management Review, 11*(4), 726–735.

Claycomb, C., Lengnick-Hall, C. A., & Inks, L. W. (2001). The customer as a productive resource: A pilot study and strategic implications. *Journal of Business strategies,* http://www.entrepreneur.com/tradejournals/article/75372920_1.html

Cline, R. J., & Haynes, K. M. (2001). Consumer health information seeking on the Internet: the state of the art. *Health Education Research, 16*, 671–692.

Davenport, T., & Prusak, L. (1997). *Working knowledge: How organizations manage what they know*. Cambridge, MA: Harvard Business School.

Fahey, L., & Prusak, L. (1998). The eleven deadliest sins of knowledge Management. *California Management Review, 40*(3), 265–280.

Feder, H. M. (2008). *Value-driven health care initiative continues to evolve*. Managed Care Outlook, January 1, 10–11.

Ferguson, T. (2002). Key concepts in online health: e-patients as medical researchers, *Ferguson Report,* Retrieved on Jan 2008 from http://www.fergusonreport.com/articles/fr00903.htm

Fottler, M. D., Ford, R. C., Roberts, V., & Ford, E. (2000). Creating a healing environment: The importance of the service setting on the new customer oriented healthcare system. *Journal of Healthcare Management, 45*(2), 91–106.

Grandinetti, D. A. (2000) Doctors and the Web: Help your patients surf the Net safely. *Medical Economics, April*, 28–34.

Gustafson, D. H., Hawkins, R., Boberg, E., Pingree, S., Serlin, R. E., Graziano, F., et al. (1999). Impact of patient-centered, computer-based health information/support system. *American Journal of Preventive Medicine, 16*, 1–9.

Gustafson, D. H., McTavish, F. M., Boberg, E., Owens, B. H., Sherbeck, C., Wise, M., et al. (1999). Empowering patients using computer-based health support systems. *Quality in Health Care, 8*, 49–56.

Halperin, A. (2007). *The wisdom of the medical crowd*, Business Week, http://www.businessweek.com/investor/content/apr2007/pi20070429_699650.htm?chan=technology_technology+index+page_top+stories

Hansen, M. T., Nohira, N., & Tierney, T. (1999). What's your strategy for managing knowledge? *Harvard Business Review, March–April*, 106–116

HHS. (2007). Retrieved on May 18, 2008 from http://www.hhs.gov/valuedriven/

Huber, G. P. (1991). Organizational learning: The contributing processes and the literatures.*Organization Science, 2*(1), 88–115.

Kelley, S. W., Donnelly J. H., Jr., & Skinner, S. J. (1990). Customer participation in service production and delivery. *Journal of Retailing, 66*, 315–335.

Liu, S. S., & Yuh-Yun Lin, C. (2007). Building customer capital through knowledge management processes in the health care context. *Health Care Management Review, 32.2*(April–June), 92(10).

Möller, K., Rajala, R., & Westerlund, M. (2008). Service innovation myopia? A new recipe for client-provider value creation. *California Management Review, 50(3),* 31–48, 18.

Nambisan, P., & Nambisan, S. (2009). Models of consumer value co-creation in health care. forthcoming in *Health Care Management Review, 34*(4).

Nonaka, I. (1994). A dynamic theory of organizational knowledge creation. *Organization Science, (5:1),* February, 14–37.

Nonaka, I. (1998). *The knowledge creating company: Harvard Business Review on management.* Boston: MA: Harvard Business School Publishing.

Nonaka, I., & Konno, N. (1998). The concept of 'Ba': Building a foundation for knowledge creation. *California Management Review, 40*(3), 40–54.

Nonaka, I., von Krogh, G., & Voelpel, S. (2007). Organizational Knowledge creation theory: Evolutionary paths and future advances. *Organization Studies, 27*(8), 1179–1208.

Orlikowski, W. J. (1992). The duality of technology: Rethinking the concept of technology in organizations. *Organization Science,* 3 (3), 398–427.

Polanyi M. (1962). Tacit knowing – its bearing on some problems of philosophy. *Reviews of Modern Physics, 34*(4), 601–616.

Porter, M. E., & Teisberg, E. O. (2006). *Redefining health care: Creating value-based competition on results.* HBS Press.

Prahalad, C. K., & Ramaswamy, V. (2004). Co-creation experiences: The next practice in value creation. *Journal of Interactive Marketing, 18(3),* 5–14.

Sawhney, M., & Prandelli, E. (2000). Communities of creation: Managing distributed innovation in turbulent markets. *California Management Review. 42*(4), Summer, 24–54.

Seicean, A., & Neuhauser, D. (2007). A value-driven approach to health care. *Nonprofit Management & Leadership, 17*(4).

Shaw, B., Han, J. Y., Baker, T., Witherly, J., Hawkins, R., McTavish, F., et al. (2007). How women with breast cancer learn using interactive cancer communication systems. *Health Education Research, 22*, 108–119.

Shaw, B., McTavish, F., Hawkins, R.P., Gustafson, D. & Pingree, S. (2000). Experiences of women with breast cancer: Exchanging social support over the CHESS computer network. *Journal of Health Communication, 5*(2), 135–149.

Solowitch, S. (2001). *The citizen scientists.* Wired Magazine http://www.wired.com/wired/archive/9.09/disease.html

Urban, G. L., & Hauser, J. R. (2004). Listening in to find and explore new combinations of customer needs. *Journal of Marketing, 68*, 72.

Walther, J. B., & Boyd, S. (2002). Attraction to computer-mediated social support. In C. A. Lin & D. Atkin (Eds.), *Communication technology and society: Audience adoption and uses* (pp. 153–188). Cresskill, NJ: Hampton Press.

Wang, M., Wang, J., & Zhao, J. (2007). An empirical study of the effect of customer participation on service quality. *Journal of Quality Assurance in Hospitality & Tourism, 8*(1), 49–73.

Windrum, P., & Garcìa-Goñi, M. (2008, May). A neo-Schumpeterian model of health services innovation. *Research Policy,* 37(4), 649–672.

# Chapter 9
# The Strength of IT-Based (Virtual) Interfirm Ties in the Development of Complex Product Systems

**Ikenna S. Uzuegbunam**

**Abstract** This chapter examines the value of "virtual embeddedness" in the context of firms that develop complex product systems (CoPS). The development of CoPS usually involves many firms working together. Firms may choose to maintain arms-length relationships with their partners. But often they must coordinate new product development (NPD) through more embedded interactions because of the intricate nature of systems development in CoPS. Although embeddedness can be socially constructed, the rise of Internet and digital technologies have given way to the emergence of a new form of embeddedness – virtual embeddedness, which provides CoPS firms with unprecedented opportunities for learning and scope economies in the process of NPD. Based on a new typology of virtual embeddedness in organizational space, I posit that virtual embeddedness is a good complementary vehicle to modularity in the management of NPD between CoPS firms. Accordingly, I draw some implications for future research.

## 9.1 Introduction

The problem of designing and coordinating the activities of large-scale complex systems is central to the management research enterprise (Ethiraj, 2007). Many CoPS innovation projects require teams of highly specialized people working in concert across company boundaries (Ethiraj, 2007; Hobday, 1998). Although teams in CoPS development projects may choose to communicate through face-to-face interaction whenever possible, most communication between team members working across firms tends to take place online (virtually), via information technology (IT).

Virtual communication between new product development (NPD) teams in CoPS has become more prevalent because of recent advances in IT and the accompanying

---

I.S. Uzuegbunam (✉)
School of Management, Gatton College of Business & Economics, University of Kentucky, Lexington, KY 40506, USA
e-mail: iuz222@email.uky.edu

The author of this chapter would like to thank Jacquelyn Thompson for excellent editorial comments

S. Nambisan (ed.), *Information Technology and Product Development*, Annals of Information Systems 5, DOI 10.1007/978-1-4419-1081-3_9,

growth of the Internet. Also, online communication flows between people involved in complex product development has increased because of the need for joint problem solving and knowledge sharing in an era where the requirements for new complex technological products can change rapidly.

This chapter explores the relatively unstudied, vast implications of virtually embedded ties in the development of CoPS. Virtually embedded ties are interorganizational linkages that are initiated and maintained through electronic technologies and that provide distinctive solutions to the same exchange-relationship problems that socially embedded ties address (Fowler, Lawrence, & Morse, 2004; Lawrence, Morse, & Fowler, 2005). Virtually embedded ties, like socially embedded ties, embody some element of trust facilitated through exchange of proprietary information and joint problem solving (c.f. Fowler et al., 2004; Uzzi, 1997).

The chapter elucidates the nature of firms' virtually embedded relationships by showing how such relationships involve formal versus informal mechanisms and shallow versus deep ties. The term *formal mechanisms* refer to linking interactions that are under the sponsoring organization's control (e.g., organizational e-mail/chat); *informal mechanisms* refer to links that are outside the sponsoring organization's control (e.g., LinkedIn, Facebook, Skype). The term *shallow mechanisms* refer to fewer IT-based opportunities for the exchange of information, and *deep mechanisms* entail greater opportunities for information to be shared through multiple channels, virtually. These characteristics of virtually embedded ties are used to describe the effects of IT on the virtual embeddedness between interfirm teams for CoPS development. The chapter also suggests some meaningful directions for further research.

The chapter is organized as follows. The following section briefly revisits the annals of collaboration between firms within the overall framework of NPD of CoPS. Specifically, virtual interfirm collaboration is considered *in the context of how it* unveils significant organizational learning implications for collaborating firms. Then the discussion turns to the potential for more interdisciplinary research between information systems and organizational theory that can bring more clarity to the research agenda of NPD in a virtual world. A key practical implication *that emerges from the proposed framework* is that virtual embeddedness is a viable complement for interfirm modularity as companies strive to effectively coordinate their CoPS projects.

## 9.2 Collaboration Among CoPS Firms

### *9.2.1 Complex Product Systems*

> It's the rare product today that doesn't contain components incorporating, wholly distinct and specialized technologies. It's the rare service today, whose performance doesn't combine several specialized skills. And it's the rare business today that doesn't rely on its raw materials, marketing, or distribution on people with diverse technological or market-specific skills. Finding and assembling all those assets under the same roof is difficult, to say the least. Often, it's not even desirable. (Gomes-Casseres, 1994: 63)

CoPS comprise high-value products, systems, capital goods, control units, networks, and high-technology constructs; tend to be produced in one-off or small batches; and emphasize systems design, project management, systems engineering, and systems integration (Hobday, 1998). Two or more companies are usually involved in developing these systems in a setting where any given firm will be responsible for developing at least one module of the CoPS. Most often, the teams that develop these systems are located throughout the world.

For instance, the team of companies that developed the Boeing 787 Dreamliner included a long list of firms that cut across geographical boundaries: General Electric (Ohio), Kidde Technologies (North Carolina), Rockwell Collins (Iowa), Honeywell (Arizona), Rolls Royce (United Kingdom), Dassault Systemes (France), Mitsubishi Heavy Industries (Japan), Kawasaki Heavy Industries (Japan), and Korea Airlines-Aerospace Division (Korea).

In addition to the companies that develop modules for the system, others are responsible for the architectural innovation and systems integration of the CoPS (Brusoni, Prencipe, & Pavitt, 2001; Henderson & Clark, 1990). For example, Boeing Commercial Airplanes served as the major systems integrator responsible for development, integration, final assembly, and program leadership for the Dreamliner. NPD teams can find designing, developing, and integrating systems such as the Boeing 787 Dreamliner to be daunting because the systems and processes involved are complex.

As a result, a main factor favoring the formation of interfirm network ties between companies is the growing complexity of products and services, and of their design, production, and delivery (Gomes-Casseres, 1994). This is because individual companies are unable to develop all the competencies required to develop CoPS. Thus, companies frequently outsource the development of systems components to other organizations. In this context, the success of the innovative firm depends pivotally on the strength of its interfirm ties (e.g., Freeman & Soete, 1997; Prahalad & Ramaswamy, 2000).

For example, MIPS Technologies and its partners, such as Toshiba, DEC, AT&T, and Siemens, co-developed reduced instruction set computing (RISC) architecture. In 1992, when most companies developed this type of product, the company at the center of each group (in this case, MIPS) usually designed the RISC technology, licensed the semiconductor firms to produce the chips, and supplied systems on an object exchange model (OEM) basis to resellers (Gomes-Casseres, 1994). Figure 9.1 illustrates the MIPS product development network.

The following section shows how embedded ties between firms as opposed to mere transactional ties could enhance the value of collaboration in product development.

### *9.2.2 The Value of Network Embeddedness*

Collaboration between firms is the cornerstone of NPD in CoPS. Companies increasingly rely on other companies for the information, resources, technologies,

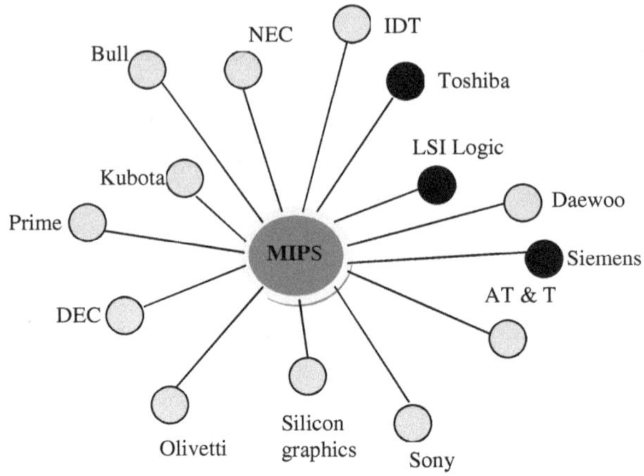


**Fig. 9.1** MIPS CoPS development network (adapted from Gomes-Casseres, 1994)

and markets that these other companies control (Gulati, 1998; Gulati, Nohria, & Zaheer, 2000; Lavie, 2006). Similarly, learning through networks has also been identified as an important motivation for collaboration (Hamel, Doz, & Prahalad, 1989; Gulati et al., 2000).

This view suggests that firms can experience learning economies related to new technologies and new markets through network relationships with other firms. For example, Japanese car companies strategically determined that they should learn through alliances with their American counterparts; as a result of the intent behind these alliances, Japanese auto manufacturing firms enjoyed superior performance (Hamel et al., 1989).

Although many firms restrict their collaborative efforts to arm's-length engagement with other firms (in a transactional form), a good many others *embed* themselves with their partners so deeply that their economic action cannot possibly be interpreted as atomistic in the neoclassical economics sense (Granovetter, 1973, 1985; Gulati et al., 2000; Uzzi, 1997). In contrast to arms-length transactional relationships, embedded relationships often involve a high degree of *trust*, which reduces transactional uncertainty, and creates opportunities for the exchange of products, services, *and knowledge* that are difficult to price or enforce contractually (Uzzi, 1996). Consequently, when firms are embedded with one another, they are likely to learn more from each other because the exchange is anchored by trust.

Thus, to fully understand the extent of embeddedness between two collaborating firms, the need exists to conceptualize the level of trust in these relationships. Although trust usually comes from frequent face-to-face interactions between individuals who represent these companies, it is also important to understand that frequent interactions can also lead to distrust between firms. However, in the spirit of Granovetter (1973), this chapter focuses on situations where frequent interactions between companies are more likely to lead to trustful relationships. This point is especially crucial here because frequent virtual interaction between people lacks the personal touch (characteristic of socially embedded relationships), which can often lead to negative affects/emotions/feelings.

Although the traditional notion of trust embodies an element of face-to-face interaction, trust can also arise from situations where IT creates a bridge between the collaborating companies. The nature of this online interaction between people from different organizations can often be ubiquitous, frequently involving many communication channels. These IT-enabled bridges can be through data, voice, or/and video media.

Although the sponsoring organization(s) have established some of these channels for their employees, some other channels may be hosted by third-party organizations that have no explicit ties with the focal organizations, ex ante. The partnering organizations may not directly sponsor these channels, but that does not mean they are unaware of them. In fact, in some cases, organizations recognize that the product development project is highly complex; thus, the company may not only endorse the channels but also encourage employees to participate in them, even during work hours. The key distinction here is that the focal organization does not *control* the channel.

These differences between the nature and extent of virtual interconnections between NPD teams in CoPS are likely to have several implications for participating firms. These implications deserve further scholarly examination.

## 9.3 The Rise of a New Type of Embeddedness

> Alenia Aeronautica, Fuji Heavy Industries Ltd., and Spirit Aerosystems Inc...; this trio of suppliers, along with 40 other global partners, is taking part in a ground-breaking development effort. Not only are they sharing the risk and design burden for their piece of the 787, they are also participating in *a virtual development world* where every aspect of the plane and its manufacturing processes is designed, created and tested digitally before anything physically moves into production...With the 787 Dreamliner program, Boeing leveraged a common digital environment to help a dispersed global design team more effectively collaborate and leverage a single 3D product definition throughout all phases of the 787's lifecycle. (*Design News*, 2007)

The notion that people and social units such as firms are embedded in a web of social relationships is not new (c.f. Granovetter, 1973, 1985; Uzzi, 1997). However, the rise of digital networking and the Internet has given way to a new kind of embeddedness that foremost researchers in the field of economic or sociological theory probably did not imagine (Fowler et al., 2004; Morse, Fowler, & Lawrence, 2007). Thus, one can imagine a world of interfirm relationships that are either arms-length (in terms of their transactional bias), socially embedded (in terms of physical ties), or virtually embedded (in terms of digitally established connections).

Prior research has highlighted the virtue of socially embedded ties (e.g., Uzzi, 1997; Uzzi & Spiro, 2005); however, we have much to learn about the value of virtually established, embedded connections. Recently, some authors have argued that these ties can be beneficial in many interorganizational contexts. Specifically, Morse et al. (2007) argue that virtually enabled ties can help an entrepreneur overcome the liability of newness typically associated with new ventures. This is because virtually

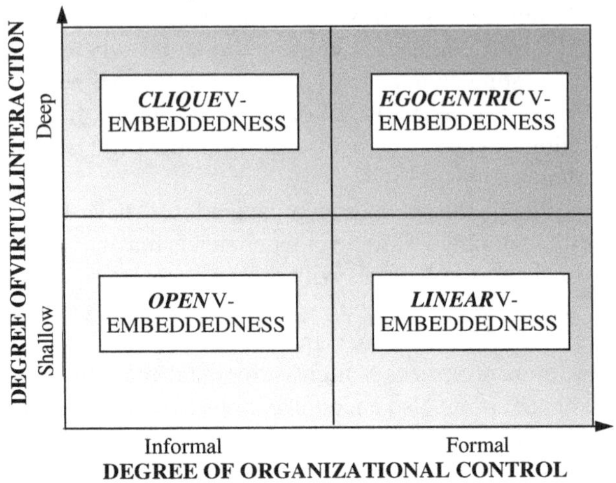


**Fig. 9.2** A typology of virtually embedded interfirm CoPS teams

embedded interfirm ties are likely to be less expensive to establish because they rely on existing technological frameworks, and they are also easier to uncouple if need be, thus overcoming the shortcomings of socially embedded ties that Uzzi (1997) and Fowler et al. (2004) highlighted.

Although some of these arguments are compelling, we still know little about how virtual embeddedness will play out in the context of NPD. To understand the role of virtual embeddedness in its full ramifications, it is beneficial to propose a typology of the IT-based or virtual ties among firms (see Fig. 9.2). This typology draws on the traditional characteristics of embeddedness in terms of frequency of interactions, but in virtual form. This typology is also anchored by the IT usage in organizations, in terms of organizational channels versus informal connections. Thus, I suggest a typology where virtual embeddedness can be defined as *linear, open, egocentric,* or *clique*. In the following sections, I discuss these types of virtual embeddedness in terms of how they apply to NPD in CoPS.

## 9.4 Linear (or Functional) V-Embeddedness

Virtually embedded interfirm teams of the linear type are typically coupled through one channel of communication (usually, e-mail or company web environment). Team members communicate through e-mails that their parent organizations usually sponsor, thereby ensuring a high degree of organizational oversight. This type of embeddedness is purely functional in the sense that the collaborating companies are concerned with resolving specific problems encountered during systems development.

An advantage of employing this approach to virtual embeddedness is that it provides "quick fixes" (easy solutions) in situations where speed to market is crucial and where organizational resources are scarce. Also, the sponsoring firm is able to appropriate a significant portion of the information value that is being exchanged through this medium. It suffices to add that this case of virtual embeddedness is analogous to the conventional notion of the strength of weak ties (c.f. Granovetter, 1973), where firms can solve problems quickly through partner firms that are acquaintances but not necessarily friends.

The obvious downside of the linear (functional) type of virtual embeddedness is that it provides only economies of learning as it pertains to the specified scenario. In other words, linear embeddedness has the potential to enhance the depth of knowledge (pertaining to specialization) as opposed to breadth of knowledge. It does not provide the focal company with possibilities for earning economies of scale and scope that could exist if more channels of communication were employed in solving NPD problems in CoPS. In these virtually embedded networks, modularity often plays a significant role in managing interfirm collaboration in CoPS.

## 9.5 Open V-Embeddedness

Open V-embeddedness in CoPS is similar to open-source movements, hence the name. Like open-source communities, the ties that govern systems development under these arrangements are *informal* in that no specific organization controls their system inputs and outputs. Furthermore, the IT connections made here may seem *shallow*, which suggests that the participating firms have chosen one or few IT connections. Although system developers that are plugged into this network are likely to be part of other communities for CoPS development, it is possible that they will spend most of their project time using this specific network because expertise is more broadly and easily available. This makes this model of virtual embeddedness suitable for research and design phases of NPD in CoPS. The approach to problem solving in this model is the community-based approach (Fowler et al., 2004).

Consider open source development labs (OSDL), a consortium of firms formed by open-source companies and developers from around the world to further the growth of the Linux operating system. This consortium includes companies such as IBM, Fujitsu, HP, Hitachi, NEC, Oracle, Intel, Novell, AMD, Google, Cisco, and Motorola. In OSDL, no single member organization controls the forums used to share information. However, because of the strategic value of this collaboration to participating firms, firms such as IBM spend about $100 million on Linux development each year, a small proportion of what the company once spent on proprietary software (Chesbrough, 2007). Each company involved in this collaboration freely shares information about developments in an open, virtual format.

## 9.6 Clique V-Embeddedness

The notion of *cliques* in network research is not new. Just as individuals do, companies can form informal cliques. A clique is generally defined as a subset of members who are more closely identified with one another than with others in a group and who exchange among themselves, for example, information, affect, and friendship (Tichy, 1973). Thus, many researchers suggest that cliques are usually established between a few players who are strongly connected to each other while excluding a majority of people who could be a part of this network. Although cliques may seem to exclude a great many actors, they often connect different clusters of other networks that the focal actors belong to. In the context of NPD in CoPS, if the NPD-involved firms are closely knit friends while they maintain memberships in other closely knit groups, such well-connected firms may be able to access information that will be beneficial for NPD.

For example, Uzzi and Spiro (2005) investigated the concept of "small worlds" in NPD in the Broadway musical setting. Their findings suggest that a moderate level of clique formation (in terms of its ability to create small worlds) is beneficial for NPD. In other words, past a certain threshold, "... cohesive cliques tend to overlook important information that is discrepant with their current thinking because members tend to exchange common rather than unique perspectives" (Uzzi & Spiro, 2005, p. 463). Although cliques in the social context can have this curvilinear effect on the outcomes of product development, cliques formed using virtual connections are likely to overcome this liability because IT affords greater reach and richness.

Acting just as socially embedded cliques do, virtually embedded cliques can be informal in terms of how actors communicate using non-company-sponsored channels. Information can be exchanged on a website for common interests such as a professional organization's website. However, *deep* proprietary information is exchanged usually through one or few means because members are intent on keeping NPD information within their limited circle of friends, their clique.

It is possible, however, that an outsider can be in another clique with a member of the focal virtual forum and can access information through that member. Herein lies the downside of this model of virtual embeddedness. If the outsider is a rival company, the company may gain access to highly proprietary information that might hurt the focal firm.

## 9.7 Egocentric V-Embeddedness

When a company is egocentric in its virtual network focus on NPD in CoPS, their search for systems knowledge may be embedded in a larger community of alter firms. Brusoni et al. (2001) studied three major system integrator firms in aircraft engine control systems and discovered that most of these systems integrator firms simultaneously outsourced production to partner firms while maintaining their knowledge of the outsourced components. Companies follow a certain logic as they maintain their knowledge of their outsourced sub-systems; that is, they monitor the interdependencies between components in terms of uneven rate of technology changes. This clearly suggests that the focal firm focuses on its competitive advantage in terms of its knowledge co-specialization activities and capabilities. Also, these virtual connections between firms operating under this mode of virtual embeddedness are made through formal channels the egocentric firm established/sponsored as a way of appropriating returns.

The design and development of the Boeing 787 Dreamliner is another good example of the egocentric virtual embeddedness model. In the past, Boeing designed 70% and produced 30% of its aircraft. With the Dreamliner, Boeing changed strategy. The company assumed the role of systems integrator, thereby allowing partner companies to design and manufacture several modules. According to Kevin Fowler, Boeing's vice-president for systems integration:

> We want to get the best collection of people to create the best airplane, so we needed to look globally. What you find is not only is it expensive, it's not feasible to have everyone come and be located in one spot. It defeats the purpose of having designers close to manufacturing. We wanted something to enable us to work as one team and be ***virtually connected.*** (*Design News*, 2007)

To set up its virtual team, Boeing created the Global Collaborative Environment (GCE). This virtual environment includes a set of computer and networking capabilities that connected every member of the 787 team, regardless of their location. This environment includes Boeing-developed applications in addition to third-party programs for simulation and design tasks. In this way, Boeing is able to maintain knowledge of the design components that it has outsourced to other firms.

## 9.8 Virtual Embeddedness and Modularity

*Modularity* refers to a systems approach where changes in components that make up a system's architecture will not change the relationships between components in the architecture. However, it is often necessary in the development of complex product development projects to account for technical changes at the niche (component) level as well as at the architectural level of innovation (Henderson & Clark, 1990). When niche (component) level innovation is required and when the technologies are reasonably well understood, lead companies involved in these complex product development projects can manage the process using modular systems approaches (Brusoni et al., 2001; Schilling, 2000). But when the change is architectural or both niche and architectural, managers must consider alternative approaches to manage changes in the architecture of the system.

Furthermore, firms do not always migrate towards modularity (Schilling, 2000). Some firms may be motivated to deemphasize modular systems design strategies in their systems architecture. In these cases, firms may chose to limit the number of firms that can interface with their product as a way of maintaining market power (Schilling, 2000). Therefore, when the motives for systems development in CoPS is focused less on modularity and more on integration, firms are more likely to rely on trust mechanisms for managing both component and architectural innovation.

A network embeddedness approach for managing NPD in CoPS can potentially help manage architectural innovation. Although social embeddedness is likely to be more costly in terms of monitoring technical changes in the architecture of the system, virtual embeddedness provides a less costly approach. Virtually embedded companies that are involved in NPD such as in the case of the Boeing 787 Dreamliner are likely to resolve product development issues that pertain to the change in technology and specifications, even in the relative absence of modularity. This is because system developers from different firms that are not co-located can access fine-grained information in a timelier and richer manner. If the modular strategies of the focal firm changes, virtual embeddedness will also allow companies to adapt their products to different customers more easily.

## 9.9 Conclusions and Suggestions for Future Research

Although significant research has been devoted to the *real/physically/socially embedded ties* between firms that participate in product development (e.g., Hansen, 1999), fewer studies have examined the value of *virtual embeddedness* in the context of NPD. Some unattended questions that could help further this research surface at this point: Can virtual ties completely substitute for physical (social) ties between interfirm teams of complex product development? If so, what characteristics distinguish between socially embedded ties and virtually embedded ties? What negative effects (if any) do virtually embedded interfirm teams have on product development? What contextual factors can enhance the value of virtual embeddedness for CoPS teams? What organizational structures within the firm can support or limit product development teams that are virtually embedded with teams from other organizations?

To be specific, one potential direction for future research is to empirically investigate how virtual embeddedness might complement and improve social embeddedness between firms. Because the cost of establishing and dissolving virtually embedded connections is relatively small compared with social embeddedness (and the benefits appear to be relatively the same), firms are likely to reap the benefits of social embeddedness if they initiate virtual connections with their prospective product development partners. A study that will investigate this research question must be survey based to disentangle the broader effects of IT spending from the more specific effect of IT investments in alliances.

Furthermore, case studies can be designed to supplement survey data. These case studies should involve multiple cases where virtual connections are used primarily in NPD of CoPS as well as cases where virtual connections are not as prevalent. Qualitative data from such a study will provide some useful nuances in understanding the limitations of virtual embeddedness in organizational environments.

Finally, systematic formal modeling can be carried out to explicate the effects of different types of virtual embeddedness on firm economies. Such an inquiry should employ a model that is sensitive to the often exponential and non-deterministic effects of virtual connections on the success of NPD in CoPS. Complementing a formal approach with empirical testing may help uncover some interesting findings for the nascent literature on virtual embeddedness as it affects new product development.

## References

Brusoni, S., Prencipe, A., & Pavitt, K. (2001). Knowledge specialization, organizational coupling, and the boundaries of the firm: Why do firms know more than they make? *Administrative Science Quarterly, 46*, 597–621.

Chesbrough, H. (2007). Why companies should have open business models. *MIT Sloan Management Review, Winter*, 22–28.

*Design News*. (2007). Boeing's global collaboration environment pioneers groundbreaking 787 Dreamliner development effort. (http://www.designnews.com/article/13616-oing_s_Global_Collaboration_Environment_Pioneers_Groundbreaking_787_Dreamliner_Development_Effort.php.)

Ethiraj, S. K. (2007). Allocation of inventive effort in complex product systems. *Strategic Management Journal, 28*(6), 563–584.

Freeman, C., & Soete, L. (1997). *The economics of industrial revolution*(3rd ed.). Cambridge, MA: The MIT Press.

Fowler, S. W., Lawrence, T. B., & Morse E. A. (2004). Virtually embedded ties. *Journal of Management, 30*(5), 647–666.

Gomes-Casseres, B. (1994). Group versus group: How alliance networks compete. *Harvard Business Review, 72*, 62–84.

Granovetter, M. (1973). The strength of weak ties. *American Journal of Sociology, 78*, 1360–1380.

Granovetter, M. (1985). Economic action and social structure: The problem of embeddedness. *The American Journal of Sociology, 91*, 481–510.

Gulati, R. (1998). Alliances and networks. *Strategic Management Journal, 19*, 293–317.

Gulati, R., Nohria, N., & Zaheer, A. (2000). Strategic networks. *Strategic Management Journal, 21*, 203–215.

Hamel, G., Doz, Y. L., & Prahalad, C. K. (1989). Collaborate with your competitors and win. *Harvard Business Review, January–February*, 133–139.

Hansen, M. T. (1999). The search-transfer problem: The role of weak ties in sharing knowledge across organization subunits. *Academy of Management Review, 44*, 82–111.

Henderson, R. M., & Clark K. (1990). Architectural innovation: The reconfiguration of existing product technologies and the failure of established firms. *Administrative Science Quarterly, 35*, 9–30.

Hobday, M. (1998). Product complexity, innovation and industrial organization. *Research Policy, 26*, 689–710.

Lavie, D. (2006). The competitive advantage of interconnected firms: An extension of the resource based view. *Academy of Management Review, 31*, 638–658.

Lawrence, T. B., Morse E. A., & Fowler, S. W. (2005). Managing your portfolio of connections. *Sloan Management Review, 46*(2), 59–65.

Morse, E. A., Fowler, S. W., & Lawrence, T. B. (2007). The Impact of virtual embeddedness on the new venture survival: Overcoming the liabilities of newness. *Entrepreneurship Theory & Practice, March*, 139–159.

Prahalad, C. K., & Ramaswamy, V. (2000). Co-opting customer competence. *Harvard Business Review, 78*(1), 79–87.

Schilling, M. A. (2000). Toward a general modular systems theory and its application to interfirm product modularity. *Academy of Management Review, 25*(2), 312–334.

Tichy, N. (1973). An analysis of clique formation and structure in organizations. *Administrative Science Quarterly, 18*(2), 194–208.

Uzzi, B. (1996). The sources and consequences of embeddedness for the economic performance of organizations. *American Sociological Review, 61*, 674–698.

Uzzi, B. (1997). Social structure and competition in interfirm networks: The paradox of embeddedness. *Administrative Science Quarterly, 42*(1), 35–67.

Uzzi, B., & Spiro, J. (2005). Collaboration and creativity: The small world problem. *American Journal of Sociology, 111*(2), 447–504.

# Part III
# Issues for Future Research

# Chapter 10
# An Agenda for Future Research on IT and Product Development

**Satish Nambisan**

**Abstract** As the nature and process of innovation have changed drastically in the past several years, so has the role of information technology (IT) in supporting the innovation activities. The objective of this book has been to examine the issues related to the application of IT in product/service development from multiple disciplinary and theoretical perspectives. The various chapters have considered a wide range of issues including the business value of IT applications, PLM implementation, virtual teams, customer co-innovation, and knowledge management systems. The discussions in these chapters identified several issues for future research related to the different topics. In this concluding chapter, I identify and discuss some of the broader research themes that have emerged from the different chapters. By identifying these broader themes, I hope to bring a sharper focus on and lay out a rich and promising agenda for future research on IT and product development.

## 10.1 Introduction

As noted in the introductory chapter, in the past one decade or so, the nature of innovation has undergone considerable change in most industries. Innovation has become much more global and collaborative in nature. New innovation models involve networks of firms and emphasize distributed innovation processes. The diversity and number of partners involved indicate the complexity of some of these emerging models. Further, the continued pressure to reduce the time and cost of innovation has forced many companies to adopt standardized product development systems and processes. These changes have in turn enhanced the importance and relevance of information technology (IT) in supporting product and service innovation. Similarly, the wider adoption of enterprise IT applications such as ERP and CRM has also enhanced the need to have similar standardized systems and applications that would not only support innovation management but also integrate it with rest of the enterprise activities more tightly.

S. Nambisan (✉)
Lally School of Management, Rensselaer Polytechnic Institute, Troy, NY 12180, USA
e-mail: nambis@rpi.edu

S. Nambisan (ed.), *Information Technology and Product Development*, Annals of Information Systems 5, DOI 10.1007/978-1-4419-1081-3_10, 

The objective of this book has been to examine the issues related to the application of IT in product/service development from multiple disciplinary and theoretical perspectives. The various chapters have considered a wide range of issues including the business value of IT applications, PLM implementation, virtual teams, customer co-innovation, and knowledge management systems. In examining these issues, the authors of the various chapters drew from multiple fields and areas including marketing, strategy, organizational behavior, and information systems. The discussions in these chapters identified several issues for future research related to the different topics.

In this concluding chapter, I identify and discuss some of the broader research themes that have emerged from the different chapters. The objective is to bring a sharper focus on and lay out a rich and promising agenda for future research on IT and product/service development.

## 10.2 Critical Themes for Future Research on IT and Innovation

### *10.2.1 IT and Network-Centric Innovation*

The increased emphasis on organic (or innovation-driven) growth strategies in many companies has also been accompanied by a growing realization regarding the need to "look outside" for innovative product ideas and technologies, i.e., the need to reach out to customers, suppliers, independent inventors, academic researchers, innovation brokers, and a host of other external entities. These different entities together represent the global brain, a vast untapped creative potential that lies beyond company boundaries (Nambisan & Sawhney, 2007). However, making such a shift from innovation initiatives that are centered on internal resources to those that are centered on external networks and communities – i.e., a shift from *firm-centric innovation* to *network-centric innovation* – is quite challenging and complex.

Network-centric innovation has been defined as an "externally focused approach to innovation that relies on harnessing the resources and capabilities of external networks and communities to amplify or enhance innovation reach, innovation speed, and the quality of innovation outcomes" (Nambisan & Sawhney, 2007).

Four key principles underlie network-centric innovation. First, the innovation network should establish and promote a set of shared goals and objectives that would give direction and bring a level of coherence to the innovation activities. Second, it is important that network partners adopt a shared "world view" or awareness of the external environment – i.e., key assumptions, evaluation methods, frameworks, etc., related to the innovation context. Third, the network will need to support social knowledge creation, i.e., knowledge creation that occurs in a collaborative and cumulative manner through interactions among the different partners. Finally, the network has to define an architecture of participation that bring clarity to the innovation work is distributed among the different network partners as well as the way the "rights" (or rewards) from the innovation are shared by the partners.

The success of network-centric innovation will be dependent on how well these four principles are upheld, and this in turn implies the critical role of IT. Specifically, IT becomes an integral part of the support infrastructure for such network-centric innovation initiatives.

Over the past few years, a wide range of IT-based applications have emerged that could be deployed to enhance the organizational readiness or preparedness for participating in network-centric innovation. Some of these tools facilitate communication and knowledge sharing among network members while some other tools enable coordination and management of collaborative innovation processes. Some of the earlier chapters considered the role IT can play in instilling structured product development processes and in brining a level of rigor and stability to innovation activities. Such a role is particularly important in the network-centric innovation context. Another critical role for IT is offer a wide range of communication support – ranging from facilities for a community of innovators to come together and interact to highly secure forums for a defined set of partner firms to share documents.

The more integrated these IT-based tools are with the underlying innovation processes in the network and the capabilities of the network members, the greater the potential returns from such tools. Thus, the key task for companies in deploying these technologies is to establish an integrated innovation environment that embraces the network members and brings coherence to their activities and contributions.

Three broad research issues assume importance in this context. The first issue relates to the need to develop *a flexible IT architecture that can support different models of network-centric innovation*. Various models of network-centric innovation exist – ranging from those that have centralized governance (dominant partners) to those in which the partners share the governance responsibilities (Nambisan & Sawhney, 2007). A critical question for future research then is how should companies devise their IT infrastructure to support their participation in different network-centric innovation contexts? Addressing this issue would potentially require integrating theoretical concepts and insights related to network governance, distributed innovation processes, and IT management.

The second issue relates to the *use of IT in enhancing the innovation reach of companies*. As companies seek out innovative ideas from their customers (as well as from independent inventors), IT plays a critical role in increasing their reach to all corners of the world. Innovation intermediary companies such as InnoCentive have demonstrated the power of Web-based platforms to increase the innovation reach to the global inventor community. Future research may focus on identifying the critical characteristics of such IT platforms and their impact on enhancing the innovation reach to different parts of the inventor community. Another related research issue is the nature of support the IT platform can offer for both structured and unstructured knowledge interactions between companies and external inventors.

The third issue relates to the *support IT can provide to integrating the external innovation opportunities with the company's internal innovation engine*. It is quite evident that to be successful companies will need to integrate their internal and external innovation activities. Future studies may focus on identifying the organizational mechanisms that would facilitate such integration and how such organizational mechanisms may be combined with the IT infrastructure to bring a high level of coherence between the company's innovation activities and that of its network partners.

Overall, network-centric innovation context provides a fertile ground for future research and the insights from such studies would likely become very valuable as more and more companies make the shift toward such collaborative innovation practices.

### 10.2.2 Product Life Cycle Management and Portfolio Management

A topic of considerable contemporary interest to both researchers and practitioners in the innovation management area is product life cycle management (PLM). As noted in two of the chapters in this book, the emphasis on PLM as a business concept has been driven by a host of internal and external factors. On the one hand, the need to accelerate innovation and become more efficient in product development has enhanced the importance of more mature product development and maintenance processes. At the same time, external factors such as globalization, product and technology complexity, and shrinking product life cycle have emphasized the need to adopt a broader product platform approach that could facilitate sharing of product components or modules as well as technologies across the enterprise.

In the 1990s and the early part of this decade, much of the focus of corporate IT departments has been on implementing ERP and CRM solutions. With the widespread deployment of these enterprise applications, many companies have realized that there is a critical gap in their corporate data model related to product and product development. It is true that some of the companies have implemented product data management (PDM) solutions in the 1980s. However, the functionalities provided by PDM systems are limited to design and manufacturing engineers, and further, they offer limited connectivity with other enterprise data. More importantly, PDM solutions have traditionally not been very user friendly and consequently, PDM adoption has been restricted to a few large engineering-oriented companies.

PLM solutions extend the functionalities of PDM systems to marketing, finance, and product support areas and enable companies to achieve seamless integration of all their product life cycle activities (from the design and development of products to their support and eventual retirement) with other enterprise processes such as customer relationship management, inventory management, and procurement.

However, as Andy Hewett notes in an earlier chapter, implementation of PLM solutions has not been easy and many firms have been struggling with both technical and managerial issues related to PLM deployment. This in turn raises several issues for future research.

In particular, there are three broad research issues that present the most promise in terms of potential insights for successful PLM deployment.

The first issue relates to *developing a deeper understanding of the broader product development context within which the IT solution is deployed.* Specifically, what is the product development strategy (and the product portfolio strategy) and how does the IT solution complement such a strategy? For example, the nature of PLM implementation in companies that have adopted a product platform strategy (Gawer & Cusumano, 2002) is likely to be different compared to that in companies which pursue more integrated product architectures. Similarly, the adoption of portfolio management practices may, in turn, place relatively more emphasis on certain functionalities of the PLM solution with implications on the ease of implementation. Thus, future research should focus on identifying the key elements of the product development context and examine their interaction effects with the IT solution. Such an approach could lead to valuable insights on strategies and practices that need to accompany PLM implementation efforts.

The second research issue relates to the *process and technological infrastructure that complements the PLM solution.* A critical task in PLM implementation is the integration of the IT solution with other enterprise applications such as ERP and CRM. Future studies should focus on examining the impact of different configurations of process and technological infrastructure on PLM implementation success. Several factors including the type of process and data standards that have been adopted by the organization will shape the relative ease of integrating the PLM solution with other enterprise applications. Thus, insights from these studies could enable organizations to ensure that the right set of process and technological infrastructure is established prior to PLM implementation.

The third and final research issue relates to the *implementation of PLM in a distributed innovation context where the PLM functionalities cross organizational boundaries.* As more and more companies embrace external partners in product development activities, the scope of the PLM solution will need to extend to include such inter-firm interactions. This raises several interesting issues for future research. For example, what are the characteristics of Web-enabled PLM solutions that are likely to be useful in such collaborative innovation contexts? How should companies integrate their product development activities with those of their external partners using PLM solutions? What are the important antecedents to the successful implementation of such cross-border integration? Studies that focus on these and other issues would likely offer valuable insights that could help extending PLM functionalities to support collaborative innovation initiatives.

As might be evident from the brief discussion of the above three issues, studies that address these issues will need to adopt an interdisciplinary approach and incorporate theoretical constructs and frameworks from different areas including product development, strategy, operations, and IT.

### *10.2.3 Experimentation in Innovation*

Experimentation has assumed considerable importance in recent years – both in business in general (Davenport, 2009) and in product/service development (Thomke, 2003). Business experimentation enable companies to test out new business strategies and processes and make more judicious decisions regarding their implementation. Simple frameworks have been suggested to organize such business experiments. For example, Davenport (2009) recommends an iterative hypothesis testing framework that organizations can employ to test out alternate solutions to business problems before roll out.

Experimentation has become critically important in product development too as the scope and the complexity of product development projects continues to increase (Dahan & Hauser, 2002). However, it is also important to make such experiments cost-effective. IT can play a key role in achieving this objective. Virtual prototyping tools help to reduce innovation costs; more importantly, they enable companies to engage a large set of stakeholders in concept testing activities, thereby reducing the innovation risks as well as the time-to-market.

Experimentation in service innovation present another set of unique challenges. As Thomke (2003) indicates it is difficult to test out new services in a traditional laboratory setting. On the other hand, "live" tests of new services that involve real-world customer while useful pose several risks including those related to customer relationships and brand image. Thus, IT-based testing tools and platforms are particularly appealing for conducting experiments in service innovation.

Several important research issues arise from this focus on experimentation and the role IT can play in supporting it. I briefly describe two broad sets of issues here.

First, given the wide range of IT-based tools that are available – from statistical tools to virtual reality prototyping and simulation tools – *developing an understanding of the characteristics of these tools is important in order to select and deploy the right set of tools in a given context.* Studies have identified a whole host of IT-based tools for experimentation, however, there has been limited attention paid to evaluating their effectiveness in different contexts. Future studies should focus on developing contingency models that elaborate on the key elements of various tools and inform on their relative effectiveness in different product development contexts.

Second, it is evident that to *derive value from the different innovation and experimentation tools available in the market, they have to 'fitted' with the innovation context* (Thomke, 2006). This implies changes in innovation systems and processes as well as the design of appropriate experiments. A critical question for future research then is how should companies design experiments so as to leverage the capabilities of these IT-based tools? What aspects of the innovation processes would need to be modified to enhance the effectiveness of the IT-based tools in experimentation?

With more and more companies adopting experimentation as the cornerstone of their innovation strategy, IT will likely come to play a critical role in enhancing the quality and value of such experiments and thereby contributing to innovation success. Future research that is targeted at the issues outlined above would thus be very beneficial to companies as they explore different types of experiments in innovation.

### *10.2.4 IT Platforms for Customer Co-innovation and Value Co-creation*

As noted elsewhere in this book, the notion of customer (or user) innovation is not new. Eric von Hippel's (1988) research over the years has led to numerous insights on how lead users can make significant contribution to product improvements as well as to the creation of new products/services. However, with the emergence of the Internet and other information and communication technologies, the scope and the depth of customer (user) involvement in innovation and value creation has undergone radical change.

As discussed in detail in Chapter 3, IT-based platforms (or virtual customer environments) have "democratized" innovation activities in many industries. While the early studies on this topic (Prahalad & Ramaswamy, 2003; Nambisan, 2002; Nambisan & Baron, 2007; Nambisan & Nambisan, 2008; Sawhney, Verona, & Prandelli, 2005; Thomke & von Hippel, 2002) have offered critical insights on the different types of such IT-based platforms and on the strategies and practices to enhance customers' motivation to contribute to innovation initiatives, several other important research issues remain to be investigated.

In particular, there are four broad topics that future studies may focus on. The first topic relates to the need for *coherence in devising IT-based platforms for hosting customer co-innovation and value co-creation activities*. In recent years, many companies have implemented several different social media technologies (blogs, wikis, online communities, etc.) to support their interactions with customers. In most cases, however, different parts of the organization have adopted or deployed different technology platforms to interact with customers. As a consequence, at the enterprise level there is often very little coherence among these different customer co-innovation initiatives. Thus, an important topic for future research in this area relates to how companies can bring coherence to the design and deployment of these IT-based platforms. In addressing this issue, there is much potential for drawing on theoretical concepts and insights from different related areas including computer-mediated communication, user innovation, and social media. A desired outcome of such studies would be a theoretically-grounded framework that could guide the selection and integration of varied IT components to support different types of customer co-innovation activities.

The second topic is related to the *establishment of complementary organizational mechanisms to support and enhance the capabilities offered by the IT platform*. While IT platforms do enable companies to interact with customers, it will require more than just a set of communication tools for such interactions to be effective. Specifically, companies would need to deploy organizational mechanisms to complement those tools and technologies. These include customer recognition programs, product knowledge centers, idea rating systems, and community manager roles. Future studies that focus on identifying and evaluating the potential effectiveness of such organizational mechanisms could offer invaluable insights to companies in ensuring that their customer co-innovation initiatives add value to the business.

However, to be really effective, *customer co-innovation platforms would need to be integrated with the organization's broader innovation system and processes too*, and this forms the fourth topic. To leverage the innovative ideas and solutions offered by customers, they need to be acted upon. And, this requires integrating the customer co-innovation initiative with the remainder of the company's innovation engine. Future studies that focus on this issue would need to adopt a broader perspective and examine what elements of the organization's innovation process infrastructure would need to be adapted to integrate them with the IT platform. For example, this might imply different processes to evaluate ideas that originate from customers. Similarly, this might also imply engaging with customer innovators as some of those ideas move through the company's product development pipeline. Thus, future research on identifying and evaluating such process accommodations to bind together the company's customer co-innovation initiative with other parts of the internal innovation system assume critical importance.

Finally, studies should also conduct rigorous empirical examination of the *impact of IT-based platforms for customer co-innovation*. As noted previously, much of the early literature in this area has focused on establishing the potential for IT to enhance the nature and scope of customer engagement in innovation and value creation. However, there has been limited number of empirical studies on this topic. Importantly, IT platforms for customer co-innovation can have both direct and indirect impact (Nambisan & Nambisan, 2008). The direct impact would likely be on the effectiveness of the company's innovation – in terms of innovation cost, time, and quality. The indirect impact would be on the company's relationship with customers as well as customer perceptions regarding the product, brand, etc. (e.g., brand image). It is important that companies deploying IT platforms for customer co-innovation are aware of these different outcomes and as such empirical studies that focus on this issue could offer valuable and timely insights.

## 10.3 Conclusions

The objective of this book has been to discuss a wide range of issues related to the application of IT to support product and service development. The four broad topics identified in this chapter as well as the varied issues discussed in the earlier chapters together lay out a rich and highly promising agenda for future research in the area of IT and product/service development. Importantly, the discussions in the various chapters have also highlighted the significance of adopting a broad inter-disciplinary perspective and drawing on theoretical concepts and frameworks from varied areas for pursuing such a research agenda.

## References


Dahan, E., & Hauser, J. (2002). The virtual customer. *Journal of Product Innovation Management, 19*(5), 332–353.

Davenport, T. H. (2009, February) How to design smart business experiments. *Harvard Business Review*, 69–76.

Gawer, A., & Cusumano, M. (2002). *Platform Leadership: How Intel, Microsoft, and Cisco drive industry innovation*. Boston, MA: Harvard Business School Press.

Nambisan, S. (2002). Designing virtual customer environments for new product development: Toward a theory. *Academy of Management Review, 27*(3), 392–314.

Nambisan, S., & Baron, R. (2007). Interactions in virtual customer environments: Implications for product support and customer relationship management. *Journal of Interactive Marketing, 21*(2), 42–62.

Nambisan, S., & Nambisan, P. (2008, Spring). How to profit from a better virtual customer environment. *MIT Sloan Management Review*, 53–61.

Nambisan, S., & Sawhney, M. (2007, October). *The global brain: Your roadmap for innovating faster and smarter in a networked world*. Pennsylvania: Wharton School Publishing.

Prahalad, C. K., & Ramaswamy, V. (2003). *The future of competition: Co-creating value with customers*. Boston: HBS Press.

Sawhney, M., Verona, G., & Prandelli, E. (2005). Collaborating to create: The Internet as a platform for customer engagement in product innovation. *Journal of Interactive Marketing, 19*(4), 4–17.

Thomke, S. (2003). *Experimentation matters: Unlocking the potential of new technologies for innovation*. Boston, MA: Harvard Business School Press.

Thomke, S. (2006, Winter). Capturing the real value of innovation tools. *MIT Sloan Management Review, 47*(2).

Thomke, S., & von Hippel, E. (2002). Customers as innovators: A new way to create value. *Harvard Business Review, 80*(4), 74–81.

von Hippel, E. (1988). *The sources of innovation*. New York: Oxford University Press.

# Index



S. Nambisan (ed.), *Information Technology and Product Development,* Annals of Information Systems 5, DOI 10.1007/978-1-4419-1081-3,

**Q**



**R**

**W**

Papier | Fördert gute Waldnutzung
FSC® C083411

Kolibri 360 GmbH
Ferdinand-Jühlke-Straße 7
99095 Erfurt, Deutschland
produktsicherheit@kolibri360.de